XHTML

BY EXAMPLE

201 West 103rd Street
Indianapolis, Indiana 46290

Ann Navarro

XHTML by Example

Copyright © 2001 by Que

International Standard Book Number: 0-7897-2385-9

Library of Congress Catalog Card Number: 00-101129

Printed in the United States of America

First Printing: November 2000

02 01 00   4   3   2   1

Trademarks

All terms mentioned in this book that are known to be trademarks or service marks have been appropriately capitalized. Que cannot attest to the accuracy of this information. Use of a term in this book should not be regarded as affecting the validity of any trademark or service mark.

Warning and Disclaimer

Every effort has been made to make this book as complete and as accurate as possible, but no warranty or fitness is implied. The information provided is on an "as is" basis. The author and the publisher shall have neither liability nor responsibility to any person or entity with respect to any loss or damages arising from the information contained in this book.

Acquisitions Editor
Todd Green

Development Editor
Sean Dixon

Managing Editor
Thomas F. Hayes

Project Editor
Karen S. Shields

Copy Editor
Sossity Smith

Indexers
Kevin Fulcher
Larry Sweazy

Proofreaders
Jeanne Clark
Megan Wade

Technical Editors
Shane McCarron
Kynn Bartlett
Benoît Marchal

Team Coordinator
Cindy Teeters

Interior Designer
Karen Ruggles

Cover Designer
Rader Design

Production
Darin Crone

Contents at a Glance

Table of Contents

About the Author

Ann Navarro is chief operating officer for the HTML Writers Guild, the world's largest organization of Web developers and Internet enthusiasts. Active in the Web Development community for more than five years, Ann is the author of three other books on HTML, XML, and related topics, including *HTML by Example* (Que, December 1999). She is an active member of the W3C's HTML Working Group, the group charged with crafting the XHTML Recommendations. Ann also provides executive direction as CEO and founder of WebGeek, Inc., a privately held Web and Internet consulting firm. She currently lives in Port Charlotte, Florida, with her husband Dave and Dizzy the cat, where they enjoy snorkeling and have spent far too many hours crawling around the attic running ethernet cable in the new house.

About the Contributor

Andrew H. Watt (chapters 12, 19) is an independent consultant who specializes in Web technologies, including XML, XHTML, Domino, and Java. Previously he wrote the XML section of *Platinum Edition Using XHTML, XML, and Java 2.*

Dedication

For Dave: Want to go for a swim?

Acknowledgments

The process of writing a book involves a great many people. As always, I am indebted to many for their assistance, advice, and support throughout the creation of this manuscript. At Macmillan USA I'd like to thank acquisitions editor Todd Green, development editor Sean Dixon, as well as Sossity Smith, Karen Shields, Jeanne Clark, Kevin Fulcher, Larry Sweazy, and the Macmillan production team.

Thanks to my agents Neil Salkind, David Rogelberg, and all of the staff at Studio B Productions, who so deftly handle the business aspects of my writing career.

Special thanks goes to Shane McCarron—my technical editor, friend and colleague on the HTML Working Group. Without his sharp eye, quick wit, and occasional firm nudge, this book would not have been nearly as accurate or complete.

And finally to my husband Dave, who watched over WebGeek while my attention was focused firmly on my laptop, writing this book at some of the oddest moments.

Tell Us What You Think!

As the reader of this book, *you* are our most important critic and commentator. We value your opinion and want to know what we're doing right, what we could do better, what areas you'd like to see us publish in, and any other words of wisdom you're willing to pass our way.

As an Associate Publisher for Que, I welcome your comments. You can fax, email, or write me directly to let me know what you did or didn't like about this book—as well as what we can do to make our books stronger.

Please note that I cannot help you with technical problems related to the topic of this book, and that due to the high volume of mail I receive, I might not be able to reply to every message.

When you write, please be sure to include this book's title and author as well as your name and phone or fax number. I will carefully review your comments and share them with the author and editors who worked on the book.

Fax:	317-581-4666
Email:	quetechnical@macmillanusa.com
Mail:	Associate Publisher
	Que
	201 West 103rd Street
	Indianapolis, IN 46290 USA

Introduction

From HTML to XHTML

If you've been on the Web for more than just a few minutes, you've probably heard about HTML. It's so pervasive that it's discussed frequently on television, and not just as an answer in a quiz show! Story lines in comedies include characters having their own Web sites. You hear "www-dot-something-dot-com" in nearly every radio advertisement. HTML is showing up in résumés outside the realm of tech workers—it's become mainstream. But you know that the Web is continuing to grow: XML, the Extensible Markup Language, is the buzzword in the halls of business today. XHTML, the Extensible Hypertext Markup Language, bridges the two worlds: HTML to XML.

What's the *By Example* Advantage?

There are two distinct advantages in learning XHTML when it's done *By Example*. First, by completing the examples as you read through each chapter, the concepts are reinforced for you immediately; much more so than just reading about a technique.

Second, with the XHTML examples that will be available for download from the Web, *XHTML by Example* gives you a great position on the cutting edge of Web development, all while allowing you to practice your new skills on today's sites. How? As you work through the examples, you can edit them to suit your immediate needs, letting you have up a working XHTML-based Web site in minutes!

Who Should Use This Book?

Most readers of this book will have some experience in writing HTML Web pages. The root of many concepts presented in Part I, "Learning XHTML," will be familiar to you through your work in HTML. You'll gain a reinforcement of your current knowledge, along with the expanded skills that come with the extension into XHTML.

Even if you've only dabbled in HTML, *XHTML by Example* provides sufficient information for you to begin your learning right here.

For all readers, you'll tour the exciting new efforts underway at the W3C that will enhance interoperability between devices, markup languages, and the custom needs of businesses, vertical markets, and public interest groups.

Why Should You Learn XHTML?

The World Wide Web has continued its record-breaking growth, and has become an integral part of modern life. On the job, it's not just programmers or technical staff that are producing Web sites: marketing personnel, administrative assistants, teachers, managers—almost any job imaginable—also can be responsible for a segment of the company Web site. Outside the workplace, families and friends stay connected through the Web. We store our calendars and address books online, make travel arrangements, buy tickets to entertainment venues, and do our Christmas shopping online. Knowing how to create and maintain these pages allows you to keep pace on the job and at home—with very little effort!

By working with XHTML in creating these Web pages, you'll be fully poised to integrate the XML-based documents and data stores that your company is developing or that your bank, creditors, or correspondents are using to streamline business processes.

What Tools Do You Need?

The only tools you'll need—besides your computer of course—is your favorite text editor and a Web browser. No special software is required to write XHTML. Windows users can use Notepad, Macs come with SimpleText, and many Unix users will be familiar with VI or Emacs. You can certainly use a more advanced editor, such as TextPad, Programmer's File Editor (PFE), or even specialized tools such as HomeSite, but nothing more than a basic editor is required.

XHTML is new enough that the visual Web tools haven't yet caught up. When they do, you might want to experiment with them. By that time, you'll have a solid grasp on creating XHTML by example, and will be able to evaluate the effectiveness of these tools.

As I mentioned previously, you will need a Web browser package or two for viewing and critiquing your own documents. I strongly recommend having both Microsoft Internet Explorer and Netscape Navigator available, as well as an "alternative" browser or two such as Opera or Lynx. You won't necessarily need an Internet connection while working through this book, but having one will allow you to visit the sites mentioned throughout the text and to download the sample code that will be available on the publisher's Web site. To get there, browse to `http://www.mcp.com/detail.cfm?item=0789723859`.

How This Book Works

Each chapter in this book begins by explaining a particular concept, giving examples in short sections of XHTML markup as you go along. After you've mastered the concept, you'll be ready to work with a full-fledged example. I encourage you to type in each of the examples, as the act of creation will reinforce the concepts that you've just read. Some of the examples also will suggest that you modify the text to make it more suitable for your personal use. When you're done, you can test and view the documents in your Web browser.

The key to the organization of this book is simple: It's progressive. You'll start out simply, by going over the fundamental concepts of XHTML and creating basic pages. From there, you'll begin working with XML concepts such as DTDs, schemas, and XML-based style sheets, and move on to the projects still being discussed at the W3C: modularization, document and device profiles, and more.

Overview of Chapters

This book is divided into logical parts and chapters to help you find the lessons that are most appropriate to your knowledge level. What follows is a description of each part of this book, including a look at each chapter.

Part I: Learning XHTML

Chapter 1, "XHTML Fundamentals," reviews the basic concepts involved in all XHTML documents. Chapter 2, "Adding Semantics to Structure," discusses the meaning that can be attached to structural elements through their use and presentation. Chapter 3, "Working with Images," walks you through the process of incorporating these popular features in your XHTML documents. Chapter 4, "Collecting Data with Forms," takes a close look at the process of retrieving input from your users. Chapter 5, "Working with Tables," guides you through the ins and outs of tabular content. Chapter 6, "Using Frames," highlights the features and cautions necessary when working with framed content. Chapter 7, "Universal Accessibility on the Web," discusses the concepts of universal design that allow access to content by those with physical limitations, as well as those browsing from devices with limited capabilities. Chapter 8, "Validating XHTML Documents," introduces you to the tools available to check the accuracy of your work, and finally Chapter 9, "Implementing XHTML Today," takes a look at how XHTML might be used in current browsers and on today's Web with very little effort!

Part II: XHTML Style and Structure

Chapter 10, "XHTML as the Bridge to XML," begins with an overview of the freedom that XML brings to markup and how you can begin to use it with XHTML. Chapter 11, "Using Cascading Style Sheets with XHTML," covers a quick review of CSS, and how it's integrated with XHTML. Chapter 12, "XSL—Style the XML Way," discusses XSL, the Extensible Stylesheet Language.

Chapter 13, "Document Type Definitions—The Syntax Rulebook," introduces you to the world of DTDs, where you define and use your own elements and attributes.

Part III: Modularization

Chapter 14, "XHTML Modularization," begins our look at the current work at the W3C, and the concepts that make XHTML so powerful: the ability to combine vocabularies. Chapter 15, "Creating a Custom XHTML Module," guides you through the process of defining your own elements and attributes that will be combined with the standard XHTML modules. Chapter 16, "Combining Custom Modules with XHTML," teaches you how to bind these modules together and use them as a new document type.

Part IV: The Future of XHTML

Chapter 17, "Subsetting XHTML: XHTML Basic," reviews an existing use-case for a subset of XHTML capabilities: the XHTML Basic DTD. Chapter 18, "XHTML Document Profiling," explores how authors can describe their documents in meaningful ways, to be cached, processed, or transformed according to the needs of various devices. Finally, Chapter 19, "Next Steps for XHTML," looks inside the plans of the broadcast community for incorporating XHTML in the broadcast stream, and ideas for embedding broadcast media on the Web itself.

Conventions Used in This Book

This books uses the following typeface conventions:

Typeface	Meaning
Italic	Variables in "pseudocode" examples and HTML terms used the first time
Bold	Text you type in
`Computer type`	Commands, filenames, and HTML tags, as well as URLs and addresses of Internet sites, newsgroups, mailing lists, and Web sites

NOTE

Notes provide additional information related to a particular topic.

TIP

Tips provide quick and helpful information to assist you along the way.

The Other Advantage

In writing computer-oriented books, I've invested not only a significant amount of time and effort, but also a sincere hope that you, the reader, find the information here to be accurate, valuable, and helpful. But if I don't hear from you, it's difficult for me to know whether these goals were met. Therefore, I want you to let me know how I did by sending me email. I will take any question, concern, praise, or complaint you have about this book and its examples, errors, or anything else that comes up. I'll do my best to provide the correct answer or refer you to a place where you can find the information you need, or someone to ask who might have more experience in the given topic than I do. Please write to me at xhtml@webgeek.com.

It is very important to me that you are satisfied with everything you come across in this book. If you get through a chapter and are still having trouble with a concept, take a peek at the Web site I'll be maintaining for this book, to see if someone else has encountered the same problem. Updated bits of errata, and anything else related to questions and problems readers have had, will be posted there. You can find it at http://www.webgeek.com/books/xhtmlbyexample/. The most important thing to remember is that I don't want you wasting time on an error or on a concept that I might have explained poorly. So do look there or email me before you spend too much time hitting yourself over the head.

If you've created something that you're particularly proud of, drop me a line about that, too! I love to hear about my readers' success stories.

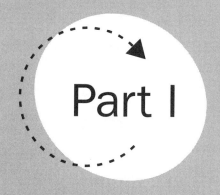

Learning XHTML

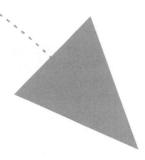

XHTML Fundamentals

At first glance, XHTML documents are very similar to HTML documents. Much of what has changed is in the background. Instead of being based on SGML (the Standard Generalized Markup Language) as HTML is, XHTML is an application of XML, the Extensible Markup Language. Because of this, several fundamental changes have been made to the way you write XHTML content as compared to how you would author content in HTML.

The W3C was actually quite concerned about the transition that needed to take place between HTML and XML. In May of 1998 they held a public workshop on the topic near San Francisco, California. During the two-day event, Web developers, software vendors, and authors of both the HTML and XML recommendations discussed how HTML could be brought into the XML world while minimizing the learning curve. The solution suggested was a transitional language that would provide a "bridge" between HTML and XML. That language is what we now know as XHTML.

XTHML conforms to the XML concept of well-formedness, which restricts the author to a complete and ordered syntax. This really isn't anything new that wasn't in HTML, just that this time it's being enforced where completeness was at times optional before. In addition to well-formedness, XML also introduces several new attributes that appear on elements in the document head section. We'll explore each of those and get a quick overview of the structural concepts for all XHTML documents.

This chapter teaches you:

- The three document types in XHTML 1.0
- XML namespaces
- How to handle language defaults
- How to add meta information
- The differences between block-level and inline elements

XHTML Document Well-Formedness and Validity

The primary requirement of XHTML documents, as with any XML-based document, is that they be well-formed. *Well-formedness* means that all elements are written using proper syntax, they are closed where they should be, attribute values are always in quotes, and so on. Validity, which is a requirement of XHTML documents but an optional state for XML documents, requires that the syntax used in XHTML documents also conform to the document type definitions (DTDs) for those documents. You can't have elements nested within each other if the DTD prohibits it, attribute values must conform to the specified range of values, and the document must conform to any other restrictions set out in the DTD.

XHTML has three different DTDs that you might use. Which one is appropriate for your needs will depend on the answers to several questions you will explore throughout the rest of this chapter.

Choosing an XHTML Document Type

Before you can begin creating an XHTML document, or an HTML 4 document for that matter, you must choose which "flavor" of XHTML you will be using. To help you decide, consider the following questions:

- Will your document use frames? If so, you must use the XHTML 1.0 Frameset DTD.

- Do you intend to use CSS or another form of style sheet (such as XSL) for your presentational information? If so, you can use XHTML 1.0 Strict if you place all of your presentational information in the style sheet. Use XHTML 1.0 Transitional if you'll be mixing presentational elements, attributes, and style sheets.

- Do you require the ability to use elements that have an intrinsic style component, such as the <i> tag for italics (versus the <em> tag for emphasis), and you cannot use style sheets to provide that instruction? If so, you must use XHTML 1.0 Transitional.

EXAMPLE

The answers to these questions can lead you through a decision tree that might look like the diagram in Figure 1.1.

These basic questions can point you in the right direction. Let's take a closer look at each of the three document types, so that your decisions will indeed be the correct ones.

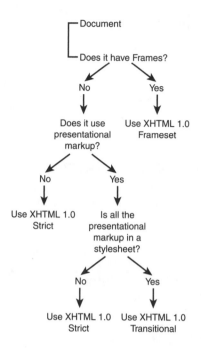

Figure 1.1: You can use this decision tree to determine the proper XHTML document type for your needs.

XHTML 1.0 Strict

As with its cousin, the strict version of HTML 4.0, XHTML 1.0 Strict documents contain no fully presentational information. If it has to do with style, look, and display, the instructions are instead given to the browser through a style sheet. Presentation can be as simple as a color choice for text or headings or the alignment of images. Beyond those options, the prescription of font faces, styles, and sizes, and the visual aspects of tables—such as the thickness of the border, cell padding, and spacing—are all considered "presentational." All of these features are removed from the language, meaning there aren't elements or attributes that govern those decisions any longer. Those instructors are instead provided to the browser via the style sheet.

EXAMPLE

The following memo has several instances where words and phrases need to be offset from the rest of the text. In the headers, the To:, From:, and Re: fields are traditionally boldface. Elsewhere, when citing the name of a magazine publication, the name is italicized.

If it were written on a word processor, you'd see it like this:

Memorandum

To: Joe Cline

From: Marshall Jansen

Re: *Business Week* article

Joe,

Attached is a copy of a recent *Business Week* article focusing on the success of e-commerce in our industry, with a mention of our award-winning Web site! Please circulate among your staff.

Best,

Marshall

In XHTML, you mark this up as shown in Listing 1.1, and the result is the memo shown in Figure 1.2.

Listing 1.1: `memo.html`

```
<!DOCTYPE HTML PUBLIC "-//W3C//DTD XHTML 1.0//EN">
<html>
<head>
<title>Memo - Business Week</title>
</head>
<body>
<h1>Memorandum</h1>
<p><b>To:</b> - Joe Cline<br>
<b>From:</b> - Marshall Jansen<br>
<b>Re:</b> - <i>Business Week</i> article</p>

<p>Joe,</p>
<p>Attached is a copy of a recent <i>Business Week</i> article focusing on the
success of e-commerce in our industry, with a mention of our award winning Web
site! Please circulate amongst your staff.</p>

<p>Best,<br>
Marshall</p>

</body>
</html>
```

OUTPUT

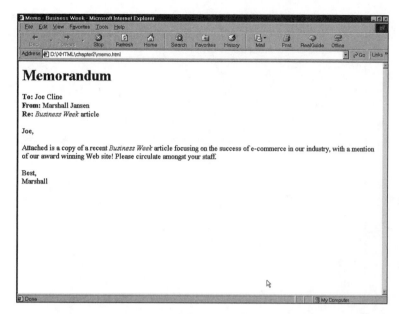

Figure 1.2: *This memo has markup that includes bold and italics tags.*

NOTE

You might have noticed that the filename in Listing 1.1 is memo.html. XHTML has not defined its own MIME-type, and retains the document naming conventions of HTML. Therefore, XHTML documents will have the .html file extension.

This sample uses the presentational tags <i> and <b> to produce the italic and boldface effects. However, remember that, with XHTML 1.0 Strict, presentation isn't allowed in the elements or attributes. We can change this passage to be compliant with Strict (as shown in Figure 1.3) by replacing <i> and <b> with <em> and <strong>, respectively:

```
<p><strong>To:</strong> - Joe Cline<br>
<strong>From:</strong> - Marshall Jansen<br>
<strong>Re:</strong> - <em>Business Week</em> article</p>
<p>Joe,</p>
<p>Attached is a copy of a recent <em>Business Week</em> article focusing on the
success of e-commerce in our industry, with a mention of our award winning Web
site! Please circulate amongst your staff.</p>
```

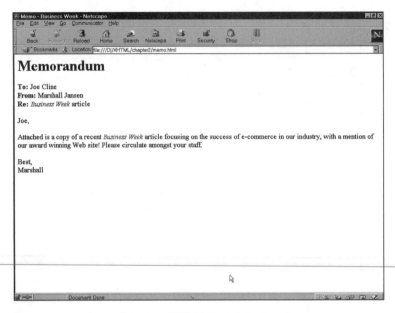

Figure 1.3: *A conforming XHTML 1.0 Strict document uses emphasis and strong emphasis rather than bold and italic elements.*

Notice in Figures 1.2 and 1.3 that both of these paragraphs look the same in Netscape Navigator. The paragraphs would look the same when viewed in Internet Explorer as well. This is because the browser programmers have adopted the conventional rendering of the emphasis and strong emphasis elements as italic and boldface, respectively.

I say traditional rendering here, in that the XHTML specification doesn't require that those elements be presented in italic or boldface. Instead, it only requires that they be given some form of emphasis that is distinct from the main body of text and from each other. So a user agent—that is, the browser or other display software—could render emphasis as purple text, or a bigger font size, or a combination of both and still be compliant with the specifications.

XHTML 1.0 Transitional

The idea of a "Transitional" doctype first appeared in HTML 4. The idea was to alert developers to the fact that the presentational elements and attributes found within it were being deprecated. *Deprecated* means that the usage has fallen officially out of favor, and that there is (usually) a different preferred method of obtaining the same result.

Though deprecated, these presentational elements and attributes are still fully compliant within the Transitional doctype. A presentational attribute handles things like color, alignment, width, and size. Consider this one line:

```
<p align=center>This would render centered in the browser</p>
```

The paragraph element is structural, as we've discussed previously. The `align` attribute, however, gives rendering instructions, and is therefore presentational. In a Transitional document, this construct is perfectly legal. If this were a Strict document, the alignment instructions would be relegated to the style sheet.

XHTML 1.0 Frameset

The Frameset document type is only used when frames are a part of the document set structure. Frameset begins with the Transitional document type, and adds the frameset, frame, and noframes elements, and associated attributes such as target.

NOTE

Only the documents that actually have the frame structure take the Frameset doctype. Other target documents can use Transitional or Strict.

Meta Information—The Document Head

Some of the most important information in your XHTML documents will be included before you begin to create what we traditionally think of as the "content." This section is made up of at least five components: the DOCTYPE declaration, and the `html`, `head`, `title`, and `meta` elements. Each of these tags provides a discrete piece of information about your document, and as such, is often referred to as *metadata*. Defined simply, metadata is data (information) about data. So metadata in your XHTML documents will be information about your document.

Of the five tags that provide meta information, four of them are required in all XHTML documents. The first required element in any XHTML document is the DOCTYPE declaration. As we discussed earlier, the doctype declares which version of XHTML 1.0 your document is based upon.

The Doctype Declaration

One of the three following DOCTYPE declarations must be used:

```
<!DOCTYPE html PUBLIC "-//W3C//DTD XHTML 1.0 Strict//EN"
    "http://www.w3.org/TR/xhtml1/DTD/xhtml1-strict.dtd"

    <!DOCTYPE html PUBLIC "-//W3C/DTD XHTML 1.0 Transitional//EN"

    "http://www.w3.org/TR/xhtml1/DTD/xhtml1-transitional.dtd">
<!DOCTYPE html PUBLIC "-//W3C/DTD XHTML 1.0 Frameset//EN"
    "http://www.w3.org/TR/xhtml1/DTD/xhtml1-frameset.dtd">
```

The DOCTYPE declaration can be broken down thusly: The tag is opened with the string <!DOCTYPE. Next is the root element for this document type, in our case, html (note that html here is in lowercase). PUBLIC declares that the next portion is a public identifier for this document type, rather than a local name, which would be noted using the SYSTEM keyword. For example, when working with the Transitional DOCTYPE declaration, the string "-//W3C/DTD XHTML 1.0 Transitional//EN" is known as the *formal public identifier*, or FPI. Each version has its own FPI, as does any XML-based language. Finally, the URI provided is the location of the document type definition file.

CAUTION

The DOCTYPE declaration is unique in XHTML in that it has mixed-case components. Doctypes must be written exactly as they are shown here—capitalization, spacing, punctuation, and all. The browser or parser's ability to recognize them (and act upon them appropriately) depends on it.

THE ROOT ELEMENT

Following the DOCTYPE declaration will always be the *root element* of your document—for us, the HTML element. This is the element within which all other elements are contained. You could think of it as the filing cabinet in which all folders and papers are held, or the suitcase in which all of your clothing and other travel necessities are stored.

NOTE

You might wonder why the root element for XHTML documents isn't xhtml, versus html. To find the answer, consider what the abbreviation XHTML stands for: the Extensible Hypertext Markup Language. Although XHTML is extensible, it's still a hypertext markup language, and for that reason, uses html as its root element.

XHTML diverges from HTML at this point, adding several attributes to the root element that you might not have seen before. These include an XML namespace, the XML language attribute, and the language attribute. These XML-based attributes are important in providing the additional detail required that allows XHTML to act as that bridge between HTML and XML that I described previously.

THE NAMESPACE

When the W3C Working Group responsible for creating the "Namespaces in XML" recommendation did so, they were likely unaware of the firestorm they were about to unleash on the development community. For a concept with such a seemingly simple definition, the debates about what it truly means have been both staggering and unending.

Put very simply, an *XML namespace* is an abstract collection of names that are used as element types and attribute names in XML documents.

To visualize this, you might think of the English alphabet. The English alphabet namespace has as members each letter (element type). The namespace is not the written list, but the collection of those letter names.

The namespace is identified by a *URI* (Uniform Resource Identifier). This was probably an unfortunate choice on the part of the Working Group, in that the use of a URI leads many people to believe that a file defining the members of the namespace will be found if they follow the URI—not necessarily so. A URI was chosen because it's unique, and universally applicable to the Internet. Nothing else should be implied or inferred by the identifier being a URI.

We'll look at namespaces in much more detail in Part II, "XHTML Style and Structure." For our purposes here, it's important to know that the XHTML namespace is identified with the URI

`http://www.w3.org/1999/xhtml`

and when expressed as the full XML namespace attribute, it is written as

`xmlns="http://www.w3.org/1999/xhtml"`

> ✔ For more on namespaces and how they impact XHTML documents, see "The Freedom of XML—Defining It All Yourself," p. 176.

xml:lang AND lang

The two *language attributes* hold the same information: an identifier for which language is used when writing the document. The first version, the `xml:lang` attribute, is the XML-conforming attribute that identifies the primary natural language that the document is written in. XHTML 1.0 also includes the HTML-based `lang` attribute for backward compatibility. If you include these attributes, you should use both for full interoperability. Although the attributes are optional for the same reason—interoperability—that you'd use both if either were present, a good argument can be made for never leaving them out. It's a small consideration toward broader acceptance and usability of your documents.

The value of the `xml:lang` and `lang` attributes are two-letter language codes. The code "en" refers to English, "fr" to French, and so on. A list of country codes can be found online at `http://www.ics.uci.edu/pub/websoft/wwwstat/country-codes.txt`. Do note, of course, that not all country codes correspond to a language code for purposes of the `lang` attribute when a country doesn't have its own unique language.

Finally, then, we have a complete opening tag for the root element of any of our XHTML documents:

```
<html xmlns="http://www.w3.org/1999/xhtml" xml:lang="en" lang="en">
```

Head, Title, and Meta Tags

Immediately after the root element is the head element. This will contain the title element and any content that will be stored in meta tags.

The title element is required of all documents. Authors should choose their document titles carefully. As with a book title, the document title should convey the contents at a glance, without resorting to lengthy sentences or the use of keywords. If this book were to be published as an XHTML document, the title would likely appear as

```
<title>XHTML by Example</title>
```

Next within the head content are any required meta elements. Meta is used to hold descriptive information about the document itself. Quite often you'll see author credit, creation date, copyright information, and other details that you might normally see in the front matter of a book, or in the masthead area of a magazine.

The meta tag has two primary attributes, name and content:

```
<meta name="author" content="Ann Navarro">
```

The value of the name attribute can be any string of characters, provided that there are no spaces. That would mean

```
name="author-name"
```

is valid, whereas

```
name="author name"
```

is not.

The content attribute, on the other hand, doesn't have that restriction, so phrases like my name, a list of comma-delimited values, and other entries are all possible values.

EXAMPLE

A full head element for this book, then, might read:

```
<head>
<title>XHTML by Example</title>
<meta name="author" content="Ann Navarro"></meta>
<meta name="publisher" content="Que"></meta>
<meta name="ISBN" content=">>0789723859<<"></meta>
</head>
```

Now you're ready to move into the actual document content.

TIP

Many document authors find it useful to practice version control within meta tags. Document version numbers, publication dates, and other authoring notes can be stored in these elements for reference by future editors.

Building Blocks of XHTML Documents

All XHTML elements fall into two categories: *block-level* elements and *inline* elements. Both types of elements look the same: They have opening tags, content, and closing tags. What's different is what is allowed to occur within that enclosed content.

Block-Level Elements

Think of block-level elements as the large concrete blocks used to build a house or other building. They provide the main structure of the document, where the inline elements provide the finishing details.

The definition of what can or can't be included within an element is known as the *content model*. The content model for each element is defined in the *document type definition*, or DTD. That is the document that is referenced by the URI in the doctype declaration. It has, in rather cryptic notation similar to the notation used to describe computer languages known as Extended Backus-Naur Form, the required syntax of all XHTML elements, attributes, and character entities.

The declaration for the body element in the XHTML 1.0 Strict DTD is seen here:

```
<!ELEMENT body %Block;>
```

This says that body is the name of the element, and it can contain what is defined in the parameter entity Block. Looking further to the definition of Block we find

```
<!ENTITY % Block "(%block; | form | %misc;)*">
```

This says that the entity Block is defined as a choice of the elements in the block entity (lowercase, differentiating it from Block), the form element, or the elements defined in the misc entity.

The block entity is defined as

```
<!ENTITY % block
     "p | %heading; | div | %lists; | %blocktext; | fieldset | table">
```

which is a choice of p, the elements in heading, div, the elements in lists and blocktext, the fieldset element, or table.

You can see that the formal description of content models can quickly become complex. For the most part, you won't need to worry about mentally parsing these formal definitions. There are tools available to you, such as the validator discussed in Chapter 8, "Validating XHTML Documents," that will help check the compliance of your document to the DTD.

Although not all do, block-level elements are the only elements that also might contain other block-level elements. In addition, they all might contain inline elements and character data.

Inline Elements

Inline elements are those that can only contain other inline elements or character data. They can never contain block-level elements. For instance, the emphasis element is an inline element. It can contain character data (the text contained within the start and end tags) and other elements, such as strong emphasis.

EXAMPLE

It's not uncommon to see text that has been both italicized and presented in boldface. To accomplish this, two inline elements are nested. You can wrap the magazine name in our previous memo within the strong element to increase its emphasis:

```
<p>Attached is a copy of a recent <strong><em>Business Week</em></strong>
article focusing on the success of e-commerce in our industry, with a mention
of our award winning Web site! Please circulate among your staff.</p>
```

The output seen in Figure 1.4 shows both emphasis styles applied to the data within those tags.

OUTPUT

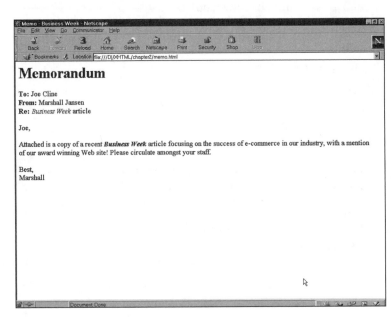

Figure 1.4: *This document uses nested inline elements: boldface and italic.*

It doesn't matter in which order most elements are nested, but once nested, they must be closed in descending order. In the previous example, the <strong> tag came first, then the <em> tag. Therefore the </em> tag must be the first closing tag, as it completes the innermost tag, then the outer </strong> tag is closed. If they are closed in improper order, the document is not well-formed.

What's Next

In this chapter, you've learned about the basic structure of an XHTML document. Each document must follow one of three document types, the choice of which is based on the type of content the document will contain.

Every XHTML document must contain at least four out of five elements before any visible content is included. These elements include the doctype declaration, root, head, and title elements. Meta tags are optional, though are contained within the head element when present.

Block-level elements are those that can, at times, contain other block-level elements, and can always contain inline elements and data. Block-level elements tend to make up the larger structures of the document. Inline elements may only contain other inline elements and data. They tend to provide the finishing touches or minor details in the overall structure of the document.

In Chapter 2, "Adding Semantics to Structure," we'll talk about adding semantics to the structure of your document. You'll learn how to provide meaning in your organization by choosing the proper heading levels, organizing data using lists, and emphasizing important content.

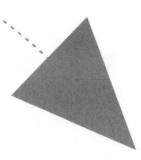

Adding Semantics to Structure

In the first chapter you spent a considerable amount of time learning about the structure of HTML, XHTML, and your documents. The purpose of this was more than just to provide you with a nice visual of building blocks, or nesting Tupperware containers. Instead, we've been leading up to the discussion in this chapter. In this chapter, you learn how the structural components of XHTML differ from each other, why those distinctions are important, and what the characteristics of each component are meant to tell us.

This chapter teaches you:

- How semantics define XHTML behavior

- Document organization using headings

- How to order and group data using lists

- How to emphasize data using structure

The Semantics of Semantics

One of the biggest difficulties Web designers can face when moving from HTML into the world of XML is getting behind the idea that elements, in and of themselves, have no *semantics*. Semantics are the collection of facts that are universally understood about a given object, especially those facts that pertain to its appearance.

For instance, the piece of furniture in your home known as a table is a structure with a flat, horizontal surface supported some distance from the floor by several supports known as legs. A table in the United States is going to be functionally equivalent to a table that is found in Kenya, Nepal, or Chile. The *semantics* of the table are the same.

Bringing this concept back into XHTML, everyone knows that a paragraph is a single block of text, separated visually from other blocks of text. In this book, the paragraphs are presented with a blank line before and after the block of text.

The paragraph element <p> carries with it the same semantics—the tag acts as a container for the text being presented.

Most elements in XHTML have semantics defined either by the XHTML Recommendation or by the earlier HTML Recommendations on which it is based.

Organizing Documents with Headings

One of the most abused elements in HTML is the heading. I believe this is more a function of easy desktop publishing methods than any real intent to abuse the structure of a document. Many authors simply don't realize what headings are intended to represent!

Headings are intended to denote structural divisions within a document. These divisions coincide with what you'd see on an outline: major headings, subheadings, and sub-subheadings, and so on.

Take a look at the table of contents for this book. It is organized in a rather basic outline fashion. Chapter numbers indicate the major headings, with subheadings indented for each level that is drilled down. For instance, the entry for Chapter 1, "XHTML Fundamentals," looks like this:

<confirm Chapter 1 TOC entry, copy here as seen in real TOC, then plug into below>

That could be converted to a more standard outline form using the following notation:

I. From HTML to XHTML

   A.

   B.

   C.

EXAMPLE

If we were to take Chapter 1 in its entirety and publish it as an XHTML page, we'd want to convey the same *structure* to the data as is shown in the table of contents. To do that, we'd use XHTML headings, beginning with the level 1 heading, <h1>:

```
<h1>From HTML to XHTML</h1>
…content…
<h2>First C Heading</h2>
…content…
etc…
```

Many HTML authors are tempted to choose their heading levels by the size or appearance of the text when it's rendered by the browser. As I've often repeated in these first chapters, avoid the temptation to do so, as it removes the structural information from the document and applies presentational semantics to elements that weren't meant to have them.

Grouping and Ordering Data with Lists

At times, semantics are attached to data that has specific structural groupings. For instance, my family structure can be represented as

- Dave
- Ann
- Linda

This structure doesn't require specific ordering, but it does depend on having a collection of individual data points that form a group. Data points within groups, then, are generally presented in list format, be that delimited by bullet points, numbers, letters, commas, spaces, or any other identifiable character or presentation.

EXAMPLE

It's important to remember here that a list has *both* semantics and structure. A list is not just about its delimiting characters. Its functionality is defined by both the bounding of the data into a group (the structure), and then by the presentation of the individual units within the group (the semantics).

In XHTML, we have the same three major list types as found in HTML 4: unordered lists, ordered lists, and definition lists.

Unordered Lists

An unordered list is a representation of a data collection where the individual members have no relative rank or position. For instance, the coins in my wallet have no specific order to them, and they could be described using an unordered list. My coins include five quarters, two dimes, a nickel, and seven pennies.

The basic unordered list syntax remains as

```
<ul>
<li>five quarters</li>
<li>two dimes</li>
<li>a nickel</li>
<li>seven pennies</li>
</ul>
```

Notice that in this example, each of the opening list item tags has a corresponding closing tag, meeting the well-formedness requirement of XHTML.

The only rendering action required of the XHTML-compliant browser is that the list items be delimited in an unordered manner. The most traditional rendering is to use a solid bullet point (disc), as shown in Figure 2.1.

CHANGING LIST ITEM DELIMITERS

When working with the Transitional or Frameset document types, document authors have the additional freedom to select presentation instructions for delimiters using the type attribute. Table 2.1 shows possible values for type.

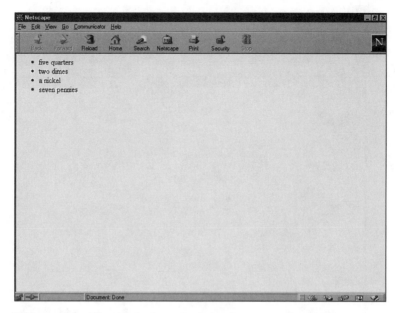

Figure 2.1: *The typical rendering of an unordered list uses solid discs.*

Table 2.1: Available Bullet Types for Unordered Lists

Attribute Value	Representation
Default (unstated type)	A filled circle
Square	A small filled square
Circle	An unfilled circle
Disc	A filled circle

EXAMPLE

The following example makes use of the default, circle, and square delimiter types:

```
<body>
<p>Default list</p>
<ul>
<li>item one</li>
<li>item two</li>
</ul>
<p>List Two - Circles</p>
<ul type="circle">
<li>item one</li>
<li>item two</li>
</ul>
<p>List Three - Squares</p>
<ul type="square">
<li>item one</li>
<li>item two</li>
</ul>
</body>
```

Figure 2.2 shows the results.

OUTPUT

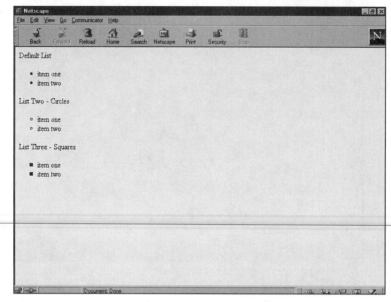

Figure 2.2: *Three different types of unordered lists.*

MAKING YOUR LIST MORE COMPACT

The second attribute available for unordered lists is the `compact` attribute. This attribute is a rendering suggestion to the user agent that essentially minimizes the line height and space between lines when presenting the list.

EXAMPLE

In HTML 4, the `compact` attribute was a Boolean attribute. Boolean attributes were turned on or off simply by their presence or absence. Therefore a `UL` tag written as

```
<ul compact>
```

was functionally equivalent to

```
<ul compact="compact">
```

XHTML does not allow attributes to be expressed using the Boolean syntax due to the necessity of all attributes having values, which is a part of well-formedness. Therefore the second example,

```
<ul compact="compact">
```

is required in XHTML.

Ordered Lists

Ordered lists, contrasted with unordered lists, attach priority and relative position to their members. What that order means isn't directly provided by the semantic of having order. Instead, the surrounding prose will provide appropriate context.

EXAMPLE

For instance, a numbered list could be used to express the members of my family. I could choose to order them as

1. Ann

2. Dave

3. Linda

The meaning of the ordering isn't apparent simply because the list is ordered. The reader could assume that I placed myself in the number one position just as a self-referential starting point. In view of the end result, they could be correct, but only coincidentally. In this case they would not be correct. The fact that I ordered this list by age would only be apparent if I expressed that in my text before or after the list.

TIP

Don't make your readers guess at the internal semantics of your ordered lists. Be sure to identify in the surrounding prose what meaning should be inferred from the ordering of your list. If no meaning should be inferred, change to an unordered list.

The rendering options for ordered lists, as with unordered lists, are set using the type attribute. The potential values for type are shown in Table 2.2.

Table 2.2: Number Sets Used in Ordered Lists

Attribute Value	Representation
1	Arabic numerals (1, 2, 3)
a	lowercase Arabic letters (a, b, c)
A	uppercase Arabic letters (A, B, C)
i	lowercase Roman numerals
I	uppercase Roman numerals

Casting a basic list in an ordered fashion is as simple in XHTML as it was in HTML. If the type attribute is not stated, the default is Arabic numerals. If we were to relist my family in an ordered list using lowercase Roman numerals, I would write:

```
<ol type="i">
<li>Ann</li>
<li>Dave</li>
<li>Linda</li>
</ol>
```

SETTING THE LIST START VALUE

A unique aspect of ordered lists is the starting value used for the list delimiter. By default, the delimiter starts at the beginning of the chosen set, that is the number 1, the letter A, or the Roman numeral I.

However, document authors are free to choose a different starting point. This is accomplished using the start attribute, placed on the OL element.

EXAMPLE

I do much of my banking online. I can request a list of recently cleared checks, which are presented as an ordered list, starting with the first check number I requested. In this situation, the list number should be the check number (see Figure 2.3). In the source, I might see:

```
<ol start="1653">
<li>Publix Supermarket - $52.96</li>
<li>Florida Power and Light - $102.39</li>
<li>Comcast of SW Florida - $59.51</li>
</ol>
```

EXAMPLE

Setting a unique starting point isn't confined to Arabic numerals. The same approach can be taken with any ordered list type. We could recast my list of recent checks using Roman numerals, for a little fun (see Figure 2.4):

```
<ol type="i" start="1653">
<li>Publix Supermarket - $52.96</li>
<li>Florida Power and Light - $102.39</li>
<li>Comcast of SW Florida - $59.51</li>
</ol>
```

Note that although I chose a non-numeric list delimiter in the second example, I still manipulated the start value using a numerical value. Despite the fact that some list representations use letters, they are indeed still a numbering system. Therefore the value of a start attribute can, if only for simplicity's sake, be represented in a single system: the Arabic numerals.

OUTPUT

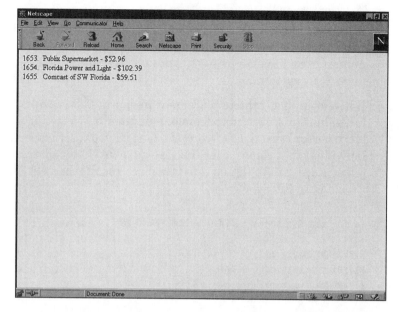

Figure 2.3: *An ordered list with a specified starting number.*

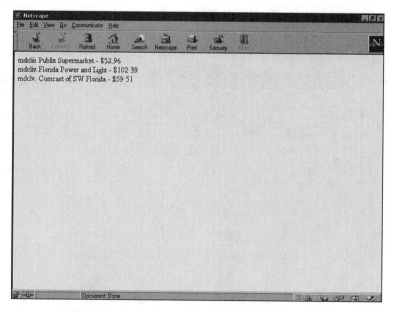

Figure 2.4: *Setting a new starting point using Roman numerals.*

MANIPULATING AN INDIVIDUAL LIST ITEM VALUE

It also is possible to change the numeric value of a list item to something other than the next sequential value. For instance, a list using Arabic numerals could begin using 1, 2, and 3, but you could force the fourth item to be 5 rather than 4.

EXAMPLE

When looking at athlete placement in sports score results, you often see individual rankings jump from one number down two or more when two or more persons are tied in score. To do this, you'd set a specific value on the individual that comes after the tie—such as Nancy and Sue tied for third place. Rather than listing a fourth place result, the next athlete is listed as finishing in fifth place:

```
<body>
<p>Top six finishers in the Ladies 100 meter Freestyle
<ol>
<li>Janet Davis</li>
<li>Stephanie Lindstrom</li>
<li>Nancy Cruz<br>Sue Clayton</li>
<li value="5">Linda Nelson</li>
<li>Suriya Khan</li>
</ol>
```

Figure 2.5 shows the result.

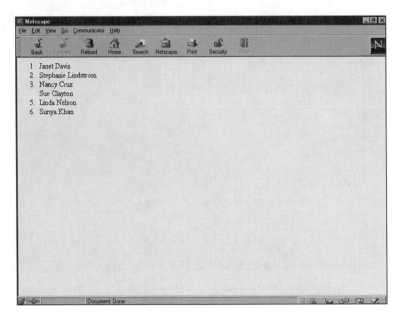

Figure 2.5: *Changing the value of a single list item.*

MIXING LIST TYPES IN NESTED LISTS

Nested ordered lists are frequently used to present information in a traditional outline form. In developing the table of contents for this book, we could retrieve the chapter title and individual section headings, and come up with a list that looks like this:

II. Adding Semantics to Structure

    1. Organizing Documents with Headings

    2. Grouping and Ordering Data with Lists

        A. Unordered Lists

            1. Changing the List Item Delimiter

            2. Compacting Your List

        B. Ordered Lists

            1. Setting the List Start Value

            2. Manipulating an Individual List Item Value

    3. Mixing List Types in Nested Lists

        C. Definition Lists

        1.Nesting Ordered or Unordered Lists within Definition Lists

    3. Emphasizing Important Content

        A. Inline Emphasis

        B. Block-level Emphasis

    4. What's Next?

To produce this in XHTML, we'd need a set of four nested lists.

EXAMPLE

The first list is an uppercase Roman numeral list, containing the chapter numbers and titles. Because we're looking only at Chapter 2, we need to set the start value of this list to 2:

```
<ol type="I" start="2">
<li>Adding Semantics to Structure
```

NOTE

The list item tag has not yet been closed. This is not a violation of the well-formedness requirement; instead this is because a nested list actually occurs within the preceding list item. The list item tag will be closed only after the nested list is closed.

Next is the list of major headings within the chapter. This list uses Arabic numerals, and begins with 1. Because 1 is the default start value, it does not need to be declared. The Arabic numeral choice is also the default for an ordered list, so we don't need to declare that either. The markup will appear as

```
<ol>
<li>Organizing Documents with Headings</li>
<li>Grouping and Ordering Data with Lists
```

Again, we'll be nesting a list within the second list item, "Grouping and Ordering Data with Lists," so this second list item remains unclosed for now.

Next are the lettered items for the chapter subheadings about individual list types:

```
<ol type="A">
<li>Unordered Lists
```

The first list item A has a further subheading, requiring its own one-item list. After this list is closed, we can close the list item for Unordered Lists, so we have

```
<ol>
<li>Changing the List Item Delimiter</li>
<li>Compacting Your List</li>
</ol>
</li>
```

Having closed the list item for Unordered Lists, we're now back within the uppercase Arabic alphabet list. By simply opening a new list item, the list will continue on at the proper value:

```
<li>Ordered Lists
```

A new nested list is now needed for the subheadings under Ordered Lists, so we open and complete a new one here:

```
<ol>
<li>Setting a List Start Value</li>
<li>Manipulating an individual list item value</li>
<li>Mixing list types in nested lists</li>
</ol>
```

The next list item is the third item "C" in the subheading list, "Definition Lists":

```
<li>Definition Lists
<ol>
<li>Nesting Ordered or Unordered Lists within Definition Lists</li>
</ol>
</li>
```

Now that each of the subheadings for "Grouping and Ordering Data with Lists" have been presented, that list item and that nested list can be closed:

```
</ol>
</li>
</ol>
```

One more major heading, for "Emphasizing Important Content":

```
<li>Emphasizing Important Content
<ol>
<li>Inline Emphasis</li>
<li>Block-level Emphasis</li>
</ol>
</li>
```

The final entry, then, is the fourth major heading "What's Next?" after which the main Roman Numeral list, and its sole list item, must be closed:

```
<li>What's Next?</li>
</li>
</ol>
```

The entire sequence then comes together as shown in Listing 2.1. Figure 2.6 shows the result.

Listing 2.1: A Set of Nested Lists

```
<ol type="I" start="2">
<li>Adding Semantics to Structure
<ol>
<li>Organizing Documents with Headings</li>
<li>Grouping and Ordering Data with Lists
<ol type="A">
<li>Unordered Lists
<ol>
<li>Changing the List Item Delimiter</li>
<li>Compacting Your List</li>
</ol>
</li>
<li>Ordered Lists
<ol>
<li>Setting a List Start Value</li>
<li>Manipulating an individual list item value</li>
<li>Mixing list types in nested lists</li>
</ol>
<li>Definition Lists
<ol>
<li>Nesting Ordered or Unordered Lists within Definition Lists</li>
</ol>
</li>
</ol>
<li>Emphasizing Important Content
<ol>
```

Listing 2.1: continued

```
<li>Inline Emphasis</li>
<li>Block-level Emphasis</li>
</ol>
</li>
<li>What's Next?</li>
</li>
</ol>
```

OUTPUT

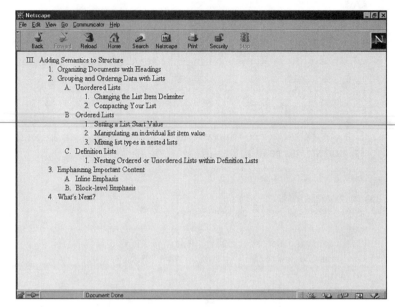

III. Adding Semantics to Structure
  1. Organizing Documents with Headings
  2. Grouping and Ordering Data with Lists
      A. Unordered Lists
          1. Changing the List Item Delimiter
          2. Compacting Your List
      B. Ordered Lists
          1. Setting a List Start Value
          2. Manipulating an individual list item value
          3. Mixing list types in nested lists
      C. Definition Lists
          1. Nesting Ordered or Unordered Lists within Definition Lists
  3. Emphasizing Important Content
      A. Inline Emphasis
      B. Block-level Emphasis
  4. What's Next?

Figure 2.6: A multi-level nested list set.

Definition Lists

Definition lists have a rather unfortunate name, in that they probably aren't used truly for definitions even half of the time they occur in documents. The idea behind them is that you have a term that is highlighted in some manner, and a corresponding definition for that term. Here, we might express that as

> **XHTML**—Extensible Hypertext Markup Language

XHTML doesn't prescribe the presentational aspects of a definition list, so authors can't count on any specific look; more so here than with other list formats. The basic syntax occurs as

```
<dl>
<dt>XHTML</dt>
<dd>Extensible Hypertext Markup Language</dd>
<dt>XML</dt>
```

```
<dd>Extensible Markup Language</dd>
</dl>
```

The results are seen in Figure 2.7.

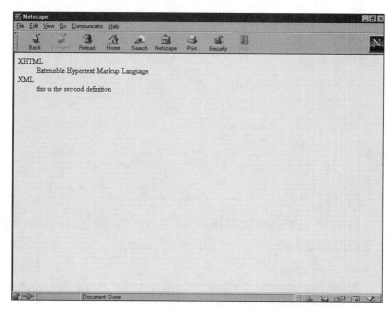

Figure 2.7: *Typical rendering of a definition list.*

NESTING ORDERED OR UNORDERED LISTS WITHIN DEFINITION LISTS

It is possible to nest other list types within a definition list. The means to do so is a little different from the other lists. The rendering of the following example is shown in Figure 2.8:

```
<dl>
<dt>XHTML</dt>
<dd>Extensible Hypertext Markup Language
<ol>
<li>XHTML 1.0 Strict</li>
<li>XHTML 1.0 Transitional</li>
<li>XHTML 1.0 Frameset</li>
</ol>
</dd>
</dl>
```

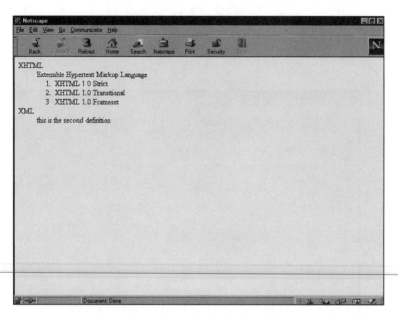

Figure 2.8: *An ordered list nested within a definition list.*

Emphasizing Important Content

Readers are familiar with conventions used to point out portions of text that the author or publisher feels deserve special attention. XHTML provides several methods of demarking such content both inline within larger blocks, and as a distinct block in and of itself.

Inline Emphasis

Two of the most common means of providing emphasis in traditional print media are the use of **boldface** or *italic*. Both of these choices have strict presentational semantics attached to them: the change in font weight and style.

Emphasis in HTML first began with the <em> element for emphasis, and the <strong> element for strong emphasis. By tradition, the major browsers would render <em> as italic and <strong> as boldface. But many developers desired some assurance that with these presentations their intentions wouldn't be tampered with. As a result, the <i> and <b> elements were introduced for italic and boldface, respectively.

However, in XHTML we're again moving away from the presentational aspects of HTML, and retaining the structural markup instead. The <i> and <b> elements are available to you, provided you use the XHTML 1.0 Transitional doctype. They remain deprecated in favor of the structural versions <em> and <strong>. Specific font weights and styles are then handled in CSS or another stylesheet language.

Block-Level Emphasis

At times, document authors will be faced with the need to offset large blocks of text, rather than just a word or phrase within a sentence. XHTML continues to provide the mechanism to do this that you're familiar with in HTML 4, namely with the <blockquote> element.

blockquote is intended to function as its name implies, a specific block of data offset as a quotation. Because blockquote is also a block-level element, you have the freedom to include additional styling at the inline level.

EXAMPLE

Suppose you were writing a term paper about Shakespeare, and wanted to quote a famous passage from *Julius Caesar*. You could do so using the blockquote element:

```
<blockquote>
Remember March, the ides of March remember:
Did not great Julius bleed for justice' sake?
What villain touch'd his body, that did stab,
and not for justice? What, shall one of us
that struck the foremost man of all this world
but for supporting robbers, shall we now
contaminate our fingers with base bribes,
and sell the mighty space of our large honours
for so much trash as may be grasped thus?
I had rather be a dog, and bay the moon,
than such a Roman.
</blockquote>
```

The actual presentation of a block quote passage isn't decreed in the HTML or XHTML specs. Instead, implementation is left to the browser programmer. Tradition has been that the text is indented on both margins (see Figure 2.9). Some browsers might go further and italicize the passage, or provide other font and color changes.

CAUTION

Avoid the temptation to use blockquote to produce the double-sided indent look for general layout purposes. As we discussed, this rendering is not guaranteed by the XHTML specification. The user agent can do anything to offset the text and still conform.

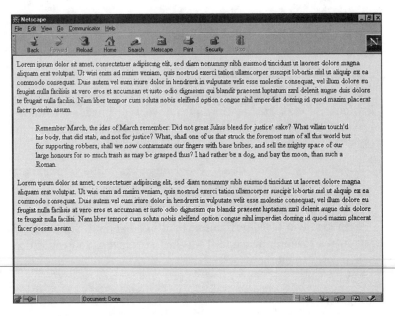

Figure 2.9: *A block quote passage rendered with indented margins between nonsense text.*

What's Next

In this chapter we've examined major structural elements provided by XHTML. You've learned how to properly organize a document using headings and create basic and nested lists that conform to the well-formedness requirements of XHTML, and we've reviewed how to emphasize words, phrases, and entire blocks of text using the appropriate emphasis elements.

Next up in Chapter 3, "Working with Images," you'll bring graphical elements into your documents using images and review the popular means of interacting with your readers—XHTML forms.

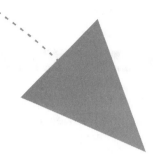

Working with Images

If the average Web user was asked to describe the World Wide Web, he might say "pictures and things on the Internet." Only people introduced to the online world before early 1995 were very familiar with the Net as a text-based medium. Desktop publishing was a major new activity and found many non-artists manipulating digital images for the first time.

Beyond the graphical skills gained in the DTP environment, digital imaging for the Web brings new concerns and constraints. The number of image formats supported by Web browsers is significantly smaller than the number you can work with in MS Publisher, or Framemaker. Additionally, the resolution and color depth available on a computer monitor change the way we see those images compared to the output you'd find in print media.

This chapter teaches you:

- What image formats work online
- Which format works best with what type of graphic
- How to incorporate images into your Web page
- How to create links using images
- How to draw hot spots on images for an interactive map

Image Formats for the Web

For many years only two image formats were supported by Web browsers: GIF and JPEG. Today, a third option, known as PNG, has been added. Each format has its own strengths and weaknesses, which we'll review here, and then we'll take a quick tour of several popular image-editing tools.

GIF Images

The most common format used for non-photographic images is GIF (Graphics Interchange Format). GIF is a *bit-map* image format, meaning that the image is "mapped" pixel by pixel. The information in the bit-map can be compressed when neighboring pixels have the same color values, using what's essentially a form of digital shorthand. This allows the resulting image file to be considerably smaller when stored, saving space on the Web server and bandwidth when the image is delivered to the site visitor.

GIF images do have some limitations, the most notable being the maximum of 256 unique colors within the image. Thankfully, this 256-color palette is not a static set of colors, but might be any 256 colors that work best within the image. This limited, though flexible, palette makes GIF the ideal candidate for graphics with large blocks of color, as often seen in logos, buttons, and banners.

Controversy over the GIF format arose in the early days of the Web, when the company that owned the patent on the LZW compression algorithm used in GIF asserted that it was owed significant licensing rights from any software publisher that produced tools that could publish GIF images. The end creator of an image generally doesn't owe any licensing fees, but in part because of the furor over this issue, the W3C began working on an open-source (royalty-free) image format known as *PNG* (*Portable Network Graphics*). Support for this image format is increasing, but PNG isn't nearly as universally supported as GIF.

NOTE

To learn more about PNG, visit the W3C Web site at http://www.w3.org/Graphics/PNG/. And see the "PNG Images—the Web's Newest Format" section later in this chapter.

JPEG Images

The JPEG format, short for Joint Photographic Experts Group, was specifically designed for digital storage of photographic images. JPEGs (sometimes referred to as JPGs) can use up to 16.7 million colors instead of GIF's relatively paltry 256. The compression algorithm used by JPEG is known as a *lossy* technique, meaning that information is literally thrown away in the process of compressing the data. A low compression rate preserves the highest quality, while a higher compression rate removes more information. With a photograph, this doesn't have much impact on image quality when using a low to moderate compression level, especially when viewed on a computer screen with the monitor's relatively low pixel-per-inch resolution.

PNG Images—The Web's Newest Format

Out of desire both to supplant the need to use image formats with proprietary, and at times costly, compression schemes such as GIF, and demand for enhanced color depth and transparency support, the W3C set out to create a new image format. The result was PNG (Portable Network Graphics).

A lossless format, PNG combines the strengths of GIF and JPEG, and provides sufficient additional features and it holds the best hope for high quality, interoperable images on the Web. Adoption has been a bit slower than many designers had hoped for, primarily due to lack of native support within the major browsers. However, such support arrived with the release of Netscape Navigator 4.5 and Internet Explorer 4, and PNG is rapidly finding its way onto the map.

Web Graphics Editors

Graphics editing tools run the gamut in price from free to well more than $500. It's certainly not necessary to spend that kind of money to produce a good-looking site, though using a free or low-end package might require a bit more effort and raw artistic talent as they'll be unlikely to offer as many features as the more sophisticated programs.

The availability of quality image editors for the Windows platform has grown rapidly over the last two to three years. No longer are PC fans stuck with last-generation software while their Mac counterparts have the cutting edge features in their versions:

- **Microsoft Paint**—This basic editor ships with the Windows operating system. It's limited in file format support (bitmap, GIF, and JPEG only), but is functional for those just getting started or the occasional doodler.

- **JASC Paint Shop Pro**—PSP had its beginnings as shareware. JASC now releases a fully functional 30-day trial that lets users test drive the package before purchasing the $99 retail version. Many Web developers favor PSP for its consistent quality and expanding features at an affordable price (Windows only).

- **Macromedia Fireworks**—Macromedia has made enormous progress in the Web development, animation, and graphics generation market.

Fireworks integrates with the entire Macromedia line of products, making it a natural for those who choose their authoring tools. It is flexible enough, however, to play nice with other publishers' systems, too. Retail price (as this book went to print) was $199.00 (Windows/Mac).

- **Adobe Photoshop**—Long the workhorse of the graphic artist world, Adobe Photoshop remains the favorite among Web developers coming from an art and design background. At a suggested retail price of $609.00, it remains out of reach of many individual developers (Windows/Mac).

Adding Graphics Using the Image Element

The image element in XHTML is considered an *inline* element. This means that it can be contained within block elements such as paragraphs. It also means that the image will quite literally be rendered "in line," right where the tag is placed within the document. The minimal required syntax for the image element includes two attributes: src for the source URL of the image file, and alt for the alternative text used to describe the image:

```
<img src="myphoto.jpg" alt="A photo of the author" />
```

Practically, at least two additional attributes are needed: height and width. These attributes hold the vertical and horizontal measurements of the image, expressed in pixels. When present, these values allow the browser to "reserve" the space required for the image as it renders the rest of the page, which results in the images appearing to "fill in" after the text has been displayed. The end result is a page that gives the appearance of loading faster, which can result in fewer impatient visitors leaving your site before the content can be displayed.

The following example puts a single image inline within a paragraph, with the image space reserved using the height and width attributes (see Figure 3.1):

EXAMPLE

```
<p><img src="fmb.jpg" height="200" width="300" alt="A view of the beach from
the 10th floor landing of my hotel." /> I recently hosted two days of
meetings at the DiamondHead Beach Resort in Fort Myers Beach, Florida.
This is the view of the beach from the 10th floor landing of the hotel.
Another day in paradise - just down the road from my home!</p>
```

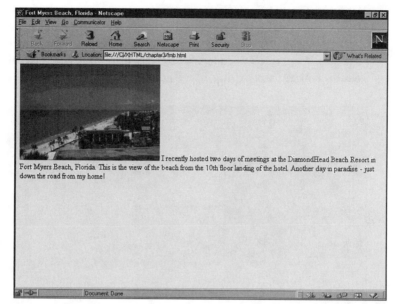

Figure 3.1: *Default inline presentation of an image within a paragraph.*

Notice that the default presentation places the bottom of the image at the baseline of the text line in which it appears. This isn't the most visually pleasing result, but it is proper behavior when an alternative alignment isn't specified.

CAUTION

Avoid the temptation to "resize" an image by setting the height and width values lower than the actual measurements. Although most browsers will attempt to compress the image into the allotted space, the result is never as clean as an actual resampling using a graphics editor—and the user must still wait for the full image to download.

Image and Text Alignment

Two adjustments can be made to the placement of an image within your page: how the image is aligned with respect to the baseline, and where the image sits relative to the entire page. Take another look at Figure 3.1 from the previous example. The bottom edge of the image sits on the baseline, which is the default behavior. Also note that the image sits on the left margin of the page, which is the alignment relative to the page as a whole.

If we change the first alignment aspect, relative to the baseline, three choices are available: top, middle, and bottom. In this case, it's important to remember that the image is considered to be entirely within a single line of text—so if we were to choose align="middle" for this attribute, you'd get results looking something like Figure 3.2.

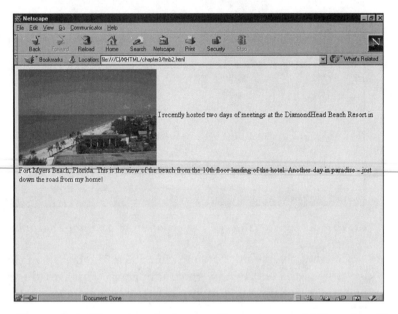

Figure 3.2: *Changing the image alignment to middle only adjusts its position relative to the baseline.*

For smaller images, this might be okay, but with something this large, the placement is awkward to say the least.

What helps in this situation is to align the image relative to the margins using align="left" or align="right". Then, the image is solidly docked at the margin, and the text will flow around it (see Figure 3.3).

Using Images as Links

Creating a graphical navigation system is one of the most popular uses of images on the Web. The links used to get around the site can then be delivered as graphical "buttons" as in the bank home page shown in Figure 3.4, or by using other metaphors like the file folder "tabs" used by the TLC site (see Figure 3.5).

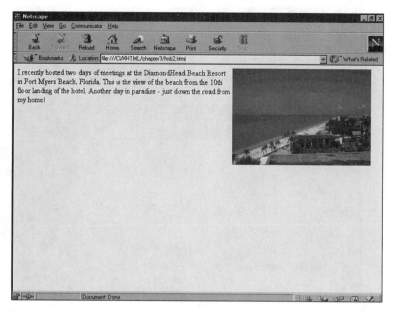

Figure 3.3: *The image is aligned to the right, with the text then flowing around it on the left side.*

Figure 3.4: *This site uses two types of "buttons" to guide users to different functions of the bank.*

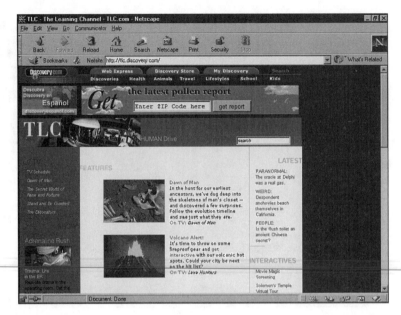

Figure 3.5: *The file folder "tabs" are a popular navigation metaphor.*

EXAMPLE

The process of linking graphics is as simple as linking text; the image element is placed inside the anchor element:

```
<a href="foo.html"><img src="bar.gif" alt="bar" /></a>
```

To simulate a navigation menu, I've created three buttons with the labels "Option 1," "Option 2," and "Option 3."

TIP

These buttons were created using the "buttonize" effect available in Paint Shop Pro 6 (shareware). Most current graphics editors have a similar effect available.

Each button will be placed inside its own anchor, linked to a corresponding option page:

```
<a href="option1.html"><img src="opt1.gif" alt="option 1" width="100"
➥height="60" /></a>
<a href="option2.html"><img src="opt2.gif" alt="option 2" width="100"
➥height="60" /></a>
<a href="option3.html"><img src="opt3.gif" alt="option 3" width="100"
➥height="60" /></a>
```

The initial results, shown in Figure 3.6, have two issues that might need to be addressed: There's a bright blue border around the images, and white-space between each of them.

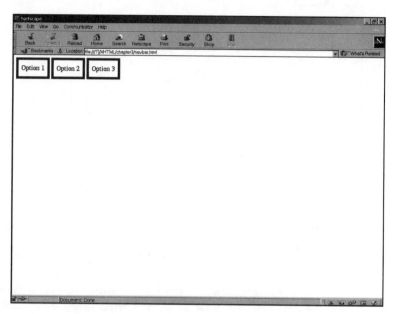

Figure 3.6: *A basic set of linked images.*

The bright blue border is the browser indicating each image is a link, just as text links are colored blue and underlined by most visual browsers. It does tend to interfere with the look of the buttons, though, so it can be removed by adding a border attribute to the image element. Setting the value to "0" (zero) tells the browser to turn the border off:

```
<img src="opt1.gif" alt="option 1" width="100" height="60" border="0" />
```

Next, to address the spacing between images, we can move each of the anchors onto the same line of text in the source HTML document. Browsers properly interpret the new line or carriage return/new line characters that many Windows- or Mac-based text editors produce as white space. Removing those by writing the links on a single line will then remove the white space (see Figure 3.7).

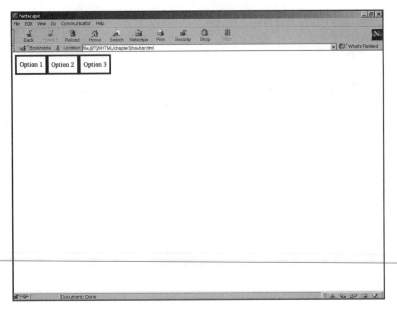

Figure 3.7: *The linked buttons with white space and bordering removed.*

Image Maps

The Web site of one of my favorite public places, the Monterey Bay Aquarium, features three separate image maps on its home page; two traditional "navigation bars," and a third based on a composite collage image (see Figure 3.8). Both versions use the same techniques; the collage image simply lets the designer break out of the grid-like effect that using individual images as links can produce.

The basic idea behind an image map is that specified regions of the image are identified as *hot spots* by mapping their coordinates to a linked URL using the <area> element. The browser captures the exact coordinates of the spot where the user mouse-clicks within the image, and activates the corresponding link.

Hot spots can be drawn in one of four ways:

- **Rect (rectangle)**—Two coordinates are used to draw a rectangle: the upper-left corner and the lower-right corner.

- **Circle**—Three values are used: the x/y coordinates of the circle's center point, and the radius length.

- **Poly (polygon)**—At least two sets of x/y coordinates, with the last set holding the same values as the first, close the polygon.

- **Default**—Not a shape so much as the set of all coordinates on the image that are not otherwise defined in a hotspot.

Figure 3.8: *An image collage used as a navigation map.*

TIP

Although it's possible to create your map definitions by hand, even the most talented Web author will need the assistance of a graphics editor to measure the coordinates of the shapes they intend to utilize. To that end, for day-to-day work, most of us use software that can produce the XHTML code for the map at the same time.

EXAMPLE

Creating an Image Map with CuteMAP

Begin by launching the map editor software. Start a new map definition by choosing File, New Map and locating the image you'll be working on within the Open dialog box. CuteMAP's interface consists of three panes (see Figure 3.9). The image is displayed in the largest pane, with a source view beneath it. To the left is a data pane, where you'll enter the URL, alternative text, and other data associated with each hot spot within the map.

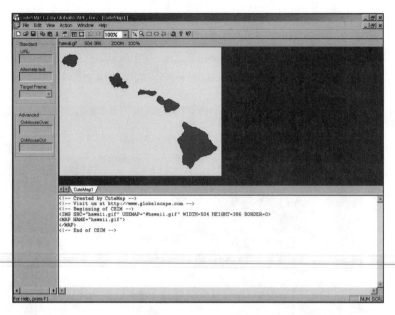

Figure 3.9: *The CuteMAP user interface.*

We'll begin with the island of Kauai, in the upper-left corner of the map. There's plenty of room around it, so a rectangle is both easy and practical here. Select the Rectangle marking tool from the toolbar (see Figure 3.10). The pointer will turn into cross hairs.

Position the pointer where you want the upper-left corner of the rectangle to be. Click and drag down to the lower-right corner of the rectangle, and then release. The area covered by the new hot spot is framed by a red cross-hatch pattern. In the data pane, enter (at a minimum) the URL and alternative text for the link—in this case, kauai.html and Island of Kauai, respectively (see Figure 3.11).

Repeat the process for each of the remaining islands, choosing the shape that fits best around the island, without overlapping with any other shapes. For Oahu, to the right of Kauai, a circle works well. Molokai can take a rectangle, as can Hawaii. Maui, on the other hand, will work best with a polygon, so we can avoid overlapping with the right side of Molokai's spot.

To create the polygon, select the Polygon marking tool. Click once where you want to begin, and again for each corner of the polygon. Notice that once you've placed two points, the polygon changes shapes as you move and place additional corners, rather like a rubber band being stretched around a set of pegs. When you're finished, right-click to indicate the final corner.

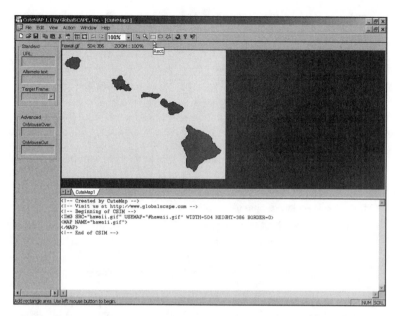

Figure 3.10: *The CuteMAP toolbar.*

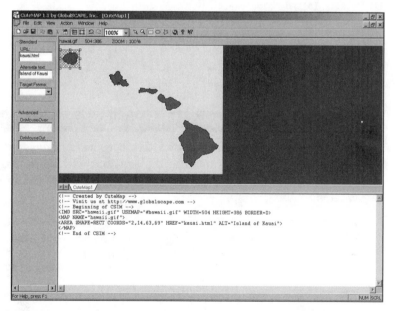

Figure 3.11: *Entering data for the newly created hot spot.*

The corresponding HTML is seen in the code pane, beneath the image. The program allows you to copy the code to the Clipboard for import into your text editor. The end result appears in Listing 3.1.

CAUTION

Most of the image mapping tools available, including CuteMAP, aren't accustomed to the case sensitivity and well-formedness requirements of XHTML. If you import the results directly into your text editor, you'll have some cleaning up to do, as you'll instantly have invalid XHTML due to the case issues. I tend to write the definitions by hand, copying over the coordinates. This situation should improve with the next versions of these tools.

Listing 3.1: An Image Map of the State of Hawaii

```
<img src="hawaii.gif" usemap="#hawaii.gif" width="504" height="386"
    border="0" alt="Image map for the state of Hawaii" />
<map name="hawaii.gif">
<area shape="rect" coords="2,14,66,69" href="kauai.html"
    alt="Island of Kauai" />
<area shape="circle" coords="178,104,43" href="oahu.html"
    alt="Island of Oahu" />
<area shape="rect" coords="238,122,303,147" href="molokai.html"
    alt="Island of Molokai" />
<area shape="poly" coords="297.157.315.138.398,173,336,214"
    href="maui.html" alt="Island of Maui" />
<area shape="rect" coords="354,223,501,374" href="hawaii.html"
    alt="Island of Hawaii" />
</map>
```

What's Next

In this chapter you've learned how to incorporate images into your Web documents, varying alignment and placement within the page. You can create links and maps using images to define visually pleasing navigation systems.

Next, in Chapter 4, "Collecting Data with Forms," you'll learn how to collect data from your site visitors using forms. A basic Perl-based CGI script for processing the form submission is supplied.

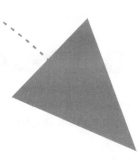

Collecting Data with Forms

As witnessed by today's booming "dot com" economy, nothing has been more vital to the success of the Web as a commercial medium as the ability to collect data from Web site visitors. The sale of information, services, and products of all kinds are contributing to the billions of dollars changing hands each year online; and each transaction begins with a simple form.

Forms combine not just XHTML elements and content, but additional scripts and programmatic actions in order to collect the data from the user and deliver it to the site owner by email, store it on the Web server, or perhaps insert it directly into a database.

This chapter teaches you:

- How to use each of the 10 form controls

- How form content is processed

- How to implement a simple CGI script written in Perl

The Components of Every Form

XHTML provides an array of 10 distinct objects that are known as *controls* used in forms. These are the boxes, buttons, and menus that the user can use to input text, make selections, and click to initiate a programmed action.

Each control has its own unique properties that you'll look at in detail in this section.

The <form> Element

Every form begins with the form element, a block-level element that will contain all form controls, any necessary accompanying data such as labels for the controls, and the location of the script or program that will process the form data. At a minimum, the form element will have two attributes: method and action. A minimal form element might look like this:

```
<form method="post" action="http://www.webgeek.com/cgi-bin/script.cgi">
…form content…
</form>
```

The method attribute takes one of two values: get or post. These values determine how the data collected in your form is sent to the server. You'll learn about the options in more detail in the "Form Processing Options" section later in this chapter. For now, you should know that "post" is the most commonly used method.

The script or program used to actually process the form data is referenced in the action attribute. This value is the full URL for the program or script.

Form Input Controls

There are 10 different types of input controls:

- Text boxes
- Password
- Checkboxes
- Radio buttons
- Select groups
- Text areas
- Hidden controls
- File upload controls

- Buttons

- Image controls

We'll look at each of these later in the chapter. Each of the 10 input control types might use the same collection of attributes. These are defined in Table 4.1.

Table 4.1: Attributes Available for the **Input** *Element*

Attribute	Use
type	Determines which input control will be created.
name	An identifying string that equates to an incoming variable name on the server.
value	Holds the content entered by the user (or preset by the author).
checked	A preselected item (used mostly for radio buttons, checkboxes, or select groups).
Disabled	Makes the control visible, yet not available for input.
Readonly	The user may not change the preselected value.
size	Usually a numeric value, used to determine the visual size of the control.
maxlength	Always a numeric value, sets the maximum number of characters allowed as input.
src	A URI.
alt	Alternative text information.
usemap	A URI for a related image map.
tabindex	A numeric value, sets the order in which the control receives the focus if the user tabs between controls.
accesskey	A single keyboard character that might be used to switch focus to the control.
onfocus, onblur, onselect, onchange	Used for scripting.
accept	Used with the file control, specifies which media types can be accepted.
align	Visual alignment of the control.

Typically you'll use the type and name attributes, and perhaps size and maxlength. As I introduce each form control type, you'll have an opportunity to use the attributes commonly associated with that control.

TEXT BOXES

Probably the most commonly used input control is the *text box* (see Figure 4.1). You see these all the time when asked to enter your name or your email address.

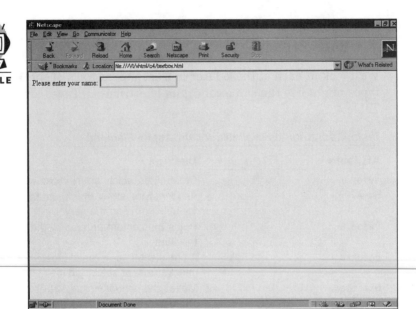

EXAMPLE

Figure 4.1: *This figure shows a simple text box input control.*

Of the attributes available to this element, only type and name are required. For practical use, however, you'll also be using the size attribute, especially when working with multiple inputs, to provide a uniform appearance while at the same time allowing the user to see his or her entire entry in most instances. The text box in Figure 4.1 was created using the following XHTML. Notice that input is an empty element, using the shorthand slash before the closing bracket to complete the tag set:

```
<p>Please enter your name: <input type="text" name="foo" size="20" /></p>
```

With a size of 20, most browsers will make the box as wide as is necessary to fit 20 characters of the default fixed-width font being used. If that's 8-point Courier, the box will be smaller than 20 characters of the text elsewhere in the document if that was done in 14-point Arial Bold.

If you'd like to control the number of characters the user can enter, the maxlength attribute can be added.

PASSWORD CONTROLS

The password control is nearly identical to the text box control. The only functional difference is that users' input is hidden behind a masking character, such as an asterisk (*), as they type. Password entry is the most common need for visual security, but you also can use passwords for credit card number entry or the collection of other sensitive information when the user might not be in a private location, such as at a Web kiosk or cyber café.

Password controls are created using the type value of "password" instead of "text":

```
<input type="password" name="foo" size="20" />
```

CAUTION

Though the user input into the password control is visually masked, the data doesn't receive additional encoding when it's sent for processing with the rest of the form input. Information that needs to be secure during that transmission will need more handling (such as a connection through SSL) than just a password control.

CHECK BOX CONTROLS: CHOOSING MORE THAN ONE OPTION

The check box control is the first of two controls that let you group options together to provide the user with a choice. Using check boxes, the user is allowed to choose zero, one, or more than one option in that group. The check box name comes from the traditional rendering by the browser—a small box that when selected, has a checkmark placed within it.

At its most basic, a check box control is written as

```
<input type="checkbox" name="box name" /> option text
```

The option text gives the user the cue to check or uncheck the box, as shown in Figure 4.2. Notice, though, that the option text *is not* contained within the input element. Instead, it is placed after the element is closed.

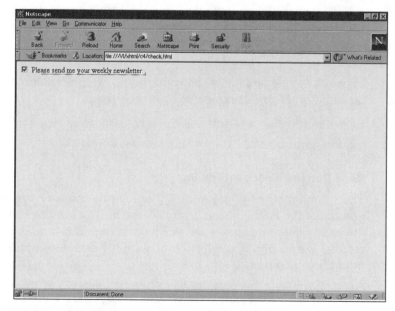

Figure 4.2: *This is a basic check box control.*

Using this configuration, if the check box is selected, the form data would be returned as

```
checkbox_name=on
```

Many times, though, you'll want a value more descriptive than "on." If you add the value attribute to the input element, that predefined text will be sent instead. For example:

```
<input type="checkbox" name="manufacturer" value="ford" /> Ford
```

would pass

```
manufacturer=ford
```

which gives the data recipient a bit more context as to the original question. You can group check boxes together by giving each of them the same name, but varying the value.

EXAMPLE

Paolo's Pizza lets local customers order their pizza online. They need to allow the user to select multiple toppings to be added to the pizza, yet they want to limit the input to the toppings they have on hand. A text box wouldn't be appropriate in this case, because that would allow free-form entry that could bring in requests they couldn't fulfill. Grouping a set of check boxes handles this task nicely:

```
<input type="checkbox" name="toppings" value="pepperoni" /> Pepperoni
<input type="checkbox" name="toppings" value="sausage" /> Sausage
<input type="checkbox" name="toppings" value="mushrooms" /> Mushrooms
<input type="checkbox" name="toppings" value="olives" /> Olives
<input type="checkbox" name="toppings" value="onions" /> Onions
<input type="checkbox" name="toppings" value="green pepper" /> Green Pepper
<input type="checkbox" name="toppings" value="extra cheese" /> Extra Cheese
```

Figure 4.3 illustrates how the check boxes are placed one after the other if no additional formatting is used between them.

Based on the user's selections, the script would return something like

```
toppings=pepperoni&toppings=extra%20cheese&toppings=onions
```

Radio Buttons: Choosing Just One

The second method of grouping options limits the user to a single selection, and that's the radio button group. These *must* have the same name to operate as a group, and the value attribute is required to make any sense of the results. For example, a selection of shipping options on an ecommerce site might be written as

```
<input type="radio" name="shipping" value="UPS Ground" /> UPS Ground
<input type="radio" name="shipping" value="2day" /> 2nd Day Air
<input type="radio" name="shipping" value="overnight" /> Overnight
```

Whichever button is selected will determine the value paired with shipping.

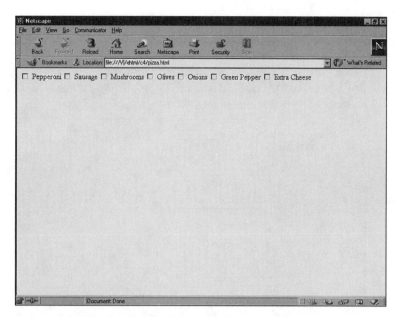

Figure 4.3: *A group of check boxes using the same name value helps logically group the information returned.*

TIP

You can provide your users a gentle nudge in a certain direction if you tell the browser to preselect one option. To do so, use the checked="checked" attribute.

THE SELECT CONTROL

This next form control has a variety of popular names; some people call it a menu, others a select box, drop-down menu, option group, or list box. I prefer to use the term *drop-down menu* to describe a control where the options are displayed (often visually "dropped down") only after the user activates the control. A *list box*, on the other hand, is a control with all or several of the choices in view at the same time. Take a look at the basic syntax.

EXAMPLE

Every select control, no matter how it's displayed visually, begins with the same collection of elements. The select element will contain individual option elements that form the content of the list inside the control:

```
<select name="size">
<option value="s"> small</option>
<option value="m"> medium</option>
<option value="l"> large</option>
<option value="xl"> extra large</option>
</select>
```

Figure 4.4 shows the traditional rendering of this control (this time in Netscape Navigator 4.72), both unactivated and after user activation.

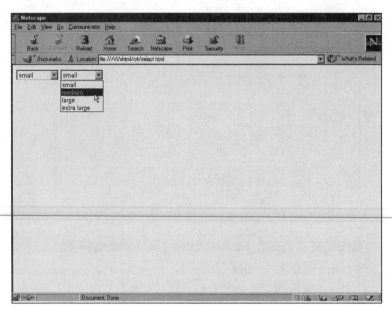

Figure 4.4: *A standard select control commonly looks like this.*

To turn this into a list box, the `size` attribute is added to the `select` element:

```
<select name="size" size="4">
<option value="s"> small
<option value="m"> medium
<option value="l"> large
<option value="xl"> extra large
</select>
```

The list box doesn't necessarily have to have a `size` attribute value that's equal to the number of option elements. If, for some reason, you wanted to create a list box with 20 elements, you could begin with 5 of them showing using a `size` attribute value of 5. A scrollbar would then appear allowing the user to see the remaining options (see Figure 4.5).

A final option for the select control is to allow the user to choose multiple options from within the list. This function is controlled with the `multiple` attribute, written as

```
<select name="foo" multiple="multiple">
…option elements…
</select>
```

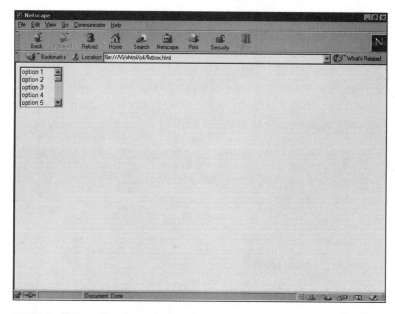

Figure 4.5: *A list box–style select control allows users to see more choices without activating the control.*

CAUTION

Although the select control has the ability to use multiple selections, take care in using this feature. The act of holding the Ctrl key when making multiple selections tends not to be intuitive to many users. Consider a set of checkboxes for multiple selections instead.

TEXT AREAS: ACCEPTING LARGE BLOCKS OF TEXT

There will be times when it is desirable to collect more than the few words or short sentence that can be entered into a reasonably sized text box. The text area control was designed to help solve that problem.

Text areas are formed a little differently from most other controls in that they are not empty elements and can accept plain text between the opening and closing tags. Additionally, they have two attributes that control the size of the control instead of one. The rows attribute manages the number rows that are visible in the control (the height measurement), and the cols attribute determines how many characters are visible horizontally (the width measurement).

EXAMPLE

A Web site that provides technical support needs to collect a detailed description of the problem their customer has encountered with the product. The service manager wants the space to be at least six lines long, and about as wide as the page allows. It also should be clear to the user that they must give as much detail as possible when describing the difficulty.

The Webmaster creates a text area control that contains the instruction "Please describe your problem in detail here." between the <textarea> tags.

```
<textarea name="details" rows="6" cols="50">Please describe your problem in
detail here.</textarea>
```

The row attribute value of 6 meets the height requirement for the control, and the cols attribute value of 50 provides a comfortable width for most users. Figure 4.6 shows the results.

OUTPUT

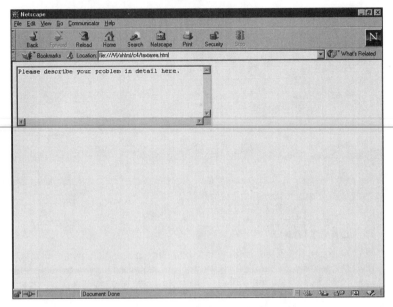

Figure 4.6: *A text area with associated instructions for the user provides a hint as to what you expect.*

TIP

Remember that the width of form controls is based on the default font in use for the browser. Fifty characters in width might appear small to a designer using a monitor set to 1024×784 (or even higher) resolution, but to a user on a 640×480 resolution monitor, it might fill the entire screen. Be sure not to set a cols value so high as to force horizontal scrolling for those users on the lower resolution machines.

HIDDEN FIELDS: PASSING ADDITIONAL INFORMATION TO THE SCRIPT

In almost any data exchange with your visitors, there is likely to be some information that is static, that is, it doesn't change with each user. Perhaps you have several different forms on your site, and you want to be able to determine at a glance which form generated the response. The hidden form control handles this for you nicely.

The hidden control will always have three attributes: `type`, `name`, and `value`:

```
<input type="hidden" name="foo" value="My value here">
```

Size or other presentational attributes aren't an issue as the form isn't visible to the end user. Although they aren't displayed, the data do still pass back and forth from the server to the user and back to the processor, so use them sparingly for important information.

FILE INPUT CONTROL

EXAMPLE

An exciting aspect of XHTML forms is the ability to accept the content of files as input within your form. The form input control generates a button with the label "browse" (on most implementations). When this button is clicked, the user can navigate through the file system on his computer until the file desired is located. After the file is accepted, the input field is populated with the path to the selected file. To add such a control, use the following syntax:

```
<input type="file" name="foo"/>
```

Figure 4.7 illustrates what the field might look like when the dialog box is generated after the button is activated. The actual implementation does vary from browser to browser.

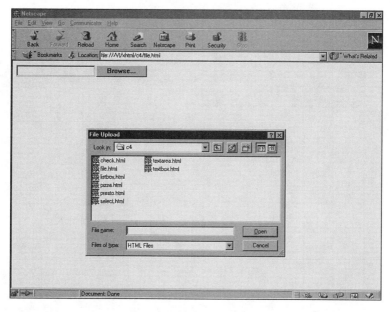

Figure 4.7: *The browse action of the file control allows users to locate the file desired.*

NOTE

If you do include a file upload option in your form, you'll need to add an additional attribute to the form element: enctype. Enctype controls the *encoding type*, or Internet Media Type of the data that is going to be passed. When a file is included, there will be two parts: the form data and the file. Therefore, the enctype value *must* be set to "multipart/form-data" to transmit both pieces successfully.

Buttons

Nearly everyone is familiar with the ubiquitous "Submit" and "Reset" buttons seen on many forms. Both of these input types have special properties. The minimal syntax for each is shown here:

```
<input type="submit" />
```

```
<input type="reset" />
```

If no value attribute is present, the browser decides what text to place on the button itself. Netscape Navigator and Internet Explorer both use "Submit Query" and "Reset," respectively.

You can change the text by introducing the value attribute. The text found there is transferred to the button (see Figure 4.8).

```
<input type="submit" value="Give it to me now!" />
```

EXAMPLE

```
<input type="reset" value="I've changed my mind" />
```

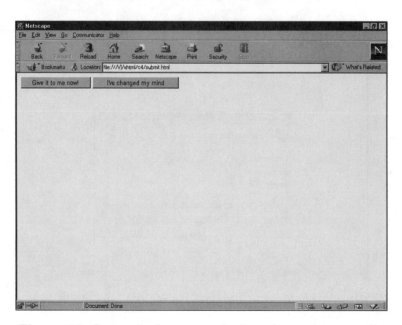

Figure 4.8: *Customized text on submit and reset buttons allows for more intuitive instructions.*

A third button type, this one without any special properties, is also available. It uses the generic type value of "button." Designed for use with scripting, the button type is supported only in some of the newer browsers, and should be used with caution.

IMAGE CONTROLS

The final input type is the image control. Used as a replacement for the "Submit" button, many designers favor it because it allows them to keep each element of their form page within the desired "look and feel." Because you're working with a separate file for the image, the input element needs an additional attribute of src. The value is the URL for the image file:

```
<input type="image" src="myimage.gif" alt="Order Now!" />
```

Putting Together a Complete Form

Now that you've taken a look at each of the available form controls, you can put them together in a complete document.

EXAMPLE

Presto Printers wants to begin taking in business over the Internet. If customers can upload camera-ready artwork, Presto can turn around their business card or letterhead order in 48 hours. Aside from the file, the customer will need to provide paper selections, quantities, shipping and billing address, payment information, and any special instructions. The manager also would like to offer customers an account registration option, so that they can save information from the initial order for one-step re-ordering.

The complete form is developed as follows in Listing 4.1.

Listing 4.1: form.html

```
<!DOCTYPE html PUBLIC "-//W3C//DTD XHTML 1.0 Transitional//EN"
    "http://www.w3.org/TR/xhtml1/DTD/xhtml1-transitional.dtd">
<html>
<head>
<title>Presto Printers Job Spec Sheet</title>
</head>
<body>
<h1>Presto Printers Job Spec Sheet</h1>
<form method="post" action="http://www.webgeek.com/cgi-bin/forms.cgi">
<input type="hidden" name="form" value="Job Spec Sheet" />
<h2>Shipping Address</h2>
Customer Name: <input type="text" name="name" size="30" /><br />
Address Line 1: <input type="text" name="add1" size="30" /><br />
Address Line 2: <input type="text" name="add2" size="30" /> <br />
City: <input type="text" name="city" size="30" /> <br />
State/Province: <input type="text" name="state" size="15" />
Zip/Postal Code: <input type="text" name="zip" size="10" /><br />
Daytime Telephone: <input type="text" name="phone" size="12" /><br />
```

Listing 4.1: continued

```
Fax: <input type="text" name="fax" size="12" /><br />
<h2>Billing Address</h2>
<input type="checkbox" name="bill-same" value="yes" /> Check here if same as
➥shipping address
<p>Address Line 1: <input type="text" name="badd1" size="30" /><br />
Address Line 2: <input type="text" name="badd2" size="30" /> <br />
City: <input type="text" name="bcity" size="30" /> <br />
State/Province: <input type="text" name="bstate" size="15" />
Zip/Postal Code: <input type="text" name="bzip" size="10" /><br />
</p>
<h2>Job Specifications</h2>
Order type: <input type="radio" name="product" value="bizcard" /> business cards
<input type="radio" name="product" value="letterhead" /> letterhead
<p>Business card stock:
<select name="cardstock">
<option value="none" />None
<option value="white" />White
<option value="cream" />Cream
<option value="tan" />Tan
<option value="blush" />Blush
<option value="grey" />Grey
</select>
Letterhead paper:
<select name="letterpaper">
<option value="none" />None
<option value="24ww" />24lb. white wove
<option value="24cw" />24lb. cream wove
<option value="24wl" />24lb. white laid
<option value="24cl" />24lb. cream laid
</select>
</p>
<p>Select your file to be uploaded here. (Please be sure to send it zipped or
➥stuffed!):
<input type="file" /></p>
<p>If you'd like to save this information for easy reordering, please enter a
➥user name and password now.
<br />
User name: <input type="text" name="user" size="10" /><br />
password: <input type="password" name="pass1" size="10" /> <br />
verify password: <input type="password" name="pass2" size="10" /> <br />
<input type="image" src="done.gif" alt="I'm done!" border="0" /></p>
</form>
</body>
</html>
```

The completed form can be seen in Figure 4.9 as viewed in Internet Explorer. It's certainly not the most aesthetically pleasing form ever created, but it contains one of each of the available form controls.

Presto Printers Job Spec Sheet

Shipping Address

Customer Name:

Address Line 1:

Address Line 2:

City:

State/Province: Zip/Postal Code:

Daytime Telephone:

Fax:

Billing Address

☐ Check here if same as shipping address

Address Line 1:

Address Line 2:

City:

State/Province: Zip/Postal Code:

Job Specifications

Order type: ○ business cards ○ letterhead

Business card stock: None ▼ Letterhead paper: None ▼

Select your file to be uploaded here. (Please be sure to send it zipped or stuffed!):

[   ] Browse...

If you'd like to save this information for easy reordering, please enter a user name and password now.

User name:

password:

verify password:

[I'm done!]

Figure 4.9: This figure shows some form controls.

✔ To learn how to make form layout more visually appealing, see "Managing Columns and Rows" p. 85.

Now it's time to actually do something with the data collected. To accomplish that, you'll need a script or program to process the information.

Form Processing Options

There are three broad categories of form processing options: by email, through scripting, or by using middleware applications. The third, middleware applications, refers to products such as Allaire's Cold Fusion, Microsoft's Active Server Pages, and other application servers that run in conjunction with the Web server software. The use of these systems for forms processing goes beyond the scope of this text, so I won't go into them any further.

`mailto:` Form Action

The processing method that's probably easiest to implement is unfortunately also the most unreliable: the `mailto:` function.

The idea behind it is simple: the email client that has been associated with clicking linked email addresses in your browser captures the form data and sends the message to the address specified in the form action. The only problem with this is that not all computers will have a browser that's set to intercept email links in this manner. To further complicate the issue, the end user can't easily change this behavior. Therefore, when the user submits the form, the browser might just "sit there," the email client might engage but perhaps only to bring up a blank email message, or any number of other unpredictable results.

That said, using a `mailto:` form action can be useful while you're learning about and planning your forms. The `form` tag would take the following form:

```
<form method="post" action="mailto:xhtml@webgeek.com">
```

CAUTION

Avoid the temptation to add additional parameters to the `mailto:` value. A popular, though flawed trend on the Web is to try to insert subject lines and even full text sections to email messages generated by forms by adding specific strings to the `mailto:` data. The use of these techniques violates accepted Internet mail protocols. Because of this, you'll likely have further difficulties in getting a `mailto:`-based form to process the data as desired.

If you do manage to get it to work, you'll get the data back in what's known as *URL-encoded* form. This is one long string of characters composed of the *name=value pairs* from each form element, and the spaces, carriage returns, and line feeds between and within those pairs converted to their equivalent ASCII character codes.

A Simple CGI Script in Perl

One of the most popular options for processing form data is known as the CGI Script. CGI stands for *Common Gateway Interface*. Exactly how this gateway works is beyond the scope of this book, but at the most basic level it acts as a doorway from the Web server to the computer on which the server resides, allowing additional computing to take place between the give and take of files.

The instructions are passed through the gateway in the form of *scripts*, which are essentially miniature programs that perform limited functions. CGI scripts can be written in quite a few different programming languages, but the most prevalent remains Perl.

Perl is an *interpreted* language, meaning that a program known as a Perl interpreter on the server processes the script. If the script were executable on its own, it would be known as a compiled program, or executable program. Perl interpreters are available for most computer platforms, including all variations of UNIX/Linux, 32-bit Windows (Windows NT, 95/98), Solaris, and almost any other popular platform that also is capable of running a Web server.

To run CGI scripts, you must have a directory within your Web site that is set up with the proper permissions. The system administrator normally does this. On a UNIX- or Linux-based system, the directory is usually named cgi-bin, and is often found at or just below the root directory of the Web site. If you have control over your own Web server, you can set this up yourself. If you use Web hosting space on an ISP or IPP, you'll need to ask your provider if they allow CGI scripts, and if so, which directories you should be using.

The following script (Listing 4.2) is a generic form handling script written in Perl. It's not important for you to know what each of the lines mean, but you will need to edit the first line of the script, known as the "path to Perl," and several of the *variables* defined in lines two through six. You'll come back to those details in a moment.

Listing 4.2: form.cgi

```
#!/usr/bin/perl                                    #Line 1
# Line 1 - enter the email address where you wish the response
# to be delivered. The @ character must be escaped, as in \@
# Line 2 - Edit the subject line between the quote characters.
# Line 3 - Enter a URL to be displayed after the form has been
# processed - Users will click this link to continue viewing
# your site.
# Line 4 - The title of the page referenced in the URL in Line 3
# Line 5 - Ask your system administrator for 'the path to sendmail' on your
➥system.
# Edit this line as necessary.


# -- edit only these variables. Do not remove quotes -

$email = "you\@yourcompany.com";                   #Line 2
$subject = "Your Subject Here";                    #Line 3
$nextpage = "http://www.yoururl.com";              #Line 4
$title = "Page title for URL in Line 3";           #Line 5
$SENDMAIL = "/usr/sbin/sendmail -t";               #Line 6
```

Listing 4.2: continued

```
# -- do not edit below this line -

read(STDIN, $formdata $ENV{'CONTENT_LENGTH'});
open (MAILOUT, "| $SENDMAIL") || die "Error, where's your sendmail?";
@response = split(/&/,$formdata);
foreach (@response) {
    tr/+/ /;
    s/=/ = /;
    s/%(..)/pack("C",hex($1))/ge;
    print MAILTOUT "$_\n";
}
close(MAILOUT);

print "Content-type; text/html\n\n";
print "\<!DOCTYPE html PUBLIC \"-\/\/W3C\/\/DTD XHTML 1.0
➥Transitional\/\/EN\"\n";
print "\""http:\/\/www.w3.org\/TR\/xhtml1\/DTD\/xhtml1-transitional.dtd\"\>\n";
print "<html><head>\n";
print "<title>Form Sent!</title>\n";
print "</head><body>\n";
print "<h1>Form Sent!</h1>\n";
print "<p>Follow this link back to <a href=\"$return\">$title;</a>.</p>\n";
print "</body></html>\n";
# end
```

EDITING YOUR PATH TO PERL AND THE SIX VARIABLES

The information stored in the six variables should be pretty self-explanatory. What you need to be careful with is how you enter them within the script.

- **Path to Perl (line 1)**—Edit this line as necessary, using the information provided by your system administrator for the "path to Perl." This line will *always* begin with the #! characters.

- **Email Address (line 2)**—This is the address to which all form responses will be delivered. It should be an address that someone will be checking frequently, and that does not have any artificial limit on the number of messages that might be stored there. Perl can only properly process the email address if the @ character is *escaped*. Escaping a character means alerting the Perl interpreter that the character should simply be passed on as text, rather than interpreted as a programming instruction (in Perl, the @ character indicates the beginning of an array name). To escape the character, a backslash must be placed in front of it. Therefore the email address I use for this book would be xhtml\@webgeek.com.

- **Subject (line 3)**—What subject should each response email have? Pick something that will immediately alert you as to what the email contains, such as

  `"Widgets Corp Web Order Form Response"`

- **Next Page URL (line 4)**—This variable holds the URL that you will make available to the user after she submits your form. It should lead back to a logical point—your site's home page, the beginning of your online catalog for an ecommerce site, or some other major division within the site. The URL must be fully qualified, that is, it must include the protocol and any fragment identifiers required. For example:

  `"http://www.mycompany.com/catalog/"`

- **Title (line 5)**—What is the title of the page you just sent your visitors to in line four? That information goes here. For example:

  `"Widgets, Inc. Online Catalog"`

- **Path to sendmail (line 6)**—Enter the information provided by your system administrator exactly as you received it, spacing, punctuation, letter case, and all. On my system, that location is `"/usr/sbin/ sendmail -t"`.

WORKING WITH NON-UNIX SERVERS

Although it's most popular on UNIX-based Web servers, Perl isn't limited to that platform. Ports of the language are available in both Windows and Macintosh versions. Small variations in syntax might be required when working on one of these other platforms, but the root language remains the same.

Of course not all CGI scripts must be written in Perl. Many are written in C, C++, various forms of BASIC, and a whole host of other programming languages. Consult your system administrator to find out which languages are available to you.

To learn more about Perl, or to download a copy of the Perl interpreter for any of these platforms, visit `http://www.perl.com`.

What's Next

In this chapter you have learned how to create XHTML pages that allow you to collect information from your site visitors through XHTML forms. You've been introduced to two methods of processing form data, `mailto:` and CGI scripts, and you can edit a simple Perl-based script for use on many Web sites.

Next up in Chapter 5, "Working with Tables," we'll look at creating XHTML tables, both for tabular content and to format content in an easier-to-read manner, such as the Presto Printing form just created in this chapter.

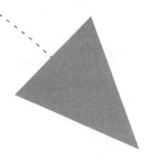

Working with Tables

In the early days of HTML, one of the most challenging page design problems dealt with the inclusion of tabular content. How could you readily structure data that was more than just a simple list? Authors needed to create grids, spreadsheets, and other information that rightfully belonged in a table if it were to be printed on paper, yet HTML didn't always have this facility. Thankfully, tables were included in HTML 3.2, and are again available in enhanced form in XHTML 1.0.

After their introduction, Web designers quickly realized that tables could be used for more than just truly tabular content. By organizing the content of a page into columns and rows, enhanced visual designs could be achieved. Some early WYSIWYG design tools went overboard with this idea, trying to give the designer "pixel perfect placement" control over page content, resulting in dozens and dozens of tables per page. I won't go so far as to tell you that you can't use tables for visual layout, but when you do, you should understand the ramifications of doing so when your pages are viewed by alternative devices.

This chapter teaches you:

- How to create a basic table
- How to merge columns and rows
- How to create tables within tables
- How to improve the usability of tabular data

Basic Tabular Structure

Every table has three essential components: the table element itself, and the rows and cells contained within it. A lot can go on in the table element, but we'll start small and build as we work through the chapter.

EXAMPLE

Let's start with a simple three-by-three grid familiar to most of us as a tic-tac-toe board (see Figure 5.1).

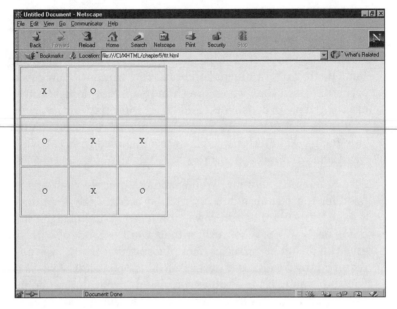

Figure 5.1: *HTML is used to create a three-by-three tic-tac-toe table.*

All contents of a table are contained within the table element. In this example, we've set just a single attribute: the border attribute. border defines the width of the edging around the table and between each cell, measured in pixels. Many browsers have a default border value of 1, though a few have been known to default to 0 (zero), which is the value used to indicate no border; therefore, it's good practice to specify exactly what you want:

```
<table border="1">
```

Structurally—that is working with just the elements that make up a table—the table only has rows and cells, not columns. Of course we see columns in the cells that line up with the cells in the rows above and below it. Each row and the cells contained within it are defined before the next row begins. Our tic-tac-toe board has three cells in the first row, each set at 100 pixels wide by 100 pixels high:

```
<tr>
<td width="100" height="100">&nbps;</td>
<td width="100" height="100">&nbps;</td>
<td width="100" height="100">&nbps;</td>
</tr>
```

NOTE

The non-breaking space character is used as "filler" in these table cells to help you visualize the outcome when viewed in the browser. Completely empty table cells are often collapsed by the browser and display as simply blank space.

The process is repeated for the second and third rows, before the table is closed:

```
<tr>
<td width="100" height="100">&nbps;</td>
<td width="100" height="100">&nbps;</td>
<td width="100" height="100">&nbps;</td>
</tr>
<tr>
<td width="100" height="100">&nbps;</td>
<td width="100" height="100">&nbps;</td>
<td width="100" height="100">&nbps;</td>
</tr>
</table>
```

The empty shell is seen in Figure 5.2.

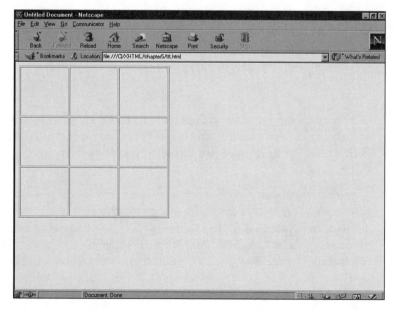

Figure 5.2: *The blank three-by-three grid is shown in the browser.*

Populate the cells with Xs and Os as you please. Figure 5.1 shows my choices. When first entered, the letters are centered vertically in the cell, but are sitting at the left border of each, which looks a little funny. To fix this, we'll need to add horizontal alignment for the cell contents.

Alignment can be added at the cell level, or for an entire row. Horizontal alignment is set using the align attribute, whereas vertical alignment is set using valign.

Because each cell's alignment within a row is the same, I can place the attributes on the table row element. I've used "center" for the horizontal alignment, and "middle" for vertical alignment:

```
<tr align="center" valign="middle">
```

Put all together, the table looks like Listing 5.1.

Listing 5.1: ttt.html

```
<table border="1">
  <tr align="center" valign="middle">
    <td width="100" height="100">X</td>
    <td width="100" height="100">O</td>
    <td width="100" height="100"> </td>
  </tr>
  <tr align="center" valign="middle">
    <td width="100" height="100">O</td>
    <td width="100" height="100">X</td>
    <td width="100" height="100">X</td>
  </tr>
  <tr align="center" valign="middle">
    <td width="100" height="100">O</td>
    <td width="100" height="100">X</td>
    <td width="100" height="100">O</td>
  </tr>
</table>
```

Much more can be done with tables than the simple alignments that we've done in this first example. Next, we'll prepare a monthly-view calendar that will utilize background color for cells, headers, a caption, and multi-column cells.

The calendar begins with a seven-column row of cells containing the days of the week. These cells act as headings for the rest of the cells in the column, so they're defined using the table head—th—element. The characteristics of each cell will be the same, with the sole exception of the actual content. Therefore the attributes can be placed on the TR element, impacting the entire row, instead of repeated seven times, once per cell.

You've used the alignment attributes already in the previous example, but the background color attribute, at least as it pertains to tables, is new. The attribute is bgcolor, just as it is with the body element. The value is a color name or hexadecimal value. I've chosen a pale yellow, with a hex value of #FFFF99:

```
<table border="1">
  <tr align="center" valign="top" bgcolor="#FFFF99" height="35" width="100">
    <th>Sunday</th>
    <th>Monday</th>
    <th>Tuesday</th>
    <th>Wednesday</th>
    <th>Thursday</th>
    <th>Friday</th>
    <th>Saturday</th>
  </tr>
```

In the next row, the first row of date cells, the first five cells don't have any data. We could simply place a non-breaking space in them as you did when creating the tic-tac-toe board. However, we want those cells to mimic print calendars, in that this leading blank area will be a single solid space, not five empty boxes. To do that, a single cell needs to occupy the first five columns. This is achieved using the colspan attribute on the td element. As you might guess, the value is the number of columns to be *spanned* by the cell in question. The alignment attributes are set to left for horizontal, and top for vertical, placing the date numbers in the upper-left corner of each cell. There is a corresponding rowspan attribute that can be used to span more than one row per cell. In this example, we only need to use colspan:

```
<tr align="left" valign="top">
    <td colspan="5" bgcolor="#CCCCCC" width="100" height="100"> </td>
    <td width="80" height="80">1</td>
    <td width="80" height="80">2</td>
  </tr>
```

NOTE

Even though the first cell in this row spans five columns, the height and width attributes are set as if the cell occupied a single column. With a colspan value of 5, the cell then occupies 500 pixels of space (100 times 5), yet the same height space, because the rowspan hasn't been manipulated.

Each of the next four rows will look the same, excepting the numeric date content of the cell:

```
<tr align="left" valign="top">
    <td width="80" height="80">3</td>
    <td width="80" height="80">4</td>
    <td width="80" height="80">5</td>
    <td width="80" height="80">6</td>
```

```
      <td width="80" height="80">7</td>
      <td width="80" height="80">8</td>
      <td width="80" height="80">9</td>
    </tr>
```

The final product is shown both in Listing 5.2 and Figure 5.3.

OUTPUT

Listing 5.2: Monthly Calendar View

```
<table border="1">
  <tr align="center" valign="top" bgcolor="#FFFF99">
    <th width="80" height="25">Sunday</th>
    <th width="80" height="25">Monday</th>
    <th width="80" height="25">Tuesday</th>
    <th width="80" height="25">Wednesday</th>
    <th width="80" height="25">Thursday</th>
    <th width="80" height="25">Friday</th>
    <th width="80" height="25">Saturday</th>
  </tr>
  <tr align="left" valign="top">
    <td colspan="5" bgcolor="#CCCCCC" width="80" height="80"> </td>
    <td width="80" height="80">1</td>
    <td width="80" height="80">2</td>
  </tr>
  <tr align="left" valign="top">
    <td width="80" height="80">3</td>
    <td width="80" height="80">4</td>
    <td width="80" height="80">5</td>
    <td width="80" height="80">6</td>
    <td width="80" height="80">7</td>
    <td width="80" height="80">8</td>
    <td width="80" height="80">9</td>
  </tr>
  <tr align="left" valign="top">
    <td width="80" height="80">10</td>
    <td width="80" height="80">11</td>
    <td width="80" height="80">12</td>
    <td width="80" height="80">13</td>
    <td width="80" height="80">14</td>
    <td width="80" height="80">15</td>
    <td width="80" height="80">16</td>
  </tr>
  <tr align="left" valign="top">
    <td width="80" height="80">17</td>
    <td width="80" height="80">18</td>
    <td width="80" height="80">19</td>
    <td width="80" height="80">20</td>
    <td width="80" height="80">21</td>
    <td width="80" height="80">22</td>
```

Listing 5.2: continued

```
<td width="80" height="80">23</td>
  </tr>
  <tr align="left" valign="top">
    <td width="80" height="80">24</td>
    <td width="80" height="80">25</td>
    <td width="80" height="80">26</td>
    <td width="80" height="80">27</td>
    <td width="80" height="80">28</td>
    <td width="80" height="80">29</td>
    <td width="80" height="80">30</td>
  </tr>
</table>
```

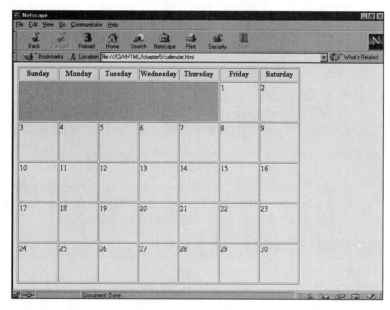

Figure 5.3: *This monthly calendar view uses merged cells and background coloring.*

Managing Columns and Rows

In the calendar example, you previewed the ability to manipulate the number of columns a particular data cell occupied. This is possible not only in the horizontal (cells spanning columns), but in the vertical (cells spanning rows), or even both. This process also is sometimes referred to as *merging* cells.

To demonstrate, let's take another look at the form developed in Chapter 4, "Collecting Data with Forms," as shown in Figure 5.4.

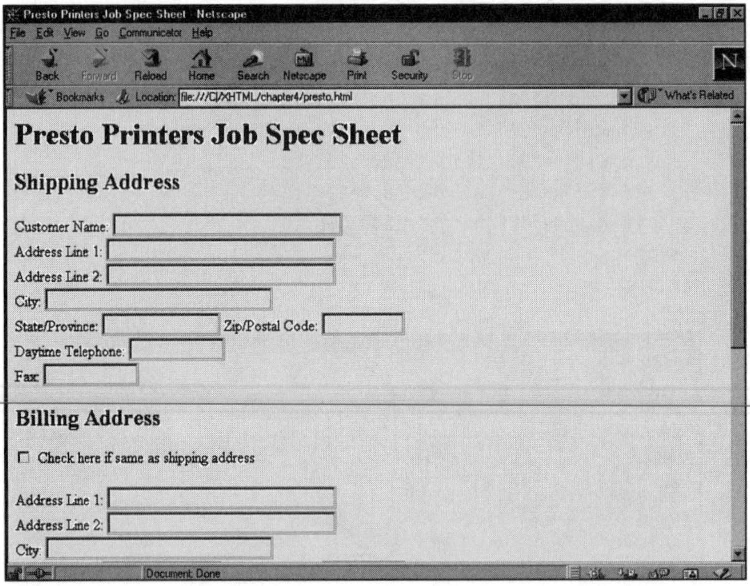

Figure 5.4: *Our previously created form needs some visual alignment.*

Looking over the form, it's clear that we can nicely line up the input fields and the labels in two distinct columns. We'll start by placing the first section (shipping address information) into our table:

```
<table border="1">
<tr>
<td align="right">Customer Name:</td>
<td><input type="text" name="name" size="30" /></td>
</tr>
<tr>
<td align="right">Address Line 1:</td>
<td><input type="text" name="add1" size="30" /></td>
</tr>
<tr>
<td align="right">Address Line 2:</td>
<td><input type="text" name="add2" size="30" /></td>
</tr>
<tr>
<td align="right">City:</td>
<td><input type="text" name="city" size="30" /></td>
</tr>
```

```
<tr>
<td align="right">State/Province:</td>
<td><input type="text" name="state" size="15" /></td>
</tr>
<tr>
<td align="right">Zip/Postal Code:</td>
<td><input type="text" name="zip" size="10" /></td>
</tr>
<tr>
<td align="right">Daytime Telephone:</td>
<td><input type="text" name="phone" size="12" /></td>
</tr>
<tr>
<td align="right">Fax:</td>
<td><input type="text" name="fax" size="12" /></td>
</tr>
</table>
```

I've set the border attribute on the table element to a value of 1 to empha-size the changes brought about by the table. For the final version, we'll take it out. Figure 5.5 shows what we've done so far.

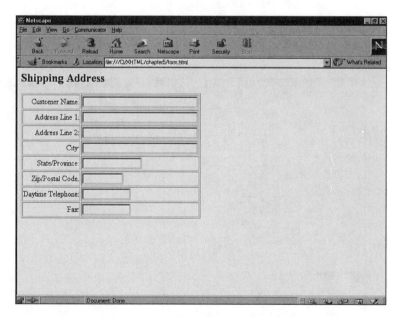

Figure 5.5: *The first section of the form is enclosed in a table for better visual alignment.*

The heading and check box for the billing address section can remain as they originally were. The actual address fields will go in another table, structured as with the shipping address (see Figure 5.6):

```
<h2>Billing Address</h2>
<input type="checkbox" name="bill-same" value="yes"> Check here if same as
➥shipping address
<table border="1">
<tr>
<td align="right">Address Line 1:</td>
<td><input type="text" name="badd1" size="30" /></td>
</tr>
<tr>
<td align="right">Address Line 2:</td>
<td><input type="text" name="badd2" size="30" /></td>
</tr>
<tr>
<td align="right">City:</td>
<td><input type="text" name="bcity" size="30" /></td>
</tr>
<tr>
<td align="right">State/Province:</td>
<td><input type="text" name="bstate" size="15" /></td>
</tr>
<tr>
<td align="right">Zip/Postal Code:</td>
<td><input type="text" name="bzip" size="10" /></td>
</tr>
</table>
```

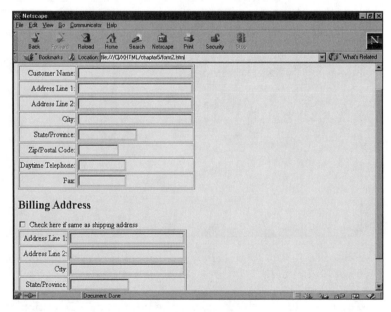

Figure 5.6: *The second address block is formatted with a table.*

TIP

The two tables in Figure 5.6 are of different sizes. To make the presentation even more visually uniform, size each of the tables to the same value using the `width` attribute on the `table` element.

Finally, the username and password sequence will be placed in a third table:

```
<table border="1">
<tr>
<td align="right">User name:</td>
<td><input type="text" name="user" size="10" /></td>
</tr>
<tr>
<td align="right">password:</td>
<td><input type="password" name="pass1" size="10" /></td>
</tr>
<tr>
<td align="right">verify password:</td>
<td><input type="password" name="pass2" size="10" /></td>
</tr>
</table>
```

Placed all together, with the borders removed and a standard submit button, the final result is shown in Listing 5.3 and Figure 5.7. Much nicer, isn't it?

Listing 5.3: The Revised Form

```
<form method="post" action="http://www.webgeek.com/cgi-bin/forms.cgi">
<input type="hidden" name="form" value="Job Spec Sheet" />
<h2>Shipping Address</h2>
<table border="0">
<tr>
<td align="right">Customer Name:</td>
<td><input type="text" name="name" size="30" /></td>
</tr>
<tr>
<td align="right">Address Line 1:</td>
<td><input type="text" name="add1" size="30" /></td>
</tr>
<tr>
<td align="right">Address Line 2:</td>
<td><input type="text" name="add2" size="30" /></td>
</tr>
<tr>
```

Listing 5.3: continued

```
<td align="right">City:</td>
<td><input type="text" name="city" size="30" /></td>
</tr>
<tr>
<td align="right">State/Province:</td>
<td><input type="text" name="state" size="15" /></td>
</tr>
<tr>
<td align="right">Zip/Postal Code:</td>
<td><input type="text" name="zip" size="10" /></td>
</tr>
<tr>
<td align="right">Daytime Telephone:</td>
<td><input type="text" name="phone" size="12" /></td>
</tr>
<tr>
<td align="right">Fax:</td>
<td><input type="text" name="fax" size="12" /></td>
</tr>
</table>
<h2>Billing Address</h2>
<input type="checkbox" name="bill-same" value="yes"> Check here if same as
➥shipping address
<table border="0">
<tr>
<td align="right">Address Line 1:</td>
<td><input type="text" name="badd1" size="30" /></td>
</tr>
<tr>
<td align="right">Address Line 2:</td>
<td><input type="text" name="badd2" size="30" /></td>
</tr>
<tr>
<td align="right">City:</td>
<td><input type="text" name="bcity" size="30" /></td>
</tr>
<tr>
<td align="right">State/Province:</td>
<td><input type="text" name="bstate" size="15" /></td>
</tr>
<tr>
<td align="right">Zip/Postal Code:</td>
<td><input type="text" name="bzip" size="10" /></td>
</tr>
</table>
```

Listing 5.3: continued

```
<h2>Job Specifications</h2>
Order type: <input type="radio" name="product" value="bizcard" /> business cards
<input type="radio" name="product" value="letterhead" /> letterhead
<p>Business card stock:
<select name="cardstock">
<option value="none" />None
<option value="white" />White
<option value="creme" />Creme
<option value="tan" />Tan
<option value="blush" />Blush
<option value="grey" />Grey
</select>
Letterhead paper:
<select name="letterpaper">
<option value="none" />None
<option value="24ww" />24lb. white wove
<option value="24cw" />24lb. creme wove
<option value="24wl" />24lb. white laid
<option value="24cl" />24lb. creme laid
</select>
<p>Select your file to be uploaded here. (Please be sure to send it zipped or
➥stuffed!):
<input type="file" />
<p>If you'd like to save this information for easy reordering, please enter a
➥user name and password now. <br />
<table border="0">
<tr>
<td align="right">User name:</td>
<td><input type="text" name="user" size="10" /></td>
</tr>
<tr>
<td align="right">password:</td>
<td><input type="password" name="pass1" size="10" /></td>
</tr>
<tr>
<td align="right">verify password:</td>
<td><input type="password" name="pass2" size="10" /></td>
</tr>
</table>
<input type="submit" value="submit" />
</form>
```

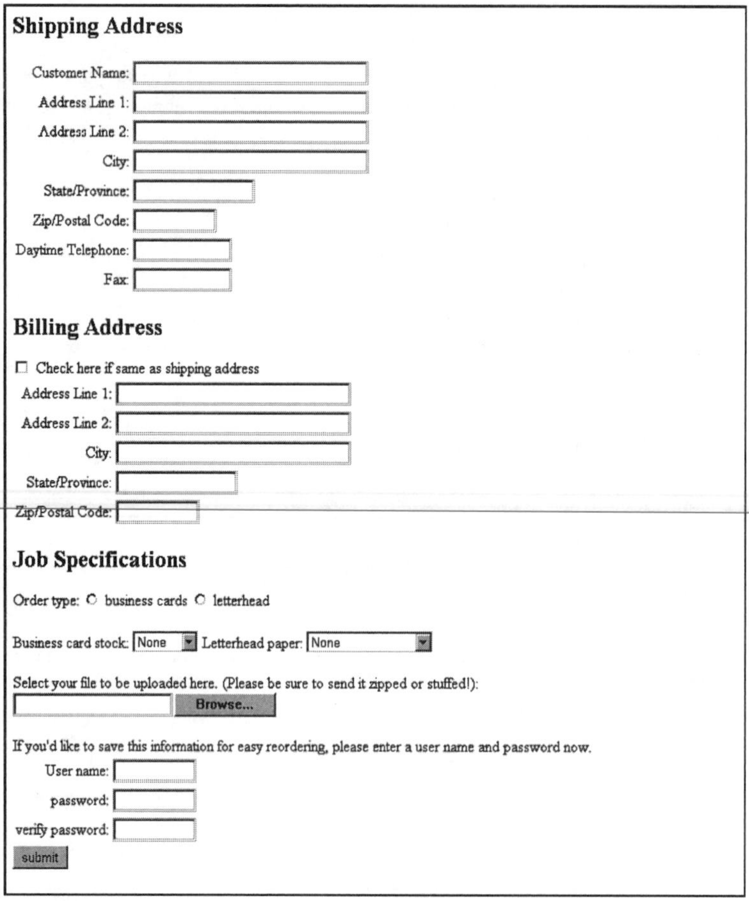

Figure 5.7: *The newly aligned table as seen in the Web browser.*

Nesting Tables

An alternative to complicated spanned layouts is available by creating entire tables within a table, a technique known as *nesting*. A common situation where you'll find nested tables is when the site layout is one large table, usually with a navigation column down the left, and the main content in a large cell on the right. Then, any tabular information in the main content area will need to be inside a table within that cell.

I've created a page on my personal Web site that details current and upcoming appearances at trade shows and other industry events. The page uses just this type of layout, beginning with a single-row, two-column table:

```
<table border="0">
<tr>
<td width="200" bgcolor="#FFFF99">
```

```
<p><strong>Getting Around</strong></p>
<ul>
<li>Upcoming Events</li>
<li><a href="books.html">Books</a></li>
<li><a href="musings.html">Musings</a></li>
</ul>
</td>
<td align="center">content goes here<td>
</tr>
</table>
```

Next we'll go back and fill in the content on the second cell, which consists of a two-row by three-column table with headers and a caption:

```
<table border="1">
<caption>Upcoming Events</caption>
<tr bgcolor="#9999FF">
<th>Event Name</th>
<th>Location</th>
<th>Dates</th>
</tr>
<tr>
<td>Y2K Pan-Pacific Conference</td>
<td>Waikiki Beach, Hawaii</td>
<td>October 19-21, 2000</td>
</tr>
<td>Builder.com Live!</td>
<td>New Orleans, Louisiana</td>
<td>December, 2000</td>
</tr>
</table>
```

Put together, the results look as shown in Figure 5.8.

Nested tables don't necessarily have to be this large or seemingly spread out. Nor are they limited to just a single table inside another. Tables can be nested to unlimited depth, although of course there is a practical limit of just a few levels.

To illustrate a third level, let's add a column to the Upcoming Events table that details the sessions in which I'll be presenting or attending:

```
<table border="1">
<caption>Upcoming Events</caption>
<tr bgcolor="#9999FF">
<th>Event Name</th>
<th>Location</th>
<th>Dates</th>
<th>Sessions</th>
</tr>
<tr>
```

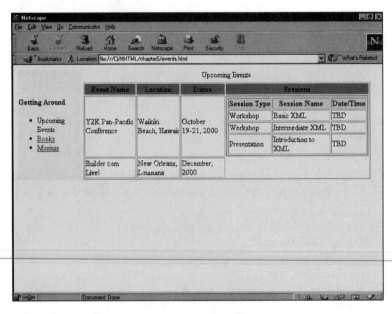

Figure 5.8: *A set of nested tables is shown here in a popular form: one large table for layout, the other has tabular content.*

```
<td>Y2K Pan-Pacific Conference</td>
<td>Waikiki Beach, Hawaii</td>
<td>October 19-21, 2000</td>
<td>new content here</td>
</tr>
<td>Builder.com Live!</td>
<td>New Orleans, Louisiana</td>
<td>December, 2000</td>
<td>To Be Announced</td>
</tr>
</table>
```

The new content in the last cell for the Pan-Pacific Conference will be a three-column, three-row table with headers:

```
<table border="1">
<tr bgcolor="#99FFFF">
<th>Session Type</th>
<th>Session Name</th>
<th>Date/Time</th>
</tr>
<tr>
<td>Workshop</td>
<td>Basic XML</td>
<td>TBD</td>
```

```
</tr>
<tr>
<td>Workshop</td>
<td>Intermediate XML</td>
<td>TBD</td>
<tr>
<td>Presentation</td>
<td>Introduction to XML</td>
<td>TBD</td>
</tr>
</table>
```

OUTPUT

The newly incorporated data is shown in Figure 5.9.

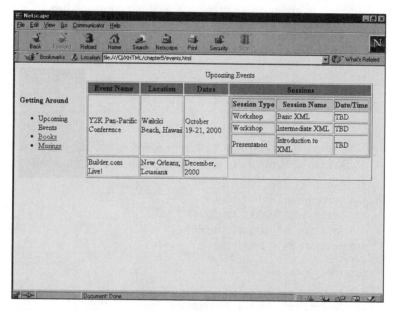

Figure 5.9: *A third table is nested inside the original nested table.*

Data Alignment—axis and id

With all the design tricks that are sometimes employed using tables, people often forget that the reason tables were developed for HTML and XHTML was to deliver *tabular content*. Rows and columns of numbers or data are presented much as you'd see them in a spreadsheet. To make sense of the information, it must be aligned in some manner. Often this is done visually by creating headers, as you did previously with the calendar page. But what if the table contains hundreds of rows? What if you can't see the table, and instead need to listen to it using a speech synthesizer? How will you be able to match the data with the header? XHTML provides several attributes that can be added to TH and TD elements to provide this identifying information.

To illustrate, let's build a small table that sorts what my family ordered the last time we went out to dinner. Each of our choices for entrée, beverage, and dessert are listed.

EXAMPLE

The table begins as all others do, with the table element and a caption:

```
<table border="1" summary="What the Navarro Family had for dinner at Los Amigos
➡Restaurant">
<caption>Dinner at Los Amigos</caption>
```

The next segment is the first table row, with the header cells. Each TH element is given an id attribute with a unique value, as all IDs are required to be unique:

```
<tr>
<th id="c1">Name</th>
<th id="c2">Entrée</th>
<th id="c3">Beverage</th>
<th id="c4">Dessert</th>
</tr>
```

Now in each subsequent row, a headers attribute is added to the TD elements, binding them to the appropriate column header:

```
<tr>
<td headers="c1">Dave</td>
<td headers="c2">Chimichanga</td>
<td headers="c3">Margarita</td>
<td headers="c4">Flan</td>
</tr>
<tr>
<td headers="c1">Ann</td>
<td headers="c2">Enchiladas</td>
<td headers="c3">Sangria</td>
<td headers="c4">Sopapillas</td>
</tr>
<td headers="c1">Linda</td>
<td headers="c2">Tostada</td>
<td headers="c3">Pepsi</td>
<td headers="c4">Fried Ice Cream</td>
</tr>
</table>
```

OUTPUT

In a traditional browser, the results are as they would be without the inclusion of the id and headers attributes (see Figure 5.10).

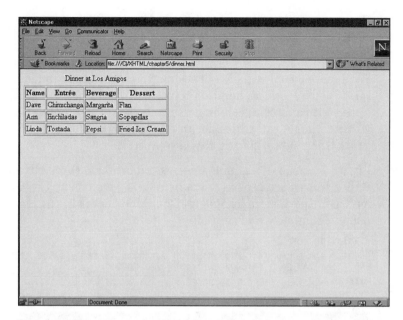

Figure 5.10: *The inclusion of* headers *and* id *attributes doesn't change the visual display of the table.*

Where the real change occurs is when a speech synthesizer or other adaptive technology reads this table for users with sight difficulties. Without the additional data, a listener might hear:

> "Dinner at Los Amigos. Name, Entrée, Beverage, Dessert, Dave, Chimichanga, Margarita, Flan, Ann, Enchiladas, Sangria, Sopapillas, Linda, Tostada, Pepsi, Fried Ice Cream."

After only a few iterations, it can become very difficult to keep track of which items apply to what header. With the addition of the id and headers attributes, the listener would hear something like this:

> "Dinner at Los Amigos. Name: Dave. Entrée: Chimichanga. Beverage: Margarita. Dessert: Flan. Name: Ann. Entrée: Sangria. Dessert: Sopapillas. Name: Linda. Entrée: Tostada. Beverage: Pepsi. Dessert: Fried Ice Cream."

TIP

If you have a particularly long value for a table header, use the abbr attribute to provide a shorter alternative for just this type of rendering. For instance, a header of "City of Departure" could take the attribute abbr="Departing".

With the example used here, you might be able to keep up, because it's fairly obvious that a Margarita belongs in the Beverage category, and not

Entrée. But if you're dealing with categories that aren't quite so obvious, such as numbers, having the headings read in place makes the difference between useful data and a stream of gibberish!

With more complex tables, it's sometimes necessary to determine the meaning of a given cell, in addition to the cell's contents, without having to listen to the entire table. A common example would be a spreadsheet dealing with various budget categories, or an expense report for a multi-stop trip, especially when subtotals or totals are present.

Figure 5.11 shows a simple expense report for a three-city business trip. Expenditures are broken down by date, as well as by category (meals, hotel, local transport, samples given). The table begins in the traditional manner, using a summary and caption:

```
<table border="1">
<summary="A summary of expenses for Marshall Jansen's sales trip for dates
September 20, 2000 through September 26, 2000.">
<caption>Expense Report: 09/20/00 through 09/26/00</caption>
```

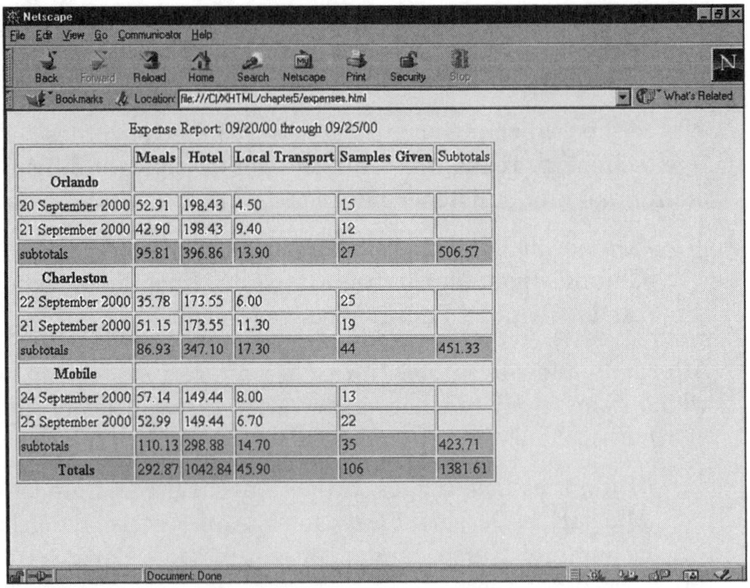

Figure 5.11: *An expense report can be formatted for the Web.*

In the first row, which contains the headers, the `id` attribute is used as before, and a new attribute, `axis`, also is defined. The value of this attribute is the category of information being defined in the cell. For the header row, this is the type of expense, so the attribute is written as
`axis="expense"`:

```
<tr>
<th> </th>
<th id="c1" axis="expense">Meals</th>
<th id="c2" axis="expense">Hotel</th>
<th id="c3" axis="expense" abbr="transport">Local Transport</th>
<th id="c4" axis="expense" abbr="samples">Samples Given</th>
<td>Subtotals</td>
</tr>
```

Each new row is for a new date and city, the city being labeled as such with an axis value of "city":

```
<tr>
<th id="city1" axis="city">Orlando</th>
<th colspan="5"> </th>
</tr>
```

The first full data row, the first date Marshall was in Orlando, introduces the headers attribute on the TD element. For instance, the amount spent on meals that first day needs to be bound to the meals category, the city of Orlando, and the date the expense was incurred. The binding is accomplished by listing each id value for those categories in a space-delimited list for the value of the headers attribute. Meals is represented by id "c1", Orlando by id "city1", and September 20 by id "d1". The headers value for this cell then becomes "c1 city1 d1". The process is repeated for each column in the row:

```
<tr>
<td id="d1" axis="date">20 September 2000</td>
<td headers="c1 city1 d1">52.91</td>
<td headers="c2 city1 d1">198.43</td>
<td headers="c3 city1 d1">4.50</td>
<td headers="c4 city1 d1">15</td>
<td> </td>
</tr>
<tr>
<td id="d2" axis="date">21 September 2000</td>
<td headers="c1 city1 d2">42.90</td>
<td headers="c2 city1 d2">198.43</td>
<td headers="c3 city1 d2">9.40</td>
<td headers="c4 city1 d2">12</td>
<td> /td>
</tr>
```

The third data row holds subtotals for Orlando:

```
<tr>
<td>subtotals</td>
<td>95.81</td>
<td>396.86</td>
```

```
<td>13.90</td>
<td>27</td>
<td>506.57</td>
</tr>
```

This entire process is then repeated for the two additional cities:

```
<tr>
<th id="city2" axis="city">Charleston</th>
<th colspan="5"> </th>
</tr>
<tr>
<td id="d3" axis="date">22 September 2000</td>
<td headers="c1 city2 d3">35.78</td>
<td headers="c2 city2 d3">173.55</td>
<td headers="c3 city2 d3">6.00</td>
<td headers="c4 city2 d3">25</td>
<td> </td>
</tr>
<tr>
<td id="d2" axis="date">21 September 2000</td>
<td headers="c1 city2 d4">51.15</td>
<td headers="c2 city2 d4">173.55</td>
<td headers="c3 city2 d4">11.30</td>
<td headers="c4 city2 d4">19</td>
<td> /td>
</tr>
<tr>
<td>subtotals</td>
<td>86.93</td>
<td>347.10</td>
<td>17.30</td>
<td>44</td>
<td>451.33</td>
</tr>
<tr>
<th id="city3" axis="city">Mobile</th>
<th colspan="5"> </th>
</tr>
<tr>
<td id="d5" axis="date">24 September 2000</td>
<td headers="c1 city3 d5">57.14</td>
<td headers="c2 city3 d5">149.44</td>
<td headers="c3 city3 d5">8.00</td>
<td headers="c4 city3 d5">13</td>
<td> </td>
</tr>
<tr>
<td id="d6" axis="date">25 September 2000</td>
```

```
<td headers="c1 city3 d6">52.99</td>
<td headers="c2 city3 d6">149.44</td>
<td headers="c3 city3 d6">6.70</td>
<td headers="c4 city3 d6">22</td>
<td> /td>
</tr>
<tr>
<td>subtotals</td>
<td>110.13</td>
<td>298.88</td>
<td>14.70</td>
<td>35</td>
<td>423.71</td>
</tr>
```

Finally, the grand totals are presented in the appropriate columns:

```
<tr>
<th>Totals</th>
<td>292.87</td>
<td>1042.84</td>
<td>45.90</td>
<td>106</td>
</tr>
</table>
```

By adding shading to the subtotals and totals columns, we also enhance usability for the sighted reader. The entire table can be seen in Listing 5.4.

Listing 5.4: The Complete Expense Report File

```
<table border="1" summary="A summary of expenses for Marshall Jansen's sales
trip for dates September 20, 2000 through September 25, 2000.">
<caption>Expense Report: 09/20/00 through 09/25/00</caption>

<tr>
<th> </th>
<th id="c1" axis="expense">Meals</th>
<th id="c2" axis="expense">Hotel</th>
<th id="c3" axis="expense" abbr="transport">Local Transport</th>
<th id="c4" axis="expense" abbr="samples">Samples Given</th>
<td>Subtotals</td>
</tr>

<tr>
<th id="city1" axis="city">Orlando</th>
<th colspan="5"> </th>
</tr>
```

Listing 5.4: continued

```
<tr>
<td id="d1" axis="date">20 September 2000</td>
<td headers="c1 city1 d1">52.91</td>
<td headers="c2 city1 d1">198.43</td>
<td headers="c3 city1 d1">4.50</td>
<td headers="c4 city1 d1">15</td>
<td> </td>
</tr>
<tr>
<td id="d2" axis="date">21 September 2000</td>
<td headers="c1 city1 d2">42.90</td>
<td headers="c2 city1 d2">198.43</td>
<td headers="c3 city1 d2">9.40</td>
<td headers="c4 city1 d2">12</td>
<td> </td>
</tr>

<tr bgcolor="#FFCCCC">
<td>subtotals</td>
<td>95.81</td>
<td>396.86</td>
<td>13.90</td>
<td>27</td>
<td>506.57</td>
</tr>

<tr>
<th id="city2" axis="city">Charleston</th>
<th colspan="5"> </th>
</tr>
<tr>
<td id="d3" axis="date">22 September 2000</td>
<td headers="c1 city2 d3">35.78</td>
<td headers="c2 city2 d3">173.55</td>
<td headers="c3 city2 d3">6.00</td>
<td headers="c4 city2 d3">25</td>
<td> </td>
</tr>
<tr>
<td id="d2" axis="date">21 September 2000</td>
<td headers="c1 city2 d4">51.15</td>
<td headers="c2 city2 d4">173.55</td>
<td headers="c3 city2 d4">11.30</td>
<td headers="c4 city2 d4">19</td>
<td> </td>
</tr>
```

Listing 5.4: continued

```
<tr bgcolor="#FFCCCC">
<td>subtotals</td>
<td>86.93</td>
<td>347.10</td>
<td>17.30</td>
<td>44</td>
<td>451.33</td>
</tr>
<tr>
<th id="city3" axis="city">Mobile</th>
<th colspan="5"> </th>
</tr>
<tr>
<td id="d5" axis="date">24 September 2000</td>
<td headers="c1 city3 d5">57.14</td>
<td headers="c2 city3 d5">149.44</td>
<td headers="c3 city3 d5">8.00</td>
<td headers="c4 city3 d5">13</td>
<td> </td>
</tr>
<tr>
<td id="d6" axis="date">25 September 2000</td>
<td headers="c1 city3 d6">52.99</td>
<td headers="c2 city3 d6">149.44</td>
<td headers="c3 city3 d6">6.70</td>
<td headers="c4 city3 d6">22</td>
<td> </td>
</tr>
<tr bgcolor="#FFCCCC">
<td>subtotals</td>
<td>110.13</td>
<td>298.88</td>
<td>14.70</td>
<td>35</td>
<td>423.71</td>
</tr>

<tr bgcolor="#CCCCFF">
<th>Totals</th>
<td>292.87</td>
<td>1042.84</td>
<td>45.90</td>
<td>106</td>
<td>1381.61</td>
</tr>
</table>
```

What's Next

In this chapter you have learned how to create a wide variety of tables, both for tabular content and basic document structure. Usability of tables can be greatly enhanced by the use of visual and informational cues as to cell content.

Next up in Chapter 6, "Using Frames," you will learn additional techniques for page layout and division by using XHTML frames.

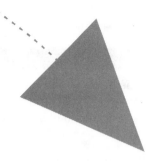

Using Frames

Mention the topic of frames to any gathering of Web developers, no matter how small, and you're bound to trigger a lively debate on the merits (and demerits!) of this controversial technology.

Frames, first introduced to the Web world in Netscape Navigator in their simplest form back in version 1.1, evolved into what we know as frames today starting with version 3.05. Frames were formally adopted into the HTML specifications with HTML 4.0, and are carried over into XHTML 1.0 with the XHTML 1.0 Frameset DTD.

This chapter teaches you:

- How to create a basic frameset
- Three methods of dividing available screen space into frames
- How to change the look of frames through attributes
- How to nest frames within frames
- How to target content into specific frames

The XHTML 1.0 Frameset Doctype

When working with frames, a fundamental change is made in the content model of the XHTML document. To manage this change, XHTML has a special DTD that includes the frame element and other associated elements and attributes necessary to create this functionality.

An interesting aspect of the Frameset DTD is that it only provides the structure into which other documents will be displayed. That is, a frameset document, when viewed in a compatible browser, offers no content of its own.

NOTE

The fact that only the structural document, the one that lays out the frameset, takes the Frameset DTD is actually quite advantageous. It means that the framed documents are written to the Traditional or Strict DTDs, allowing them to function either as framed documents or standalone documents for systems that don't support frames.

Building a Frameset

Frames divide the browser window space into two dimensions: horizontally in *rows* and vertically in *columns*. Each portion of the window space, the *frame*, is defined by its size. Sizes are set in fixed measures of pixels, by a percentage of the available space, or by relative sizing.

One of the simplest framesets to create is to divide the browser window into four equal quadrants. The basic syntax looks like this:

```
<frameset rows="50%, 50%" cols="50%, 50%">
</frameset>
```

The frameset element, then, provides the spatial relationship between each frame. However, you still need to populate each frame with content documents. To do this, each defined space will need its own frame element:

```
<frameset rows="50%, 50%" cols="50%, 50%">
<frame src="frame1.html" name="f1" />
<frame src="frame2.html" name="f2" />
<frame src="frame3.html" name="f3" />
<frame src="frame4.html" name="f4" />
</frameset>
```

Notice that each of the frame elements has a name attribute. The value of this attribute must be unique within the frameset, and must follow two important naming rules: The name must start with an alphabetic character, and cannot be _blank, _self, _parent, or _top. Those names are reserved for specific behavioral semantics you'll learn about later in this chapter in the "Linking Between Frames: The target Attribute" section.

Each of the four XHTML documents referenced in the `frame` elements are created using either the XHTML 1.0 Strict or Transitional document types. Figure 6.1 shows this frameset with a simple identifying heading in each of the framed documents.

You can re-create each of the framed documents by editing this basic document:

```
<!DOCTYPE html PUBLIC "-//W3C//DTD XHTML Transitional 1.0//EN"
    "http://www.w3.org/TR/xhtml1/DTD/xhtml1-transitional.dtd">
<html>
<head>
<title>Frame 1</title>
</head>
<body>
<h1>Frame 1</h1>
</body>
</html>
```

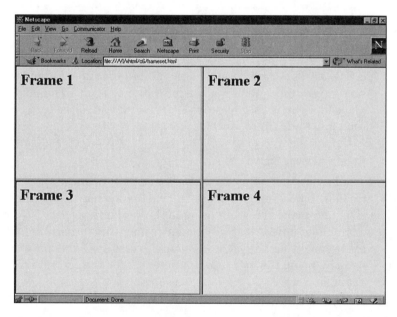

Figure 6.1: A basic four-quadrant frameset is displayed in the browser.

Managing Frame Sizes

As you discovered earlier, the size of each frame can be measured in three ways: by absolute pixel values, as a percentage of the available space, and through relative sizing.

Sizing by Pixels

The only method that allows a frame to be given an *absolute size* that will be the same no matter what type of system or monitor resolution is in use is to size it in pixels. The tricky part about working in pixels is that even though it's an absolute size, meaning the size doesn't change based on the user's monitor settings or other factors, its *apparent size* does vary.

Consider this: Many computer systems ship with a default monitor resolution setting of 640×480 pixels high. This means that if you create a frameset that divides the height of the screen into two rows, and use a size of 200 pixels for the first frame, you've taken up nearly half of the vertical screen space. However, if you're looking at a system with screen resolution set to 1,024×768, a 200-pixel frame will only take *one-fifth* of the available vertical space.

Accordingly, fixed width frames work best when the size of the contents is known in advance. For instance, some sites keep a small frame at the top of the screen to hold banner advertising or other images of a known size.

Size as a Percentage of Available Space

Probably the most popular way to size frames is to divide the space by percentages. This method allows the designer to specify things like "half the screen," or "one quarter of the left-hand column." The only restriction placed on you is that for each dimension, horizontal and vertical, the figures must add up to 100%.

Relative Frame Sizing

EXAMPLE

The last method of measuring frame space is known as *relative sizing*. At its most basic, relative sizing allows the author to say "make one frame X size, and make the other assume the remaining space." Continuing with the example of a fixed size ad banner frame, the author might reserve 100 pixels in height for the ad, and leave the rest available for content. This is done by using the asterisk character (*) for the second size value. For example

```
<frameset rows="100, *">
```

This type of design is seen on the Geek Cruises Web site (see Figure 6.2).

This can be taken even further, expressing values as a ratio. If you wanted three rows instead of two, you could write

```
<frameset rows="100, 4*, 1*">
```

which creates the initial 100-pixel high frame, and then divides the remaining space into two additional frames, the first having four pixels for every one that goes to the last frame.

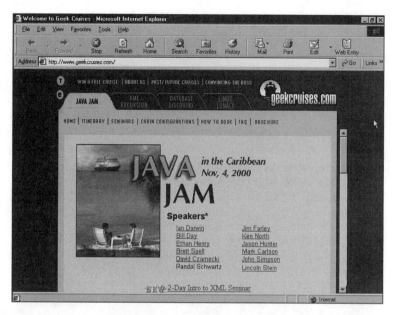

Figure 6.2: *A fixed size frame holds navigation at the top of this site, with content displayed in lower frames.*

Presentational Attributes for Frames

Authors can control the look and behavior of frames with several attributes that control scrolling, resizing, margins, and more. These attributes and their accepted values are detailed in Table 6.1.

Table 6.1: Attributes Used on the **Frame** *Element*

Attribute	Values	Effect
noresize	noresize	A boolean attribute in HTML 4.0, this instructs the browser not to let the user resize the frame at will.
scrolling	yes, no, auto	auto is the default value and will allow scrolling if needed by the contained document. If "no" is chosen, the frame will not scroll, regardless of content size.
frameborder	0, 1	Using "0" turns the default frame border off. "1" explicitly requests the border.
marginwidth	pixels	Defines a gutter, or margin, on the left and right sides of the frame.
marginheight	pixels	Defines a gutter, or margin, on the top and bottom sides of the frame.

Nesting Framesets: Frames Within Frames

The rows and columns method of instantiating frames works well, provided that you're content with dividing the space contained within the entire browser window. But what happens when you want to split the space in a single frame? To achieve this effect, you need a *nested* frame.

EXAMPLE

Begin with the frameset document that provides the initial divisions. For this example, you'll use the "6 pack" layout of two rows and three columns (see Figure 6.3).

```
<frameset rows="50%, 50%" cols="1*, 1*, 1*">
<frame src="frame1.html" name="f1" />
<frame src="frame2.html" name="f2" />
<frame src="frame3.html" name="f3" />
<frame src="frame4.html" name="f4" />
<frame src="frame5.html" name="f5" />
<frame src="frame6.html" name="f6" />
</frameset>
```

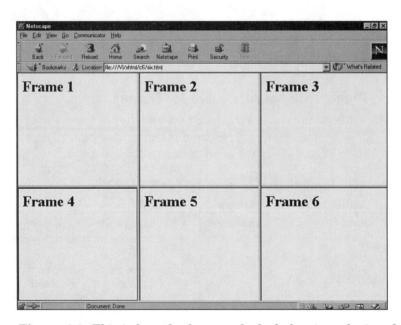

Figure 6.3: *This is how the frameset looks before introducing the nested frame.*

Next you'll take the document in frame 1 (upper-left corner) and split it into two rows:

```
<frameset rows="50%, 50%">
<frame src="frame1a.html" name="f1a" />
<frame src="frame1b.html" name="f1b" />
</frameset>
```

The result can be seen in Figure 6.4.

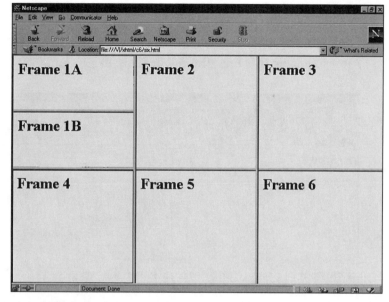

Figure 6.4: *One frame within a larger frameset also defines additional frames.*

TIP

You can nest frames to nearly unlimited levels. Think twice, however, before doing it more than once. The visible space for each frame will become increasingly smaller, and managing the hierarchy of frames becomes correspondingly more difficult.

Linking Between Frames: The `target` Attribute

Now that you're able to create the structure of a framed site, you need to be able to populate it with content and provide links between content in the individual frames. To that end, a mechanism is needed to target content to a specific frame; that's where the *target attribute* comes in.

You've noticed that each frame created so far has its own name. As noted previously, these names must be unique within a browser instance. That uniqueness is the key to success in cross-frame linking. Consider again the initial four-quadrant frameset created at the beginning of this chapter:

```
<frameset rows="50%, 50%" cols="50%, 50%">
<frame src="frame1.html" name="f1" />
<frame src="frame2.html" name="f2" />
<frame src="frame3.html" name="f3" />
<frame src="frame4.html" name="f4" />
</frameset>
```

To allow a page in the f1 frame to contain a link to a document that should be displayed in the f2 frame, the link must be targeted at f2:

```
<h1>Frame 1</h1>
<p>This link will generate <a href="frame2new.html" target="f2">new document
for frame 2</a>.</p>
```

After following this link, the results look like Figure 6.5.

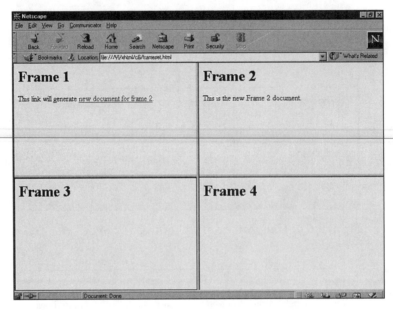

Figure 6.5: *A new document is loaded into a separate frame using the target attribute.*

EXAMPLE

A Navigation System Based on Frames

As you've seen previously in this chapter, two of the most popular uses for frames are to position banner information in a static space, and to provide a fixed navigation system. This next example will combine the two techniques while creating a Web-based recipe archive. The general layout of the site is sketched in Figure 6.6.

The best practice for any frames-based site is to begin by constructing the "shell" for the site, which is the frameset document. In this case, we'll be using nested frames, so we have two documents to create.

EXAMPLE

To begin, we'll divide the screen into the fixed banner frame and the lower portion. The banner frame should be 100 pixels in size, should not be resizable, nor should it have a scrollbar. The second row should assume all remaining available space:

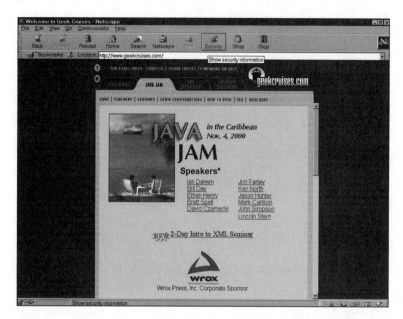

Figure 6.6: *This is the basic framed design for our recipe site.*

```
<?xml version="1.0"?>
<!DOCTYPE html PUBLIC "-//W3C//DTD XHTML 1.0 Frameset//EN"
      "http:// www.w3.org/TR/xhtml1/DTD/xhtml1-frameset.dtd">
<html xmlns="http://www.w3.org/1999/xhtml" xml:lang="en" lang="en">
<head>
<title>Navarro Family Recipes</title>
</head>
<frameset rows="100, *">
<frame src="banner.html" name="banner" noresize="noresize" scrolling="no" />
<frame src="main.html" name="main" />
</frameset>
```

Remember that the first frameset document must contain not only the
`frameset` and `frame` definitions, but also the `noframes` content that provides
alternative access for those browsers that don't support frames. To that
end, you need to provide the content that will be initially placed in each of
the three frames in a single `noframes` section:

```
<noframes>
<body>
<div align="center"><img src="banner.gif" height="90" width="500" alt="Navarro
➥Family Recipes" />
</div>
<h1>Welcome!</h1>
<p>This Web site was created as convenient way to share my family's favorite
➥recipes.
```

```
They have been arranged by category in the list below. Feel free to use as many
➥as you
wish, but if you send them along, please do give the original author
(noted in each file) attribution. </p>
<p>Bon Appetit!</p>
<ul>
<li><a href="soups.html">Soups</a></li>
<li><a href="bread.html">Bread</a></li>
<li><a href="veggies.html">Vegetables</a></li>
<li><a href="beef.html">Beef</a></li>
<li><a href="poultry.html">Poultry</a></li>
<li><a href="desserts.html">Desserts</a></li>
</ul>
</body>
</noframes>
</html>
```

The completed file is shown in Listing 6.1.

Listing 6.1: recipes.html

```
<?xml version="1.0"?>
<!DOCTYPE html PUBLIC "-//W3C//DTD XHTML 1.0 Frameset//EN"
        "http://www.w3.org/TR/xhtml1/DTD/xhtml1-frameset.dtd">
<html xmlns="http://www.w3.org/1999/xhtml" xml:lang="en" lang="en">
<head>
<title>Navarro Family Recipes</title>
</head>
<frameset rows="100, *">
<frame src="banner.html" name="banner" noresize="noresize" scrolling="no" />
<frame src="main.html" name="main" />
</frameset>
<noframes>
<body>
<div align="center"><img src="banner.gif" height="90" width="500" alt="Navarro
➥Family Recipes" />
</div>
<h1>Welcome!</h1>
<p>This Web site was created as convenient way to share my family's favorite
➥recipes.
They have been arranged by category in the list below. Feel free to use as many
➥as you
wish, but if you send them along, please do give the original author
(noted in each file) attribution. </p>
<p>Bon Appetit!</p>
<ul>
<li><a href="soups.html">Soups</a></li>
<li><a href="bread.html">Bread</a></li>
<li><a href="veggies.html">Vegetables</a></li>
<li><a href="beef.html">Beef</a></li>
```

Listing 6.1: continued

```
<li><a href="poultry.html">Poultry</a></li>
<li><a href="desserts.html">Desserts</a></li>
</ul>
</body>
</noframes>
</html>
```

Next we need to divide the lower portion of the screen, referred to in the first file as "main.html", into its two columns; the navigation frame on the left, and the main content frame on the right. These will be sized at 20% and 80%, respectively. Listing 6.2 shows the code used.

Listing 6.2: main.html

```
<?xml version="1.0"?>
<!DOCTYPE html PUBLIC "-//W3C//DTD XHTML 1.0 Frameset//EN"
        "http:// www.w3.org/TR/xhtml1/DTD/xhtml1-frameset.dtd">
<html xmlns="http://www.w3.org/1999/xhtml" xml:lang="en" lang="en">
<head>
<title>Navigation and Content: Navarry Family Recipes</title>
</head>
<frameset cols="20%, 80%">
<frame src="nav.html" name="nav" />
<frame src="content.html" name="content" />
</frameset>
</html>
```

Now that the shell is finished, we need to populate the initial frames. That means we still need to create the following files:

- banner.html

- nav.html

- content.html

The banner file consists of a single image centered within the page, and is found in Listing 6.3.

TIP

Remember that the content pages in a framed site take either the Strict or Transitional doctypes, not Frameset.

Listing 6.3: banner.html

```
<?xml version="1.0"?>
<!DOCTYPE html PUBLIC "-//W3C//DTD XHTML 1.0 Transitional//EN"
        "http:// www.w3.org/TR/xhtml1/DTD/xhtml1-transitional.dtd">
<html xmlns="http://www.w3.org/1999/xhtml" xml:lang="en" lang="en">
<head>
```

Listing 6.3: continued

```
<title>Navarro Family Recipes</title>
</head>
<body>
<div align=center><img src="banner.gif" height="90" width="500" alt="Navarro
➥Family Recipes"></div>
</body>
</html>
```

The links that will be provided in the navigation frame are connected to documents that will be displayed in the content frame. Accordingly, the target attribute must be set to focus the link on that frame (see Listing 6.4).

Listing 6.4: nav.html

```
<?xml version="1.0"?>
<!DOCTYPE html PUBLIC "-//W3C//DTD XHTML 1.0 Transitional//EN"
        "http:// www.w3.org/TR/xhtml1/DTD/xhtml1-transitional.dtd">
<html xmlns="http://www.w3.org/1999/xhtml" xml:lang="en" lang="en">
<head>
<title>Navarro Family Recipes</title>
</head>
<body>
<p><b>Recipe Categories</b></p>
<ul>
<li><a href="soups.html" target="content">Soups</a></li>
<li><a href="bread.html" target="content">Bread</a></li>
<li><a href="veggies.html" target="content">Vegetables</a></li>
<li><a href="beef.html" target="content">Beef</a></li>
<li><a href="poultry.html" target="content">Poultry</a></li>
<li><a href="desserts.html" target="content">Desserts</a></li>
</ul>
</body>
</html>
```

Finally, the initial page for the content frame must be supplied, which is content.html (see Listing 6.5).

Listing 6.5: content.html

```
<?xml version="1.0"?>
<!DOCTYPE html PUBLIC "-//W3C//DTD XHTML 1.0 Transitional//EN"
        "http:// www.w3.org/TR/xhtml1/DTD/xhtml1-transitional.dtd">
<html xmlns="http://www.w3.org/1999/xhtml" xml:lang="en" lang="en">
<head>
<title>Navarro Family Recipes</title>
</head>
<body>
<h2>Welcome!</h2>
<p>This Web site was created as convenient way to share my family's favorite
```

➥recipes.

Listing 6.5: continued

```
They have been arranged by category in the list to your left. Feel free to use
as many as you wish, but if you send them along, please do give the original
author
(noted in each file) attribution. </p>
<p>Bon Appetit!</p>
</body>
</html>
```

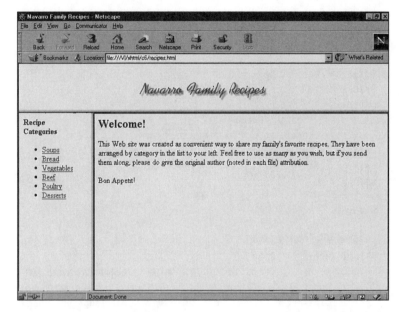

Now you're ready to view the initial Web page, as seen in Figure 6.7.

Figure 6.7: *This is the opening view of the recipe site.*

Each of the subdocuments, the ones linked from nav.html, are created in the same manner, using the XHTML 1.0 Transitional document type. These are found in Listings 6.6 through 6.11.

Listing 6.6: soups.html

```
<?xml version="1.0"?>
<!DOCTYPE html PUBLIC "-//W3C//DTD XHTML 1.0 Transitional//EN"
      "http:// www.w3.org/TR/xhtml1/DTD/xhtml1-transitional.dtd">
<html xmlns="http://www.w3.org/1999/xhtml" xml:lang="en" lang="en">
<head>
<title>Soup Recipes</title>
</head>
<body>
<h2 align="center">Soups</h2>
```

Listing 6.6: continued

```
<ul><li><a href="ccchowder.html">Chicken Corn Chowder</a></li>
<li><a href="pea.html">Split Pea</a></li>
<li><a href="cnoodle.html">Mom's Chicken Noodle</a></li>
</ul>
</body>
</html>
```

Listing 6.7: bread.html

```
<?xml version="1.0"?>
<!DOCTYPE html PUBLIC "-//W3C//DTD XHTML 1.0 Transitional//EN"
     "http:// www.w3.org/TR/xhtml1/DTD/xhtml1-transitional.dtd">
<html xmlns="http://www.w3.org/1999/xhtml" xml:lang="en" lang="en">
<head>
<title>Bread Recipes</title>
</head>
<body>
<h2 align="center">Bread</h2>
<ul><li><a href="sour.html">Sourdough</a></li>
<li><a href="7grain.html">Hearty Seven Grain</a></li>
<li><a href="rye.html">Jewish Rye</a></li>
</ul>
</body>
</html>
```

Listing 6.8: veggies.html

```
<?xml version="1.0"?>
<!DOCTYPE html PUBLIC "-//W3C//DTD XHTML 1.0 Transitional//EN"
     "http:// www.w3.org/TR/xhtml1/DTD/xhtml1-transitional.dtd">
<html xmlns="http://www.w3.org/1999/xhtml" xml:lang="en" lang="en">
<head>
<title>Vegetable Recipes</title>
</head>
<body>
<h2 align="center">Vegetables</h2>
<ul><li><a href="creamedcorn.html">Creamed Corn</a></li>
<li><a href="glazedcarrots.html">Glazed Carrots</a></li>
<li><a href="asianbeans.html">Asian Roasted Green Beans</a></li>
</ul>
</body>
</html>
```

Listing 6.9: beef.html

```
<?xml version="1.0"?>
<!DOCTYPE html PUBLIC "-//W3C//DTD XHTML 1.0 Transitional//EN"
     "http:// www.w3.org/TR/xhtml1/DTD/xhtml1-transitional.dtd">
<html xmlns="http://www.w3.org/1999/xhtml" xml:lang="en" lang="en">
<head>
```

```
<title>Beef Recipes</title>
```

Listing 6.9: continued

```
</head>
<body>
<h2 align="center">Beef</h2>
<ul><li><a href="tritip.html">Monterey Tri-Tip</a></li>
<li><a href="fajitas.html">Steak Fajitas</a></li>
<li><a href="ribroast.html">Standing Rib Roast</a></li>
</ul>
</body>
</html>
```

Listing 6.10: poultry.html

```
<?xml version="1.0"?>
<!DOCTYPE html PUBLIC "-//W3C//DTD XHTML 1.0 Transitional//EN"
      "http:// www.w3.org/TR/xhtml1/DTD/xhtml1-transitional.dtd">
<html xmlns="http://www.w3.org/1999/xhtml" xml:lang="en" lang="en">
<head>
<title>Poultry Recipes</title>
</head>
<body>
<h2 align="center">Poultry</h2>
<ul><li><a href="hmchicken.html">Ann's Honey Mustard Chicken</a></li>
<li><a href="tchicken.html">Teriyaki Chicken</a></li>
<li><a href="picatta.html">Chicken Picatta</a></li>
</ul>
</body>
</html>
```

Listing 6.11: desserts.html

```
<?xml version="1.0"?>
<!DOCTYPE html PUBLIC "-//W3C//DTD XHTML 1.0 Transitional//EN"
      "http:// www.w3.org/TR/xhtml1/DTD/xhtml1-transitional.dtd">
<html xmlns="http://www.w3.org/1999/xhtml" xml:lang="en" lang="en">
<head>
<title>Dessert Recipes</title>
</head>
<body>
<h2 align="center">Desserts</h2>
<ul><li><a href="chocmouse.html">Chocolate Mousse</a></li>
<li><a href="peanutpie.html">Peanut Butter Pie</a></li>
<li><a href="peaches.html">Peaches and Cream</a></li>
</ul>
</body>
</html>
```

NOTE

In the interest of brevity, the actual recipe files have not been provided here. The functionality of the site—loading documents in the content frame when linked in the nav frame—is the desired result being illustrated.

After you have each of these files written, your site is complete. Test your implementation of the frames by clicking any of the categories in the navi-

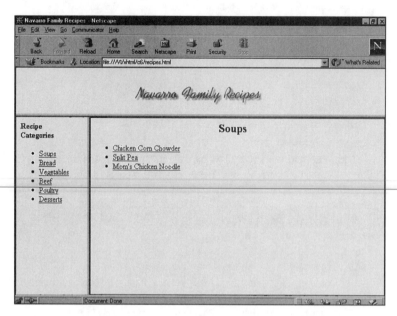

gation menu, and the new page should load in the right-hand content frame (see Figure 6.8).

Figure 6.8: *Clicking a link in the navigation frame loads the document in the content frame.*

Design Tips for Frames

Web users for the most part either love frames or they hate them. There's very little middle ground on the subject. Although some people think they've gotten a bit of a bad rap, most of the complaints about frames are firmly grounded in usability issues.

Interoperability

Nearly by definition, frames suffer from a lack of interoperability. Support is limited to the major browsers designed for desktop computer use. Limitations in screen size, processing power, or rendering methods (in the case of screen readers and Braille devices) make much of framed content unreachable by a considerable portion of the Web audience.

Additionally, some authors tend to find it cumbersome to maintain alternative access methods, or find the noframes syntax confusing or difficult to implement.

User Manipulation

One of the highest compliments a Web page can get is to find itself on a user's bookmark or favorites list. After all, that's what you're after, isn't it, visitors who find your information to be a valuable resource?

But what happens when they try to bookmark a framed site? The bookmark is made to the main site, not the individual page the user has navigated to. When working in a knowledge base or other system where users can find themselves many levels into a site, this can be an extremely frustrating experience for them to not be able to locate the document again using the bookmark.

A second problem comes up when users try to print framed material. Most browsers do not support the printing of the entire window, instead printing only the frame that currently has the system focus. Those browsers that do attempt to print the entire window (such as Internet Explorer 4 or 5), often generate inconsistent results when content in any of the frames is out of view. Sometimes content will be cropped to the visible area, and other times users find themselves with page after page of partially blank paper as the printer tries to recreate the framed look on the screen although it's only scrolling through a single frame.

Users can, to some extent, work around this problem by clicking within the frame they want to print, and most browsers will acknowledge the change in focus and print the desired area. However, without the remaining context provided by the other frames, some data might be lost when the printed version is read at a later date.

Size with Care

When working with fixed frame sizes, as you did in the recipe site, be very careful to measure your content accurately. If a frame is of a fixed size, and you prevent scrolling and resizing in the frame element, your users might not be able to view all of the content you intended if it requires more than the visible space. Figure 6.9 shows what happens when you change the banner frame to a size of 60 (versus the original 100) on the recipe site. As you can see, the banner image is chopped off just below its top.

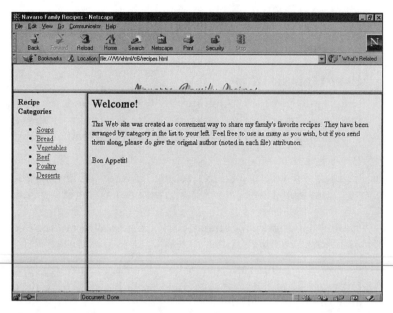

Other size issues can include frames that scroll horizontally (perhaps because of an overly large image or table that forces the scroll) that don't necessarily have to be that way, or frames so small that they result in a column of text just a word or two wide.

Figure 6.9: An improperly sized fixed frame can result in content being forced out of view.

What's Next

In this chapter you've explored the possibilities available when you frame several documents within a single browser window. You can create fixed frames with content that doesn't change, and other frames that can load new documents within their own borders or manipulate the documents within other frames. You've also learned some of the hazards of working with frames and can watch out for accessibility and interoperability problems.

Next up in Chapter 7, "Universal Accessibility on the Web," you'll take a close look at how Web designers can promote interoperability and accessibility in their Web site by authoring valid XHTML. Additional techniques that enhance accessibility for users with disabilities or those using today's

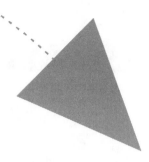

Universal Accessibility on the Web

When the topic of access to the Web for people with disabilities comes up, the discussion can often take on a very moral and righteous tone. This chapter is not going to lecture you on morality, or how to make the world a better place by adding a few attributes to your XHTML code. What we will discuss in this chapter is the realities that face many Web users, and how—by keeping a few simple issues in mind while developing your pages—you can improve your chances of disseminating the information you desire to as many people as possible.

This chapter teaches you:

- How the Web can be inaccessible
- That accessibility can help traditional users, too
- About the Web Accessibility Initiative
- How to implement the Web Content Authoring Guidelines

The Scope of Accessibility

The Web is sometimes described as the most enabling technology to become available for disabled users, while at the same time often possessing more barriers to access than most other media.

Before discussing ways to make the Web more accessible, we must first understand how it can be *inaccessible*, something that's not always easy for an able-bodied person to imagine. Disabilities that can impact the Web can be placed in four major groups:

- **Visual Disabilities**—Users might be fully or partially blind, have impaired color vision, or simply need the use of corrective lenses. Graphics that aren't labeled or described, a lack of keyboard-based navigation support, or even small print and low-contrast colors can result in barriers to information.

- **Hearing Disabilities**—A lack of captioning, transcripts, or other alternative distributions of audio-based content can leave hearing-impaired users without important information.

- **Physical Disabilities**—Some users might have limited skill or dexterity for typing, operating a mouse or trackball, or other selection pointer. Devices are available that do amazing things, such as allow a user's gaze to be tracked to "type" on a light-activated keyboard or "sip and puff" tubes that can be used by quadriplegics to turn on and off switches for simple binary decisions regarding the computer. Less drastic difficulties such as dealing with very small links within very small font sizes might be difficult for some users to accurately hover over and select, preventing full access to the site.

- **Cognitive and Neurological Disabilities**—A lack of clear and consistent labeling, navigation systems, and other visual cues can confuse many users. Excessive use of jargon on sites that will be accessed by the lay-public, or highly technical information presented to such an audience without illustration, can inhibit comprehension. Additionally, flashing, flickering, or other high-frequency movements can have serious consequences for users dealing with epilepsy or other light- and motion-sensitive conditions.

Estimates have been made that 10 to 20% of the population in most developed countries have one form of disability or another. Some of them won't affect Web access, whereas other conditions that are typical of advancing age will impact nearly all of us at one stage or another in our lives. The combination of users who fit a classical definition of disabled and those who have age-related issues constitutes a significant percentage of the potential online audience.

Advances in technology originally intended to serve a disabled audience frequently benefit the general public as much or, as a percentage of use, even more than the intended recipient of aid.

Two of my favorite examples are the sidewalk curbcut and closed-captioned television broadcasts. Not that many years ago, perhaps 10–15 years in most places, finding the curbs cut down to street level on corners throughout a city was rare, as were ramps used to bypass outdoor stairways.

Both curbcuts and ramps were originally incorporated into public works projects to assist wheelchair-bound citizens in crossing streets and gaining access to buildings previously only reachable by stairs. But look around the next time you take a walk outside or go for a drive. Who is using those features? You'll undoubtedly see several grateful parents pushing baby strollers, a postal worker pushing a delivery cart, even roller-skaters using them for a smooth transition between sidewalk and roadway. These concrete features are easily used 9 out of 10 times (or even more) for other-than-intended, but very convenient, purposes.

Closed-captioning can often be seen in sports bars or busy airport lounges—places where there's a television broadcasting the news or a game, but the ambient noise level is high enough that hearing the audio track is difficult to impossible. These establishments turn on the closed-captioning text track available on most television broadcast streams, and hearing users can happily sit across the room and still "hear" the information that accompanies the pictures, no lip-reading required.

Now I'm not intending to suggest that all of the accessibility design techniques you'll learn will be life enhancing or even convenient to the traditional user. Instead, I remind you of these situations to encourage you to remember that enhancements have a way of finding usefulness in the mainstream world as they also serve the needs of those with disabilities.

The W3C Web Accessibility Initiative

In 1997 the World Wide Web Consortium began research into what is now termed "universal accessibility" on the Web. A program office was established under the auspices of the W3C, funded in part through grants and cooperative efforts with the United States National Science Foundation, the U.S. Department of Education's National Institute on Disability and Rehabilitation Research, the European Commission, the Canadian Government, Industry Canada's Assistive Devices Industry Office, IBM/Lotus, Microsoft, Bell Atlantic, and many more.

The WAI program has five primary goals:

- Ensure that new Web technologies support accessibility.

- Develop guidelines for implementing accessibility features.

- Develop tools to evaluate and facilitate accessibility.

- Publish materials and conduct events that educate the public and Web-development community about accessibility, and perform other outreach tasks.

- Coordinate with research and development, reviewing adoption rates of accessible techniques, collaborating with outside research projects, and doing other tasks as required.

We'll be focusing on several documents published by the WAI program throughout the rest of this chapter.

The Web Content Authoring Guidelines

One of the first documents produced by the program aimed at the Web developer was the Web Content Authoring Guidelines (WCAG). Fourteen guidelines describe general principles of accessible design. Several checkpoints are provided for each guideline, giving practical applications for each design principle. The checkpoints are assigned one of three priorities:

- **Priority One**—This checkpoint *must* be satisfied, or at least one group will be *unable* to access the information.

- **Priority Two**—This checkpoint *should* be satisfied; otherwise, at least one group *might find it difficult* to access the information. Unresolved issues might represent significant (though not impossible) barriers.

- **Priority Three**—This checkpoint *might* be satisfied, or at least one group will find it somewhat difficult to access the information.

Conformance to the guidelines is rated as Level-A, Double-A, or Triple-A. Level-A conformance occurs when a site meets all Priority One checkpoints. Double-A sites meet all Priority One and Two checkpoints, and Triple-A meets all checkpoints, regardless of priority.

The full WCAG document can be found online at
`http://www.w3.org/TR/WAI-WEBCONTENT/`.

There has been controversy surrounding the WCAG document on several levels. First, many designers, even those with significant experience, find the document very dense and difficult to understand. The design principles tend to be worded vaguely (a by-product of consensus-in-committee authoring of documents), and the presentation of checkpoints and priorities can be overwhelming.

To ease the learning curve, the WAI program has published several "techniques" documents with solid examples for implementing the design principles. This has been somewhat helpful, although the result still has a tendency to be more academic than practical. Another tool is a "checklist of checkpoints" that can be printed and used as an evaluation and record-keeping tool in the post-design phase. The checklist can be accessed at `http://www.w3.org/TR/WAI-WEBCONTENT/full-checklist.html`.

Second, the conformance levels provide no leeway in implementation. If a site developer cannot meet a single Priority Two checkpoint, the site cannot be labeled Double-A conformant, no matter if every other Priority Two checkpoint is met. Many feel this results in discouraging implementation of the checkpoints sites *can* meet, because the effort will not be "rewarded" with the more desirable conformance ranking. The cost of implementation is something every company or individual will have to evaluate when planning their design techniques.

Techniques for Web Content Authoring Guidelines

In this section we'll look at each of the 12 HTML techniques discussed in the Techniques for WCAG document published by the W3C. Additional examples and issues beyond what are presented here are included in the document online at `http://www.w3.org/TR/WAI-WEBCONTENT-TECHS/`.

Designing Documents Structurally

The concept of designing documents based on their structure versus their visual look is something we've talked about in nearly every chapter so far. Even so, it's worth repeating here, with a slightly different perspective.

EXAMPLE

Think for a moment about how this chapter is presented. On the first page, it has a chapter number, then on the next line a chapter title. There's a paragraph or so of text, and then a bulleted list of things you'll be reading about. On the following page, there's a heading written in white letters on a black background. Each of these items represent a specific structural portion of the chapter. In the initial manuscript I submitted to the publisher, it didn't just say "write the number 7," and then "Universal Accessibility on the Web," leaving the reader to *interpret* the structural significance of those items. Instead, both were clearly labeled as heading Level-A (the topmost) and heading level B, respectively.

If we were to mark up the chapter using XHTML, those structures would be mapped to the h1 and h2 elements. By using the elements for their hierarchical structure, I can give the content of the elements the proper semantic importance. If I were to begin with the chapter number in an h2 element, versus an h1 element, simply because I preferred the default size and font weight, I'd lose the structural cue as to its place in the document.

Defining Languages

Language definition is one type of meta information most frequently over-looked by Web designers. Many authors will assume their site visitors will read and speak the same language they do (an affliction, I'm sad to say, that is more commmon among Americans than residents of other countries).

Begin by indicating the base language for the document using the `xml:lang` and `lang` attributes on the `html` element. Screen readers or other aural presentations can select the appropriate pronunciation, perhaps even distinguishing between U.S. English traditions and British practices.

Additionally, to name just a few advantages, indexing systems such as search engines can provide the additional data of language when cataloging sites, tactile readers (for example, Braille devices) can insert the right accent characters, or a user can automatically run a document through a translation utility if the base language isn't his preferred tongue.

EXAMPLE

Just as important as setting the base language is bounding the presence of secondary languages embedded within the document. Place names, addresses, and phrases are frequent candidates for language annotation:

```
<p>Our hotel was located on the Avenida Rafael E. Melgar Sur, just off the
dazzling white beaches of Cozumel. As we stepped out of the cab we were met
with a friendly greeting, "Holas, Amigas!"</p>
```

Both the street name and the greeting can be marked as Spanish, using the span element and the `lang` and `xml:lang` attributes:

```
<p>Our hotel was located on the <span lang="es" xml:lang="es">Avenida Rafael E.
Melgar Sur</span> just off the dazzling white beaches of Cozumel. As we stepped
out of the cab we were met with a friendly greeting, <span lang="es"
xml:lang="es">"Holas, Amigas!"</p>
```

Emphasizing Text with Additional Structure

As presentational markup crept into HTML, visual designers began using visually specific tags to emphasize phrases and other inline elements. Instead of using

```
<strong>This sentence is important.</strong>
```

they'd write

```
<b>This sentence is important.</b>
```

For the visual browser, the intended result generally came through. Sighted readers have learned to associated boldface text with something important. But what about the user who can't see the boldface treatment? By using the structural approach of strong, screen readers or tactile devices have the opportunity to give strong emphasis to the contained text in their own unique way.

A List Is a List Is a List

Another early frustration for visually oriented designers was the lack of ability to control margins and indentation within the Web browser. Someone noticed that basic lists were traditionally presented not only with bullets or numbers, but with at least a tab-stop-worth of indentation. Soon "indents" were being created by placing content within a `<ul>` or `<ol>` tag set (without including any list items).

Unfortunately, not only is this not valid code (as you learned in Chapter 2, "Adding Semantics to Structure," the content model of both `ul` and `ol` allows only `li` elements inside), the intended result wasn't always achieved.

Although many popular browsers treated lists in that indented manner, the HTML and XHTML recommendations don't require them to. A visual user agent might simply start the list at the left gutter, but a screen reader or tactile browser might directly tell the user that an ordered or unordered list is about to be presented. When no list items follow, the presentation is likely to be confusing.

The bottom line here is easy: Use lists for lists. Control indentation and other layout treatments using style sheets.

Tables: Tabular Data or Layout?

In Chapter 5, "Working with Tables," you worked through several examples that provided both tabular structure for data, and contextual information through the use of scoping, headers, IDs, and axis. Captions, summaries, headers, and footers also add utility to tabular presentations. Many of these features were added specifically to enhance accessibility, as we discussed, and should continue to be practiced.

✔ To review the use of these elements and attributes in your tables, see "Data Alignment—`axis` and `id`," p. 95.

To create the most accessible pages, tabular content is all that tables should be used for. But even the most evangelistic supporter of accessible, structural design will often concede that tables do have their uses for basic layout purposes. One of the most frequently cited cases is that of the left column of navigation information, with the main document presented in a wider column on the right.

When using this form of table, you can take several steps to ensure usability through alternative clients. The contents of each cell should make sense, whether read cell to cell from left to right, top to bottom, or some other combination. Readability can be enhanced by enclosing the content within headings, paragraphs, and other structural elements, so that the cellular content can stand on its own. This specifically precludes using tables to create a newspaper-column effect for text.

Links

Hyperlinks provide dual functionality within a Web page. They create the mechanical function of linking one document to another. But when written correctly, they also provide contextual information about the link. Where will the link take me? Is it something I'm interested in seeing? Sadly, there are thousands of Web pages online that only tell you to "click here!":

```
<p>I live in Port Charlotte, Florida. <a
href="http://www.charlottecountyfl.com">Click here</a> to visit resources for
visitors, residents, or potential residents.
```

This type of link makes two assumptions that won't always hold true. First, it assumes that the link is activated by clicking, which means a mouse or a trackball is in use. Laptop users might tap their fingers on a touch-pad. PDA owners press a stylus against the screen. Listeners using a screen reader might press a single letter or number their program has associated with the link, or perhaps they'll even speak a number to follow the link. Second, not all users will see where "here" is, and if they don't click, what do they do with "here"?

EXAMPLE

Instead, you can rewrite the hyperlink in the previous example to create a link that gives context to the hyperlink:

```
<p>I live in Port Charlotte, Florida. The <a href="http://
www.charlottecountyfl.com">Charlotte County Web site</a> has dozens of
resources for visitors, residents, or potential residents.</p>
```

Provide Alternative Information for Images

Dealing with graphical content on a non-graphical user agent is, in my opinion, one of the most difficult aspects of Web design. The best advice I've been given is to look at the page and pretend you must read and describe it to someone who is blind. What images are important? What do they represent? Should they be described literally or for the function they serve?

After those questions are answered, you have a good start on filling in the required ALT attribute for each image.

TIP

Sometimes designers use images that aren't intended to convey information. One design technique makes heavy use of blank graphics to force a particular layout (a technique I don't recommend, but it is out there). These images, often referred to as "spacer images," and other non-essential graphics can validly be given an empty ALT attribute value—for example, alt="".

TIP

An empty ALT attribute is actually preferable to one holding an asterisk, space, or other "filler" character. Screen readers will speak each asterisk if used that way. Far better to leave it empty than to have a lot of garbage read to you.

EXAMPLE

Lengthy or complex descriptions should be stored in a secondary document, referenced by the longdesc attribute:

```
<img src="Q1expenses.gif" alt="First Quarter Expenses" longdesc="q1.html" />
```

The content of q1.html would be a fully developed XHTML document (meaning doctype declaration, head, and so on), along with a detailed description:

```
<p>This pie chart shows the distribution of first quarter operating expenses.
Payroll was the largest expenditure at 48%…</p>
```

Applets and Objects

Applets and other embedded content such as QuickTime movies, Flash animations, and even sound files, can be inserted in a document using either the applet or object element.

EXAMPLE

The object element is preferred for its generic syntax and the ability to provide a text equivalent for the object as the content of the element, as well as a cascade of alternative objects to present to the user:

```
<object data="trussing.mpeg" type="video/mpeg">
<object data="trussing.gif" type="image/gif">
<p>To truss the turkey, pull the legs together and tie around the bones with
➥string…</p>
</object>
</object>
```

If the user agent supports mpeg movies, the content of the outermost object element, the movie will be played. If it doesn't, the still image will be offered. If a still image cannot be rendered, the text content will be given.

Audio and Video

Audio presentations, and the audio track portion of video presentations, should have a text-based transcript available or, if the format allows it (as with *SMIL*, the Synchronized Multimedia Integration Language), provide the text-track as a synchronized alternative to the native audio track (a la closed-captioning services for television).

If You Must Frame...

Chapter 6, "Using Frames," introduced you to the uses of frames. Still controversial to use, they are doubly problematic for non-traditional browsers. I won't review the techniques to provide alternatives again here, but will caution you to consider all other alternatives before settling on a framed presentation.

Collect Data with Forms

Forms can be given enhancements, again useful not only for accessibility purposes but for the mainstream user as well. Two techniques we'll feature here are the use of the `tabindex` attribute and access keys.

Available as an attribute on all input controls, `tabindex` sets the order in which the browser should shift the focus between controls when the Tab key is pressed. The value is a number, beginning with 1 for the first tab stop, increasing by one whole number as you go.

The `accesskey` attribute is a single specific letter on the keyboard that is bound to a given form control. By pressing or otherwise activating that letter, the user will be taken to the associated control.

This short form uses labels to provide context for each input control, `tabindex` order, and access key:

EXAMPLE

```
<form action="submit" method="post">
<label>User Name</label><input type="text" name="user" size="20" tabindex="1"
➥accesskey="u" />
<label>Password</label><input type="text" name="password" size="20" tabindex="2"
➥accesskey="p" />
<input type="submit" tabindex="3" accesskey="s" />
</form>
```

This form can now be navigated by pointing and clicking inside each control, by using the Tab key to cycle through each control, or by activating a single keyboard entry to directly access a specific control.

Script Management with Non-Traditional Browsers

Scripts can be written to interact with the browser in a device-independent manner. Rather than capturing the `onmouseover` event, instead look for `onfocus` or `onselect`. If you must use device-dependent code, consider redundant scripting—for example, if using `onmousedown`, also use `onkeydown` for keyboard activation.

For the device or browser that can't support scripts at all, a non-script alternative can be provided using the `noscript` element. The `noscript` element should contain a fully functional alternative to the script, similar to the `noframes` content on framed sites.

The Checkpoints

Each of the checkpoints defined in the WCAG document are presented here in one of three tables; Tables 7.1 through 4.4 show the checkpoints for each priority level. The tables are organized by priority and include the feature that the checkpoint covers (general issues, images, and so on) and the instruction.

Table 7.1: Priority One Checkpoints

XHTML Feature	Checkpoint
General	Provide a text equivalent for every non-text element(includes images, image maps, animations, applets and programmatic objects, ascii art, frames, scripts, sounds, audio, and video).
	All information conveyed with color is available if the color were removed.
	Clearly identify any changes in natural language for both documents and text-equivalent sections.
	Documents must be readable without their associated style sheet.
	Equivalents for dynamically generated content must be updated when the dynamic content changes.
	Avoid causing the screen to flicker until all user agents allow user-initiated control over the flicker.
	Use the clearest and simplest language appropriate for the site's content.
Images or image maps	Provide redundant text links for active areas of server- side image maps.
	Provide client-side image maps in favor or server-side maps, unless available geometric shapes cannot be defined as necessary.
Tables	For data tables, provide row and column headers.
	Use markup to associate data cells with header cells when two or more logical levels of headers exist.
Frames	Each frame must have a meaningful title attribute.
Applets and scripts	Pages should be usable when scripts or applet support is turned off. If this is not possible, an alternative page must be provided.
Multimedia	Provide an auditory version of the visual tracks of multimedia presentations.
	For any time-based multimedia presentations, also synchronize equivalent alternatives.
"If all else fails"	Provide an alternative page that uses W3C technologies, that *is* accessible, and that is updated as often as the main page.

Table 7.2: Priority Two Checkpoints

XHTML Feature	Checkpoint
General	Foreground and background colors should have sufficient contrast.
	When markup is available, use markup and text rather than images to convey information.
	Create documents that validate against published DTDs.
	Use style sheets for layout and presentation.
	Use relative rather than absolute units in attribute values.
	Use header elements to convey structure, and use them according to specification.

Table 7.2: continued

XHTML Feature	Checkpoint
	Mark up lists and list items properly.
	Mark up quotations. Do not use quotation markup to produce indentation or other visual effect.
	Ensure that dynamic content is accessible or provide accessible alternatives.
	Allow the user to turn off blinking (until user agents provide a user-adjustable setting).
	Do not create auto-refreshing pages (until user agents allow user-control of this feature).
	Do not use markup to provide auto-redirects. Use server controls instead.
	Do not create pop-up windows or cause the current window to change without informing the user.
	Use W3C technologies when available, and the latest version that is supported.
	Avoid deprecated features in W3C technologies.
	Divide large blocks of information into more manageable units where appropriate.
	Clearly identify the target of each link.
	Provide metadata as necessary to add semantic information to pages and sites.
	Provide information about the general layout of a site (site map, table of contents, and so on).
	Use consistent navigation schemes.
Tables	Do not use tables for layout unless the content can be sufficiently linearized.
	If you do use tables for layout, do not then use structural information for visual rendering.
Frames	Describe the purpose of a frame and how it relates to other frames if this is not obvious in the frame titles.
Forms	Position labels clearly in relationship to their input controls, until all user agents allow explicit binding.
	Associate labels explicitly with their controls when possible.
Applets and scripts	Use event handlers that are device independent.
	Avoid movement in pages until user agents allow the user to freeze content.
	Programmatic applets or scripts should be directly accessible or compatible with assistive technologies. (If functionality is critical, this becomes a Priority One checkpoint.)
	Any element that has its own interface must be operated in a device-independent manner.
	For scripts, specify logical event handlers rather than device-dependent handlers.

Table 7.3: Priority Three Checkpoints

XHTML Feature	Checkpoint
General	Expand the first instance of abbreviations and acronyms.
	Identify the primary natural language of each document.
	Create a logical tab order between links, form controls, and objects.
	Provide keyboard shortcuts to important links, form controls, and grouped form controls.
	Until user agents render adjacent links distinctly, provide non-linked printable characters between adjacent links.
	Provide information so that users can receive information according to their preferences for language, content type, and so on.
	Highlight navigation systems to heighten access to them.
	Group related links, identify the group, and, until user agents do so, provide a means to bypass the group.
	If search functions are provided, enable different search techniques to serve all skill levels and differing preferences.
	Place distinguishing information at the beginning of headings, paragraphs, lists, and so on.
	Provide information about document collections (for example, note when documents span more than one file).
	Provide a means to skip over multi-line ASCII art.
	Supplement text with graphical or auditory information if it will facilitate comprehension.
	Be consistent in style of presentation across related pages.
Images and image maps	Provide redundant text links for each active area of client-side image maps.
Tables	Provide summaries for tables.
	Provide abbreviations for header labels.
	Provide a linear text alternative for all side-by- side, wrapped columnar text layouts.
Forms	Include default, placeholding text in all empty form controls.

What's Next

In this chapter, you have learned how people with disabilities might face barriers when accessing online content. You've been introduced to Web Content Authoring Guidelines and techniques for creating accessible Web pages.

Next up, we'll take a look at implementing XHTML in today's Web sites, both on the Web and in the intranet or extranet, and how authors can smooth the transition between HTML 4 and XHTML.

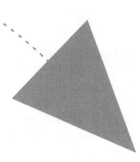

Validating XHTML Documents

Before making your Web pages accessible to the public, you'll want to take several steps to make sure they're in the best shape possible. They should be run through a spell-checker, a proofreader can help with grammar, a copy editor might be employed to help out, and your pages might need to go through several levels of managerial approval if you're working on a company site. All of these tasks are necessary in many cases, but one more check should be made before "going live": validation.

This chapter teaches you:

- What validation means
- How to use the W3C HTML Validation Service
- How to interpret and correct errors

Grammar Checking for the Web

Two of the basic rules governing how XHTML documents are created are defined as being *well-formed* and *valid*. Well-formed means that the document is complete; that is, tags that have been opened are closed, attribute values are fully quoted, and other structural components are complete. Using a grammar analogy, a well-formed document could be compared to a complete sentence. It has, at a minimum, a subject and a verb.

Validity takes the analogy one step further. A valid document is not only well-formed, but also meets all the additional grammar rules laid out in the DTD. The elements used must be defined in the DTD, the attributes must have appropriate values, the content model of elements must match the model defined, and so on. In essence, the validator makes sure you haven't misplaced your modifiers or used the wrong verb tense.

Why Validate?

Because XHTML requires that documents be both well-formed and valid, and validity itself requires well-formedness, one check can ascertain that a document conforms to both. Practically, validating your documents provides the experienced Web author benefit in finding errors that were unintentional, such as typos or a forgotten closing tag.

Typo Control

One of the most rudimentary uses of validation is to catch some of the simple problems, such as typographical errors. Any developer who's not using an authoring tool that creates tags for him is bound to make a few typos in any given document. Rather than having to painstakingly read each page for problems, a quick pass through the validator can point them out in seconds (see Figure 8.1).

TIP

Web authors from outside the United States should be aware that XHTML has adopted U.S. English standards of spelling. Terms such as "colour" and "centre" are spelled as "color" and "center." Validators will consider the Queen's English versions as erroneous.

Beyond the spelling of words used as element and attribute names, the validator can check the accuracy of your typing when quoting values, entering slashes and brackets, and any other characters necessary to make tags complete.

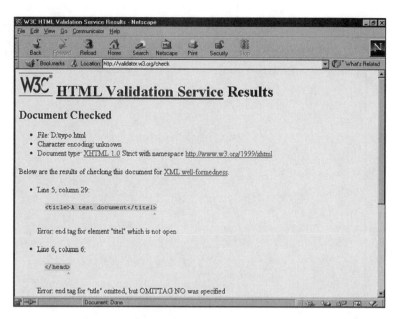

Figure 8.1: *Validator reports can point out typographical errors.*

What You See Is What You *Intended* to See

Many errors in well-formedness are apparent when you view an XHTML document in a Web browser for the first time. If you've forgotten to close a hyperlink with the requisite </a> tag, you'll quickly notice the entire paragraph (or more!) that's treated as a link rather than the word or small phrase that was intended (see Figure 8.2).

Although some errors—such as the runaway link or mismatched heading tags—are nearly universally obvious to the eye, not all well-formedness errors can be immediately spotted. This is because many Web browsers have been taught to try and interpret what the document author *intended* to do rather than what the author really did. Some might argue this programmatic "help" is a good thing, but it can lull authors into complacency and cause unnecessary frustration for site visitors.

EXAMPLE

As a test, try editing one of your table exercises from Chapter 5, "Working with Tables," and leaving off the closing </table> tag. View the file in both Netscape Navigator and Internet Explorer. What do you see?

If your system is like mine, you'll see the table as you intended in Internet Explorer, which "helped" you and assumed you did close your table (see Figure 8.3). However, in Navigator, the page is blank! A blank page is certainly not what you intended. If you only "spot checked" your work in Internet Explorer, you might never have known there was a problem until someone pointed it out to you.

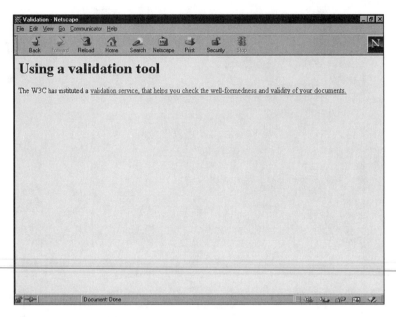

Figure 8.2: *Well-formedness errors can be easy to spot on your own; in this case, a missing </a> tag.*

 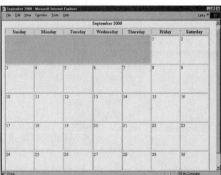

Figure 8.3: *A single missing tag can have drastically different results!*

TIP

Feedback on the Web tends to mimic that of any service industry. You're far more likely to have dissatisfied visitors just go away and never return, rather than complain and tell you what's wrong. Therefore, relying on user feedback to know if there's a problem can be a dangerous practice.

Interoperability

One issue that's becoming more and more important as the Web is expanding beyond the desktop computer is that of interoperability. What works on your desktop, a computer with a Pentium III processor and 128MB of RAM, is not necessarily going to work on your 8MB Palm Vx, or on your cell-phone with an even smaller memory allotment. In fact, we can almost guarantee that much of it *won't* work.

Now of course I'm not suggesting that a cell-phone should be able to visit all Web sites. We know that's simply not possible, nor is it even desirable. However, making sure that your Web pages are well-formed and valid can increase the likelihood that less powerful devices can make use of the sites you do produce.

Smaller devices simply don't have the computing power to handle the complex process required to anticipate what a document author might have intended to write. Browsers that don't attempt to do this are smaller and can run on less powerful machines, which means that your Web pages, when well-formed and valid, have a higher likelihood of success on those same devices.

Using the W3C Validator

There are several validation services available online, but the most accurate service is inevitably found right at the source: the W3C. The W3C service is derived from the work of Gerald Oskoboiny, who first debuted his site as the "Kinder, Gentler Validator" in the mid-1990s. Gerald later went to work for the W3C, revamping the project to be a formal service offered by the W3C. Now known simply as the W3C HTML Validation Service, it can be found at http://validator.w3.org (see Figure 8.4).

NOTE

Although the service is called the "HTML Validation Service," it can validate XHTML as well. A link on the site details which DTDs the service has access to and can validate against.

How the Process Works

The W3C HTML Validation Service provides an SGML-based validation. The ideas that we've discussed previously in this chapter, specfically validity, are carried over into HTML and XHTML from SGML.

The first step to validating your page is to enter its URL in the form provided by the service. The page must be accessible via the Web. If it's on an intranet or behind any system that controls HTTP access, the service can attempt username and password authentication based on data you provide when prompted.

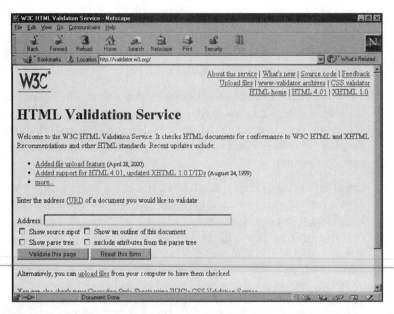

Figure 8.4: *The W3C HTML Validation Service Web site is used to check conformance to the XHTML specifications.*

The CGI script activated by your form submission will retrieve your document from the URI specified, and then parse the file looking for errors. The validator uses the DTD specified in your doctype declaration to determine just which grammar it's validating against. As it parses the document, it makes note of any errors found and where they are, and compiles them for the report back to you when it's finished.

The Meaning of Success

If you've been very careful in creating your document, you could get a clean bill of health the first time through on the validator. Your success report will look something like Figure 8.5.

Four items are listed with bullet points, detailing several characteristics of the page. Those are

- The URL of the page retrieved

- The type of Web server the page was found on (in this case, Microsoft Internet Information Server 4.0)

- What character encoding the document uses (if declared)

- The DTD referenced by the document type declaration and its accompanying namespace

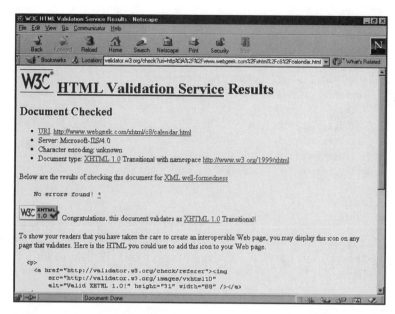

Figure 8.5: *The Validator reports a successful document.*

Next, the validator lets us know that it checked the document for XML well-formedness, because we're working with an XML application (XHTML). Finally, the end result is no errors found!

The icon displayed is one that many authors choose to add to their pages to show that they have indeed checked the validity of their documents, and that they believe in caring about such matters. It would be easy for me to begin evangelizing about the value of validity at this point, but I'll refrain. By investigating XHTML through this book and other efforts that you're making, you've already taken a step toward working in a well-formed and valid manner with all your documents!

Interpreting Error Reports

EXAMPLE

Although it's certainly nice to get a "no errors" report on the first pass through the validator, not every document will succeed. Your next task, then, is learning how to interpret the error reports given by the validator. Listing 8.1 is a simple XHTML document that contains a few well-formedness errors.

Listing 8.1: `trip.html`

```
<!DOCTYPE html PUBLIC "-//W3C//DTD XHTML 1.0 Strict//EN"
    "DTD/xhtml1-strict.dtd">
<html>
<head>
```

Listing 8.1: continued

```
<title>Shopping List
</head>
<body>
<h1>Things to get before the trip</h2>
<p>Before we leave, we need:
<ul>
<li>Beach towels</li>
<li>Sunblock</li>
<li>New snorkels
<li>Flippers for Linda</li>
</Ul>
</body>
</html>
```

Type up and upload this page to your Web site, and you can run it through the validator and see the results yourself. We'll also step through them here.

The first two bullet items in the error report (see Figure 8.6) refer to the same problem.

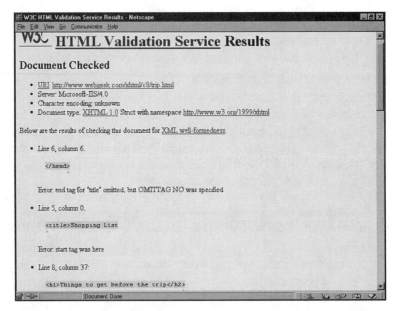

Figure 8.6: Well-formedness errors are reported by the validator.

The first bulletted item says "Error: end tag for "title" omitted, but OMITTAG NO was specified". Jump to the second bullet point, and the validator helpfully shows you where the title tag began. The first part of this error report makes sense; the end tag for the title element is missing. The second half of this sentence, "but OMITTAG NO was specified," isn't anything you really need to pay attention to. It simply means that the validation service script was told that XHTML 1.0 Strict doesn't allow end tags to be omitted (no XML end tags can). To fix this error, simply add the closing title tag.

Point three (see Figure 8.7) tells us that there is an end tag for the "h2" element, but there isn't an open "h2" to go with it. If you look carefully at the line of markup quoted to you, you'll see that the phrase started out being opened with an "h1" element. I apparently mismatched my tags on this one. Changing the closing </h2> to an </h1> fixes this problem.

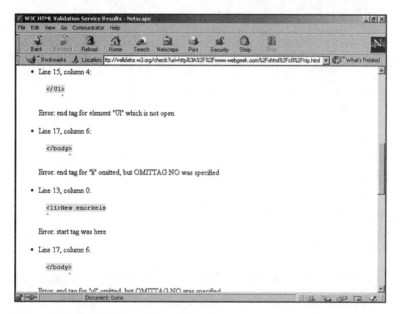

Figure 8.7: *Additional validator errors are reported.*

Next up, the validator tells us that we have another end tag for an element that's not open; this time the "Ul" element. I can do two things to correct it, I can look at line 15 of my source code and backtrack to find the opening tag. But, there's a more immediate solution in sight. Carefully look at the element being quoted; it says "Ul". If you'll remember the rules about XHTML 1.0 elements, you should remember that they all must be written in lowercase. There's the error! I opened the element with a <ul>, but tried to close it with </Ul>. In HTML, this would be valid, because HTML is case insensitive. This time around, however, we do have to write all lowercase tags. Changing this to </ul> fixes the problem.

The next error might be a bit confusing at first glance. It reports that the end tag for "li" was omitted, but the code section highlighted is for the closing body tag. For more help, look at the next bullet point, which shows you the position of the start tag for the "li" element in question. Adding the closing tag will fix the error. What the validator did was note that the "li" tag was open, and continued along in parsing the document until it hit a tag that would have been a problem occurring inside an open "li" tag, and that was the closing body tag. At that point it stopped and said "oops, that "li" element back there never got closed. Here's where I stopped, and this is why (the closing body tag, and because the end tag for "li" was omitted), and I'll be helpful and show you where it started."

The next two points, shown in Figure 8.8, have already been corrected.

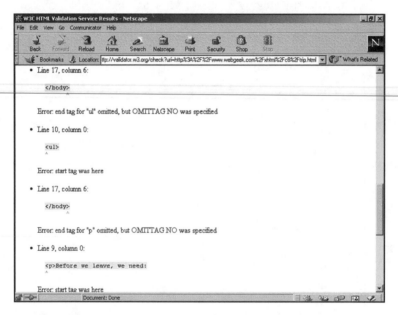

Figure 8.8: *Additional validator errors are found.*

When we corrected the case-sensitivity typo in the </Ul> tag, we fixed the fact that there wasn't a </ul> tag present.

One last error to correct (see Figure 8.9) is a missing </p> tag. The validator reports in its standard format that the end tag was omitted, and shows you where it began in the next line.

The last entry on this report (also refer to Figure 8.9) is that the original h1 element wasn't closed. We corrected this situation when we changed the closing </h2> to an </h1>.

The key to success when working with the validator is to remember that it's essentially stupid. The validator doesn't know that the h1 not having a closing tag is the same error as the h2 not having an opening tag. It will report all phases of a single problem. To help narrow down error reports, you might want to revalidate your documents after fixing each error. It will cut down on the number of remaining issues, and can help fight any feelings of being overwhelmed!

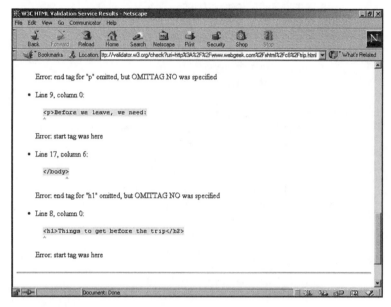

Figure 8.9: *Additional validator errors show up.*

When an Error Isn't an Error

The error reports you've seen so far in this chapter have been fairly simple to sort out. The process of validation can become more difficult when the validator gets "confused", or gives you strange and almost irrelevant looking reports. In this section, we'll take a look at some errors that generate responses that at first glance, don't make any sense.

EXAMPLE

Listing 8.2 is similar to the calendar file created back in Chapter 5, "Working with Tables." I've introduced three specific errors into it for the validator to catch. (Can you spot them?)

Listing 8.2: `calendar.html`

```
<html>
<head>
<title>September 2000</title>
<meta name="author" content="Ann Navarro
</head>
<body>
<table border="1">
```

Listing 8.2: continued

```
<caption><b>September 2000</b></caption>
  <tr align="center" valign="top" bgcolor="#99FFFF">
    <th width="100">Sunday</th>
    <th width="100">Monday</th>
    <th width="100">Tuesday</th>
    <th width="100">Wednesday</th>
    <th width="100">Thursday</th>
    <th width="100">Friday</th>
    <th width="100">Saturday</th>
  </tr>
  <tr align="left" valign="top">
    <td colspan="5" bgcolor="#CCCCCC" height="50"> </td>
    <td width="100" height="100">1</td>
    <td width="100" height="100">2</td>
  </tr>
  <tr align="left" valign="top">
    <td width="100" height="100">3</td>
    <td width="100" height="100">4</td>
    <td width="100" height="100">5</td>
    <td width="100" height="100">6</td>
    <td width="100" height="100">7</td>
    <td width="100" height="100">8</td>
    <td width="100" height="100">9</td>
  </tr>
  <tr align="left" valign="top">
    <td width="100" height="100">10</td>
    <td width="100" height="100">11</td>
    <td width="100" height="100">12</td>
    <td width="100" height="100">13</td>
    <td width="100" height="100">14</td>
    <td width="100" height="100">15</td>
    <td width="100" height="100">16</td>
  </tr>
  <tr align="left" valign="top">
    <td width="100" height="100">17</td>
    <td width="100" height="100">18</td>
    <td width="100" height="100">19</td>
    <td width="100" height="100">20</td>
    <td width="100" height="100">21</td>
    <td width="100" height="100">22</td>
    <td width="100" height="100">23</td>
  <tr align="left" valign="top">
    <td width="100" height="100">24</td>
    <td width="100" height="100">25</td>
    <td width="100" height="100">26</td>
    <td width="100" height="100">27</td>
    <td width="100" height="100">28</td>
```

Listing 8.2: continued

```
    <td width="100" height="100">29</td>
    <td width="100" height="100">30</td>
  </tr>
</table>
</body>
</html>
```

Just looking at the file in your Web browser should give you a clue that there's something wrong; here's how it rendered for me using Netscape Navigator 4.72 (see Figure 8.10).

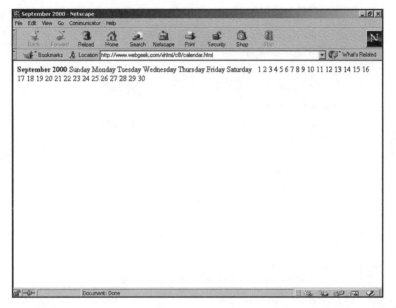

Figure 8.10: *This is not the presentation we expected for this table.*

The first pass the validator takes at the document looks like Figure 8.11.

The first item that should catch your eye in this report is that the document type is listed as HTML 4.0 Transitional! We're writing XHTML; what happened? The clue is in the first bulletted error—the doctype declaration is missing. This document needs the XHTML 1.0 Transitional doctype, so we'll add that in:

```
<!DOCTYPE html PUBLIC "-//W3C//DTD XHTML 1.0 Transitional//EN"
   "DTD/xhtml1-transitional.dtd">
```

Before revalidating, let's look at the next two errors. This first one is a little obtuse, saying "literal is missing closing delimiter", with the caret pointing at my name in the meta tag. The second error says that the CAPTION element isn't allowed to be where it is, and that the validator has assumed that the opening table tag is missing. Let's take a look at the section of code between these two elements:

```
<head>
<title>September 2000</title>
<meta name="author" content="Ann Navarro
</head>
<body>
<p>
<table border="1">
<caption><b>September 2000</b></caption>
```

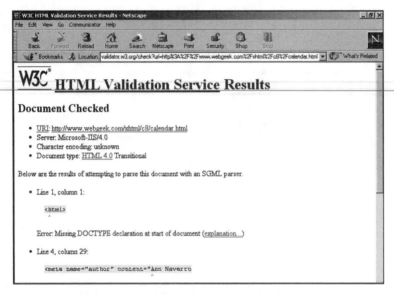

Figure 8.11: *An unexpected result is generated: HTML 4.0?*

Clearly the opening table tag is there, so the validator must be a bit confused. If you look back at the first error, the "literal missing a closing delimeter" problem, you might begin to understand why.

In the meta tag, the content attribute is missing the closing quote ("), which is the literal that was mentioned. But there's another problem: no end bracket for the meta tag itself! Remember that the validator is rather stupid. What occurred here, is that the validator saw the content attribute in the meta tag, and the quote that denoted the beginning of that attribute value. It continued along looking for another quote to close out the attribute value, and didn't run into one until it was inside the table tag (and hit the border attribute). It then thought it was finally done with the content attribute on the meta tag. The next tag it encountered was the caption element, and it said, "Hmm. This can't go there, the author must have forgotten the table tag!" Well, no, clearly we didn't. What happened is that the validator ignored the data between the "real" end of the meta tag and the caption element because it thought it was processing attribute value information. If we close up the meta tag, this "error" will go away.

Revalidate the file, and let's look at any remaining errors (see Figure 8.12).

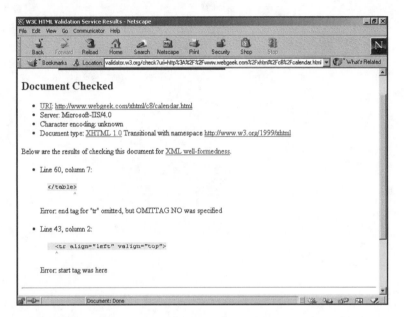

Figure 8.12: *We're down to a single error.*

This time, we've got the right document type, and only one error is being reported, a missing `</tr>`. Add that back in, and revalidate one more time, after which we should earn a "no errors!" report.

What's Next

In this chapter you have learned how validation serves as a "grammar checker" for Web documents. You've learned how to use a popular and trusted validation service provided by the W3C. Errors can be simple things to locate and fix, or you might need to "read between the lines" in what the validator is reporting to find the real problem.

Next up in Chapter 9, "Implementing XHTML Today," we'll take a look at implementing XHTML in today's Web site, including issues surrounding updating existing sites, remaining compatible with older browsers, and finding authoring tools that support XHTML.

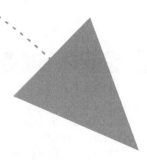

Implementing XHTML Today

One of the most delightful aspects of XHTML is that you can begin using it immediately with near perfect results. The well-formedness and validity requirements of XHTML, when followed, create highly interoperable documents that can be viewed on nearly any devices that accesses the Web.

You might have noticed that I said "near perfect" results. In the transition between HTML and XML, there are several areas that deserve special attention from authors. The W3C has outlined these for us in the XHTML 1.0 Recommendation, and we'll be reviewing each of them here.

This chapter teaches you:

- How to manage XML-based techniques in an HTML-browser world

- How to position your XHTML documents for success in XML parsers

- The tools for converting HTML to XHTML

- Automated systems for applying features in the Compatibility Guidelines

Smoothing the Transition

Using the XHTML 1.0 Compatibility Guidelines Steps can be taken to author your XHTML documents in a way that is compatible with as many HTML user agents as possible. These can be as basic as some of the original Web browsers including NCSA Mosaic, Cello, and Lynx, or the next generation of browsers that included Netscape 1.1, 2.0, Microsoft Internet Explorer 1.0, 2.0, and of course, the successive versions of each up to Netscape 6 and IE 5.0 today. We also need to be aware of browsers in use on other devices when we talk about authoring guidelines.

A common statement heard in some corners of Web design is "If it works in IE and Netscape, then I'm finished." This might cover a large majority of the desktop Web surfing market, but of course doesn't fully address the issue of backward compatibility. In this section we'll take a look at each of the guidelines suggested in the XHTML 1.0 Recommendation.

One key issue to remember when discussing how XHTML, and to some extent any XML application, will perform in today's Web browsers is that these applications were written based on the HTML Recommendations. HTML has presentational and behavioral semantics associated with it that can only be rendered if the browser has a built-in knowledge of what those semantics are. In other words, the programmers who write the browser software have taught it how to deal with each of the elements and attributes. As a result, any markup behavior that deviates from that pre-programmed expectation will have an unpredictable outcome from the authoring perspective.

XML Processing Instructions

XHTML documents formally begin with an XML declaration. This declaration is written in the form of a processing instruction that might look like this:

```
<?xml version="1.0" encoding="UTF-8"?>
```

The encoding attribute value can be modified when necessary to incorporate extended character sets. Most documents will do fine with the UTF-8 and UTF-16 character sets, which are accepted defaults on most systems.

A backward compatibility issue arises in how user agents deal with markup they don't understand. The recommendation has always been that the browser should pass through the content of the markup as raw data (essentially plain text). Most browsers interpret the processing instruction as an empty element, and therefore don't pass anything through to the browser because by definition, empty elements have no content.

Testing has shown a few browsers either mistakenly pass through unknown empty elements (the processing instruction) to the document, or simply don't recognize PIs as an element at all, and pass it through as PCDATA. These browsers include Netscape Navigator 3.0 and earlier, HotJava 1.1.5 and 3.0, Opera 3.6, Internet Explorer 3.x and 4.x/Mac. Luckily, all these have newer versions available and the number of visitors seeing such a declaration should be negligible. Still, to avoid passing it through completely, forgo the XML declaration when serving the documents as text/html.

Working with Empty Elements

HTML element syntax takes an opening tag, the element name enclosed within angle brackets (`<element>`); any contained data; and then a closing tag composed of a left angle bracket, forward slash, the element name, and a right angle bracket, for example, `</element>`. When there's no data to be contained between the tags, we have an *empty* element. HTML constructs these simply by using only the opening tag, as is done with this image element:

```
<img src="graphic.gif" alt="My Graphic">
```

The rules found in the XML 1.0 Recommendation don't allow for empty elements so a change in syntax is required moving from HTML to XHTML. Two options for managing empty elements are available to the author. The more straightforward solution is to simply add a closing tag:

```
<img src="graphic.gif" alt="My Graphic"></img>
```

However, the presence of a closing tag on an element where the browser isn't expecting one can lead to unpredictable results. To avoid that unpredictability, a syntactical shorthand developed in XML, sometimes referred to as *element minimization*, is the preferred treatment of empty elements in XHTML. XML allows authors to write

```
<br/>
```

which means the same as

```
<br></br>
```

The shorthand is nice, but introduces another problem: recognition of the element name. We said earlier than HTML syntax defines the opening tag of an element (without any attributes) as a left angle bracket, the element name, and a right angle bracket. When evaluating elemental content, browsers are likely to interpret the element name of a tag using this shorthand as `br/` rather than `br` with a slash next to it.

Because the browser doesn't have pre-programmed knowledge of the `br/` element, it's likely to do nothing with it, as seen in Figure 9.1. The text in the first segment should be broken into two lines by the `br` element that has a corresponding closing tag. The second text segment was written to be broken using the XML shorthand <br/>, as seen here:

```
<h1>Segment 1</h1>
<p>Mary had a little lamb,<br></br>with fleece as white as snow</p>
<h1>Segment 2</h1>
<p>Everywhere that Mary went,<br/>the lamb was sure to go.</p>
```

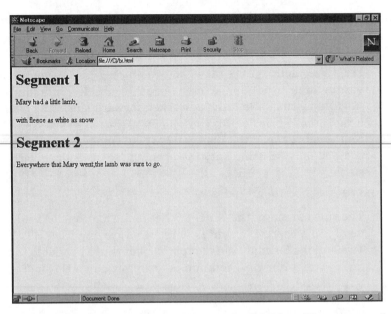

Figure 9.1: *The two XML-based methods of handling empty elements have uneven results in Navigator 4.73.*

In Figure 9.1 you see that the results are uneven. The closing-tag method has the results we were after, but the slash-shorthand, doesn't.

XHTML explored possible alternatives to these methods, looking for something that would be both XML compliant and backward compatible, producing the results that we've come to expect from these elements. Luckily, a solution was found. It is recommended that authors use the slash-shorthand version, but only after inserting a space character between the end of the element name and the slash, so that

```
<br>
```

becomes

```
<br />
```

Elements Instances with Empty Content

There are situations where a document author might need to use an element that has been defined to allow content in a manner that leaves that content empty. For instance, when working with tables, authors will often need to denote empty table cells by writing:

```
<td></td>
```

Care needs to be taken to recognize that this is an *instance* of an element that has no content, rather than an *empty element* by definition. Therefore the syntax for this element cannot be minimized. Only elements that are defined as having an empty content model are candidates for minimization.

✔ For more information on element content models, refer to "Defining Elements," p. 227.

Working with Embedded Scripts

EXAMPLE

It has become customary for Web authors to hide JavaScript (or any scripting segment for that matter) embedded in a document using the HTML commenting facility. A quick way some authors indicate the date a file was last modified is to use a small JavaScript snippet like this one:

```
<script type="text/javascript" language="JavaScript">
<!--
        document.write(" on  " + document.lastModified + " ");
// -->
</script>
```

The actual script code is hidden between the HTML comments <!-- and --> with a JavaScript comment indicator, //, thrown in for good measure before the closing HTML comment.

For HTML browsers, this technique has become a tried and true method. No current browser has any substantial problem with the technique; the script gets passed to the scripting engine appropriately, and the raw script code is hidden from view in the rendered document.

However, XML parsers handle comments a bit differently from an HTML-based Web browser. Instead of passing on the code to the scripting engine, an XML parser ignores the contents of the comment completely, in essence just throwing it into the proverbial bit bucket. To avoid this problem, scripting code needs to be wrapped in a CDATA section that the XML parser *will* recognize as something it's supposed to ignore, yet retain for use by another program. The CDATA wrapper is written as follows:

```
<![CDATA[ script here ]]>
```

The cue for the XML parser to stop ignoring the code is the string]]>. Although it's possible for that string to appear in JavaScript code, it's generally rare and certainly avoidable.

The previous JavaScript snippet would then be inserted as:

```
<script type="text/javascript" language="JavaScript">
<![CDATA[ document.write(" on  " + document.lastModified + " "); ]]>
</script>
```

Unfortunately, if you're planning on serving your XHTML documents, none of today's HTML browsers know how to handle XML CDATA sections (remember, most were written before the advent of XML). To ensure the best chances of success with scripting, consider using an external script file. The external file, which doesn't need any adjustment to the scripting code, is simply referenced with an src attribute on the script element:

```
<script type="text/javascript" language="JavaScript" src="myscript.js"></script>
```

TIP

A happy byproduct of using an external script file is that you can comment the code to your heart's content without needing to worry about nested or dropped comments. This makes reuse of your script code far more accessible.

White Space in Attribute Values

XML has strict rules on the processing of white space. All white space characters, defined in XML as one or more of a space, tab, newline character, or linefeed character, are *normalized* within attribute values. Normalization is the process of condensing white space down to at most a single white space character when found between words, and stripping any leading or trailing white space. As an XML application, XHTML also follows this process of white space normalization, both within attribute values and elsewhere in the document. Authors should take care not to rely on extraneous white space within attributes because the value will be modified by the normalization process.

Using the `isindex` Element

The isindex element was designed as a quick way to generate a single line text input control, which avoided the need to use the form element, an input element, and a second input for a submit button. This element has been deprecated in favor of the input element. Beyond that deprecation, only one isindex element should be included inside head if it is to be used.

Identifying the Natural Language of a Document or Element

It's possible to identify the natural language of a document or element using the lang attribute. The natural language is simply the original language of the word, phrase, or document. The natural language of this book would be English (U.S. English to be specific). If I were to insert a foreign language word, the lang attribute allows us to identify that language which can provide the additional context and, in some cases, even pronunciation hints to certain user agents.

XML uses the special xml:lang attribute for this language identification task. It has been recommended that authors use *both* versions of the attribute in XHTML documents to cover processing by either an HTML-based browser or an XML parser. Such usage on an element would look like

```
<p>Jack had a strange sense of <span xml:lang="fr" lang="fr">deja vu</span> the
➡moment he entered the room.</p>
```

TIP

If there is a discrepancy between the values of the xml:lang and lang attributes, the value of the xml:lang attribute takes precedence.

Managing Fragment Identifiers

A fragment identifier is the portion of a URI referenced as #fragment. Typically these are used to provide intra-document linking, or a link from one document to a specific portion of a second document (other than the top of the page). Such a link could look like

```
<a href="newpage.html#spot">Go directly to the spot!</a>
```

The corresponding spot is identified using a named anchor element:

```
<a name="spot">This is the Spot!</a>
```

A problem arises in that XML requires the fragment to be identified using an attribute of type ID, which would be found in the id attribute in HTML 4.01. However, existing Web browsers operate using the name attribute to make this identification. To allow both types of systems to make the appropriate connection, XHTML authors should use both the name and id attributes when working with fragment identifiers. Accordingly, the markup would look like

```
<a name="spot" id="spot">This is the Spot!</a>
```

Notice that the value of the name and id attributes are identical in this example.

Some additional restrictions come into play for the value of these attributes. The XML requirement of using an attribute type ID is in conflict with the HTML name attribute, which allows any CDATA in the attribute value. To help normalize these differences, the type of the XHTML name attribute has been changed to NMTOKEN. Essentially, this requires the value to be a single string of characters composed of any letters; numbers; and the characters ., -, _, and :.

TIP

XML further restricts NMTOKENs from beginning with the characters "XML" in any variation of case. Those are reserved for special tokens developed in the XML Recommendation itself.

Finally, the value of each id attribute needs to be unique within the document (note that this does not forbid the matching name attribute value).

Specifying Character Encoding

In HTML character encoding is set inside the head element using a meta element with the http-equiv attribute. For instance, to set the character encoding of the document to Japanese, you would write

```
<meta http-equiv="Content-type" content='text/html; charset="EUC-JP"'>
```

XML, on the other hand, uses the encoding attribute on the XML declaration to store this information. Previously in the "XML Processing Instructions" section of this chapter, we discussed the fact that the XML declaration must be present if the encoding is to be anything other than UTF-8 or UTF-16. So in the case here of a Japanese encoding, the XML declaration must be present, and would look like

```
<?xml version="1.0" encoding="EUC-JP"?>
```

However, to retain backward compatibility with HTML-based user agents, the meta element should also be used, with the proper handling for empty elements in XHTML. As a result, the beginning of such a document would appear as

```
<?xml version="1.0" encoding="EUC-JP"?>
<!DOCTYPE html PUBLIC "-//W3C//DTD XHTML 1.0 Strict//EN"
     "http://www.w3.org/TR/xhtml1/DTD/xhtml1-strict.dtd">
<html xmlns="http://www.w3.org/1999/xhtml" xml:lang="en" lang="en">
<head>
<meta http-equiv="Content-type" content='text/html; charset="EUC-JP"'>
<title>My Document Title</title>
</head>
```

As with the natural language declarations, the value of the encoding attribute in the XML declaration takes precedence over the value supplied in the meta element.

TIP

You've probably realized that the requirement to use the XML declaration for character encodings other than UTF-8 and UTF-16 is contradictory when faced with an audience for XHTML documents using older HTML-based browsers. In this scenario, the author is indeed forced to make a choice here. I believe a proper character encoding is far more valuable than avoiding the possibility of the stray text presentation of the XML declaration at the beginning of a document.

Expanding Boolean Attributes

EXAMPLE

A Boolean attribute is an attribute that is active simply by its presence, without a stated value. A common example is that used when pre-selecting an option in a set of check boxes inside a form, such as:

```
<input type="checkbox" name="box1" value="boxvalue" checked />
```

The rules of well-formedness in XHTML don't allow this sort of attribute presentation. The attribute, therefore, must be expanded, taking a value the same as the attribute name

```
<input type="checkbox" name="box1" value="boxvalue" checked="checked" />
```

This technique must be used for all Boolean attributes, including `checked`, `compact`, `declare`, `defer`, `disabled`, `ismap`, `multiple`, `noresize`, `noshade`, `nowrap`, `readonly`, and `selected`.

Current Web browsers, those written to be aware of and compliant with the HTML 4 Recommendation, shouldn't have a problem understanding these expanded attributes. Earlier browsers, notably of the era of Netscape Navigator 3 and Internet Explorer 3, might ignore the attribute as it would other "unknown" markup.

Accessing the Document Object Model (DOM)

The Document Object Model (DOM) is used, among other things, for accessing specific nodes in the parse tree of an XHTML document when processing scripts. The DOM used with HTML 4, known appropriately as the HTML DOM, returns element and attribute names in uppercase. The DOM used with XML specifies that elements and attributes are returned in their original case. Both these positions can be in conflict with the requirement of XHTML that elements and attributes be written only in lowercase.

Despite these apparent conflicts, the situation can be managed while retaining backward compatibility. XHTML provides for two methods of serving documents. The first is as Internet media type text/html. When this is done, applications can reliably expect that the document will be processed using the HTML DOM, with elements and attributes being returned accordingly in uppercase.

XHTML documents served as XML will likely be set to an Internet media type of text/xml, application/xml, or another media type that might soon be developed. Applications that parse these documents can use the XML DOM with confidence that the lowercase input (in keeping with the requirements of XHTML 1.0) will be returned as lowercase.

Attributes That Contain Ampersands

Any attribute that contains an ampersand character (&) must be written using the character entity for the ampersand instead of the character itself. For example, a copyright statement for Chandler & Sons, Inc. might be written in a meta element as

```
<meta name="copyright" content="Copyright 2000, Chandler &amp; Sons, Inc." />
```

This prescription also includes attribute values that hold URI values. Some Web authors mistakenly believe that ampersands included in URIs cannot be written using the & character entity because the link or source reference will no longer function. This actually isn't the case. The URI will contain & in the source document, when it's displayed in the browser the character entity is rendered, and the URI will look and function just as if it were written using the & character directly.

Using CSS with XHTML

When working with style sheets, authors are encouraged to make use of the excellent support for external style sheets both with HTML Web browsers and XML parsers. Should there be a compelling reason to embed the style sheet within your XHTML document, carefully review it for the inclusion of any < or & characters. Both types of parsers will treat these as the beginning of markup sections; the < indicating the beginning of a new element and & signaling the start of a character entity. Should either character necessarily appear within the style sheet and you can't move to an external file, you'll need to wrap the CSS in a CDATA section as described earlier in this chapter in the "Working with Embedded Scripts" section.

Remaining Compatibility Issues

Not all issues regarding compatibility or backward compatibility can be handled by a relatively simplistic set of authoring guidelines. Contradictions and collisions between HTML and XML, the technologies being blended in XHTML, are almost inevitable.

Internet Media Types for XHTML

For XHTML to be served on the Web today, authors will use the text/html Internet Media Type, with a corresponding .html file extension.

Tools That Support XHTML

It's a bit early in the development of XHTML for authoring tools to directly support output as XHTML. However, there are utilities available that can aid in the conversion of HTML to XHTML, or simply to error check and polish up XHTML files written by hand or HTML-based authoring tools. Three such utilities incorporating the same base program are featured here.

HTML Tidy

The W3C has published a tool that helps authors clean up HTML files and format them for XHTML (as well as XML). It's a very powerful utility, yet one that can be somewhat opaque when you're first trying to learn how to use it. Written by engineers, in the command-line format that so many of them love, it's not the most user friendly of programs for those who view DOS as something out of the history books and who rarely if ever encounter a Unix system. In other words, quite a few of us!

NOTE

The supporting Web site for HTML Tidy, including links for downloading the various ports of the program, can be found at `http://www.w3.org/People/Raggett/tidy/`.

EXAMPLE

A fairly standard usage has Tidy modifying the source document in place as necessary, and recording the changes and errors present in a separate text output file. To initiate this operation, the following instruction is given at the command line:

```
tidy -f errors.txt -m file.html
```

Taking this command apart piece by piece, we start by invoking the program itself with `tidy`. The *flag* or *switch* `-f` before `errors.txt` tells Tidy that it needs to create a file named `errors.txt`, to which the output of the program will be written. The second flag `-m` tells Tidy to modify the input file, represented above by `file.html`. A successful run through Tidy will result in the report seen in Figure 9.2.

To do anything more than basic tidying of your source files, you'll need to create a configuration file. This text file consists of a list of properties separated by their corresponding value by a colon. Listing 9.1 shows a basic configuration file that could be used for converting HTML source documents to XHTML.

Listing 9.1: `config.txt`, A Configuration File to Be Used with HTML Tidy

```
wrap: 72
markup: yes
output-xhtml: yes
uppercase-tags: no
uppercase-attributes: no
char-encoding: utf8
error-file: errors.txt
```

```
show-warnings: yes
```

Figure 9.2: *HTML Tidy reports a successfully tidied file.*

These configuration options tell Tidy to create a "pretty" output of the XHTML, with text that will wrap within the output document at 72 characters per line. Elements and attributes will be written in lowercase, the character encoding of the XML declaration will be set to UTF8, with warnings shown during processing, and the errors written to a secondary file named errors.txt.

To invoke tidy using the configuration file, a new argument is added to the command:

```
tidy -config config.txt file.html
```

TIP

Notice that the Errors Report and Modify In Place flags aren't necessary when a configuration file is in use, provided those options are annotated in that file.

TidyGUI

For those of us more comfortable in a graphical user interface than the command line, Andre Blavier has written a GUI overlay for HTML Tidy. An external configuration file is generated to control Tidy's options, just as with the command-line version, but a familiar set of tabbed dialog boxes are used to produce it, saving the user from having to remember property names and the syntax used to store them (see Figure 9.3).

Links to obtain TidyGUI can be found on the Tidy home page noted previously, or directly from the author's site at

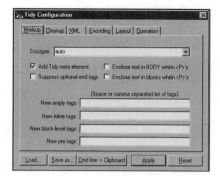

http://perso.wanadoo.fr/ablavier/TidyGUI/.

Figure 9.3: *The TidyGUI configuration dialog box provides easy access to all Tidy's options.*

EXAMPLE

To run TidyGUI, locate the source file using the Browse dialog box (see

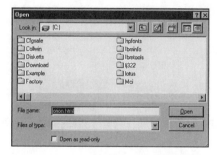

Figure 9.4), or type the path directly into the source file box.

Figure 9.4: *Locate the source file to be tidied using the Browse dialog box.*

All that's left to do is select the Tidy! button and watch the program go to work. After processing you'll see a list of warnings and errors along with the location of their occurrences in the lower pane of the main TidyGUI window, and a single description of the situation per warning type in the upper pane (see Figure 9.5).

The rewritten output is accessible using the Output button, which instantiates a new window where the markup is displayed (see Figure 9.6). I've found it a bit inconvenient that you can't simply select and copy the output directly from this window. Instead, you must use the Save dialog box to save the file locally before opening it again with the text editor of your

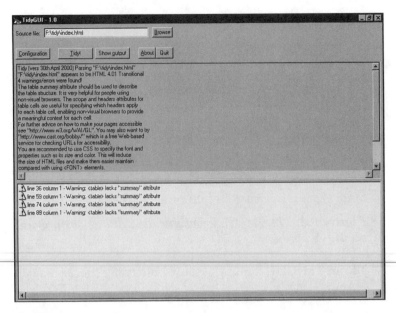

choice.

Figure 9.5: *Warnings listed in the lower pane are explained in the upper pane.*

Figure 9.6: *Output is accessed and then saved from a new window.*

HTML-Kit

HTML-Kit isn't an XHTML editor per se, but is a fully functional HTML authoring environment that has integrated the HTML Tidy features into the program. Of the available tools for using Tidy, HTML-Kit is my favorite in that it provides immediate access to the source and tidied document via a split-file view, options to perform specific Tidy tasks one at a time without

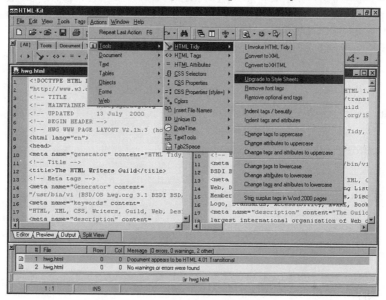

need for detailed configuration files, and a convert to XHTML feature (see Figure 9.7).

Figure 9.7: *HTML-Kit provides single-operation choices for using Tidy on your documents, including convert to XHTML.*

HTML-Kit is available and supported through the Chami.com Web site, located at `http://www.chami.com/html-kit/`.

Writing XHTML with HTML-Based Tools

It should be apparent to you by now that XHTML can be developed using any tool that you desire, from the ubiquitous Notepad or SimpleText to full featured programs designed for HTML such as Macromedia Dreamweaver, Adobe GoLive!, and even Microsoft FrontPage. Whichever method is used, even authoring directly in a plain text editor, some review and touchup will be required. Armed with Tidy (or another program that incorporates Tidy), and the W3C Validation Service your XHTML authoring can be expedited and simplified using the programs of your choice.

What's Next

In this chapter you have reviewed each of the guidelines published by the

W3C for retaining compatibility in XHTML documents for both HTML- and XML-based processors. You've used one of several tools available for tidying your source files and converting HTML-based source to XHTML.

Next, in Chapter 10, "XHTML as the Bridge to XML," we'll explore how XHTML serves as the "bridge" between HTML and XHTML, adding the freedom to define new elements and attributes to the familiar and trusted structure and semantics of HTML.

Part II

XHTML Style and Structure

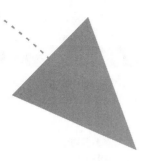

XHTML as the Bridge to XML

Back at the beginning of this book, in Chapter 1, "XHTML Fundamentals," we talked about how the W3C recognized it needed some sort of transition between the HTML most Web authors were used to working with, and XML, the new language that provided a framework for customized language definitions and new markup vocabularies. The job of making that transition was given to XHTML. XHTML 1.0 takes on many of the traits of XML, while retaining backward compatibility with HTML 4, acting as that metaphoric bridge between the two technologies.

This chapter teaches you:

- How XML provides more freedom for document authors

- What constitutes well-formedness

- How languages can be defined using document type definitions

- How a new XML-based technology, schemas, can also define XML-based vocabularies

The Freedom of XML—Defining It All Yourself

In HTML, and even now with XHTML 1.0, document authors are limited to the structures and presentation that have already been defined. But what if you want to do something else?

EXAMPLE

We can force existing elements to do what we want by using them in unconventional or even invalid ways, but doing so also compromises interoperability. Back in Chapter 1, you were introduced to one of my favorite examples of forcing meaning upon vague structure in an XHTML-based memorandum. The Web page author essentially has two choices when creating the document: use heading elements for each addressing component (see Listing 10.1), or simply use a paragraph and some line breaks with a liberal dose of emphasis (see Listing 10.2).

Listing 10.1: A Memo Using Heading Elements for Address Structures

```
<html>
<head>
<title>Memorandum</title>
</head>
<body>
<h1>Memorandum</h1>
<h2>To: Stacey Baker</h2>
<h2>From: David Angeles</h2>
<h2>Subject: Vacation Request</h2>
<h3>Date: September 22, 2000</h3>
<p>Stacey,</p>
<p>This note confirms my requested vacation dates, in order of preference, for
➥the 2001 calendar year:
<ol>
<li>March 19, 2001 through March 30, 2001</li>
<li>October 8, 2001 through October 19, 2001</li>
<li>December 17, 2001 through December 28, 2001</li>
</ol>
<p>Regards,</p>
<p>David</p>
</body>
</html>
```

Listing 10.2: A Memorandum Using Paragraphs and Strong Emphasis for Addressing Components

```
<html>
<head>
<title>Memorandum</title>
</head>
<body>
<h1>Memorandum</h1>
<p><strong>To:</strong> Stacey Baker<br />
```

Listing 10.1: continued

```
<strong>From:</strong> David Angeles<br />
<strong>Subject:</strong> Vacation Request<br />
<strong>Date:</strong> September 22, 2000<br />
<p>Stacey,</p>
<p>This note confirms my requested vacation dates, in order of preference, for
➥the 2001 calendar year:
<ol>
<li>March 19, 2001 through March 30, 2001</li>
<li>October 8, 2001 through October 19, 2001</li>
<li>December 17, 2001 through December 28, 2001</li>
</ol>
<p>Regards,</p>
<p>David</p>
</body>
</html>
```

Neither approach does much to impart any significance to the information contained within the elements other than presentation. The structures are generic enough to work with just about any text, not specifically the to, from, subject, and date content indicated in the text.

XML enables document authors to create their own elements, using names that do have meaning. An XML approach to the memo might look like Listing 10.3.

Listing 10.3: A Memo Written Using Customized XML Elements

```
<memo>
<label>Memorandum</label>
<to>Stacey Baker</to>
<from>David Angeles</from>
<subject>Vacation Request</subject>
<date>September 22, 2000</date>
<body>
<salutation>Stacey<salutation>
<p>This note confirms my requested vacation dates, in order of preference, for
➥the 2001 calendar year:
<ol>
<li>March 19, 2001 through March 30, 2001</li>
<li>October 8, 2001 through October 19, 2001</li>
<li>December 17, 2001 through December 28, 2001</li>
</ol>
</body>
</memo>
```

Today's Web browsers don't have inherent knowledge of what to do with these elements, as they do from having rendering information programmed into them for HTML elements and attributes. Style sheets provide the presentational cues to the browser instead.

From just a human-readability standpoint, the XML approach is a bit cleaner; it's clear from well-chosen element names what each of them is supposed to contain. From a machine-processing standpoint, the processor won't really care. But if the intention is to build a document management system or build dynamically generated documents out of database systems, these customized elements make all the difference in the world for ease of use and clarity of purpose.

The Concept of Well-Formedness

Well-formedness sounds very stiff, and perhaps even a little mysterious. In practice, it's a very simple concept to implement; you simply have to be *complete* when writing your documents.

The formal definition of well-formedness, as used by the W3C, can be found in the XML 1.0 Recommendation at `http://www.w3.org/TR/1998/REC-xml-19980210#sec-well-formed`. It's a bit of a circular definition, saying that a well-formed document must:

- Meet the definition of a document.

- Conform to all well-formedness constraints mentioned in the XML Recommendation.

- Any parsed entity referenced in the document also must be well-formed.

That helps, sort of, but still doesn't tell us what *well-formed* means. What comes next in this section of the XML Recommendation is what we're really looking for:

- **The document must have a DOCTYPE declaration.** XHTML user agents must be able to tell what kind of document they are receiving. Validating parsers by definition also must have access to the document type definition to process the document.

- **The document must contain one or more elements.** This one is pretty easy. Any XHTML document is going to have at least four elements: `html`, `head` with a `title` element inside, and the `body` element.

- **There is one root element.** All XHTML documents begin with the `html` element as their root element.

- **No part of the root element can appear as content in any other element.** This essentially says that the root element really has to be the root element. In other words, it's the first element to open, and the last element to close. This is well-formed:

```
<html>
<body>
```

```
...more content...
</body>
</html>
```

But this is not:

```
<body>
<html>
...more content...
</html>
</body>
```

- **For all elements, if the start tag is within another element, so must the end tag be.** What this means is that if tags are nested, one must be wholly inside the other. You might think of them as a set of graduated-size mixing bowls. You begin with the largest bowl, then put the next-smaller size bowl inside the larger one, and so on and so on until you've nested each of them inside the larger bowl. Obviously the middle-sized bowl can't be half inside the large bowl and half inside the smallest bowl; it must fit wholly within the bowl one-step larger than itself. In XHTML this means the following is correct:

```
<p><strong><em>Wow!</em></strong></p>
```

But the following is not:

```
<p><strong><em>Wow!</p></strong></em>
```

NOTE

In the formal vocabulary of markup languages, you'll often hear elements that can be nested referred to as *child* elements. The element that contains the nested element is the *parent* element. This relationship becomes more important when you begin working with scripting and the Document Object Model.

The well-formedness definition in the XML Recommendation stops here, but there are several more issues that are worthy of attention as it pertains to XHTML well-formedness:

- **The root element must declare the XHTML namespace using the xmlns attribute.** The XHTML namespace identifier is `http://www.w3.org/1999/xhtml`.

✔ To review more about the xmlns attribute, refer to "The Root Element," p. 16.

- **All attribute values must be fully contained within quotes.** A pretty simple requirement, this means that it is no longer allowable to write

```
<p align=center>
```

Instead, the attribute value must be quoted

```
<p align="center">
```

In HTML, the quotes were optional if you were working with attribute values *other than* URIs or non-alphanumeric characters, such as the # symbol in hex-based color codes. In XHTML (as well as XML), *all attribute values* must be quoted for the document to be considered well-formed.

- **Boolean attributes must be expanded.** Stated another way, this says "every attribute must have a value." A Boolean attribute is one which is "on" just by its presence. In HTML 4 an example could be the `checked` attribute on the `input` element of type `checkbox`:

```
<input type="checkbox" name="mybox" checked>
```

In a well-formed XHTML document, every attribute must have a value, so the checked option on this input would be written as

```
<input type="checkbox" name="mybox" checked="checked">
```

- **Non-empty elements must have a closing tag.** This means closing tags that were previously optional in HTML 4 must now always be present. For example, it is very common to see paragraphs written in HTML 4 in the following manner:

```
<p>This is the first paragraph.
<p>This second opening p tag opens the second paragraph, and by default,
➥closes the first.
```

In XHTML 1.0, the two elements would have to be written as

```
<p>This is the first paragraph.</p>
<p>Since the first paragraph has its own closing tag, nothing additional is
➥inferred by the start of the second paragraph element.</p>
```

- **Empty elements also must be closed.** Empty elements can be closed by either including a closing tag, or by using a shorthand notation. Both of the following examples would be well-formed:

```
<img src="myphoto.gif" alt="a picture of the author"></img>
```

or

```
<img src="myphoto.gif" alt="a picture of the author"/>
```

Both of these options create some backward compatibility problems with HTML-based Web browsers.

✔ Options to improve backward compatibility are addressed in Chapter 9, "Implementing XHTML Today," p. 157.

Improving on Well-Formedness with Schemata or DTDs

As you learned in the previous section, a well-formed document ensures that the parser can complete the rendering of the document. But well-formedness is really only the first step. The effective exchange of data not only requires a successful parsing of a document and data, but some assurance that the content of the document structures conform to any desired constraints.

EXAMPLE

For instance, the ordered list element (ol) used previously in the memo found in Listings 10.1–10.3 is designed to contain only one or more list item elements (li). That constraint can't be checked nor can it be enforced through the state of being well-formed.

What's needed, then, is a second set of rules that a document can be judged against. Historically, beginning with SGML and moving on through HTML, this rule set is provided by the document type definition. This document provides a formal description of the elements, attributes, and allowed content for each segment of a document that might be written in the language being defined.

Beginning in 1998, the W3C has been working on a second method of describing and defining languages. This effort is known as XML Schemas. The desire is to end up with a definition mechanism that is simultaneously more flexible than a document type definition, but also more expressive. The expressiveness comes with the ability to constrain element content not only down to the level of simple text data, but to say "the content must be a 10-digit whole number," or "a string of five lowercase letters." The additional constraints possible with schemas are viewed as a significant advancement in Internet commerce and automated data exchange. Just how well these efforts work remains to be seen, as the XML Schema specifications are solidified and ratified by the W3C.

Overview of Document Type Definitions

The DTD, or *document type definition*, has been the traditional means of constructing the formal grammar of a markup language. Every element is defined in terms of what other elements might be contained inside, and whether any raw data also is allowed.

For instance, the definition of the root element for all documents, the html element, allows just two other elements inside: head and body. If anything else were found within the html element, perhaps a sentence, or an image, the document wouldn't conform to the rules of grammar defined in the document type definition and would then be declared *invalid*.

A valid document, then, is one that fully conforms to all the rules in the document type definition. You've been exposed to this at a basic level already in Chapter 8, "Validating XHTML Documents," when you checked your documents using the W3C Validation Service.

For most documents that Web authors will work with, inserting the DOCTYPE declaration at the beginning of your pages and running them through the validator is the closest you'll come to the document type definition. But some of you, at least a small part of the time, will begin working with DTDs to customize portions of the language and use XHTML Modularization to create new languages.

✔ For more information on creating custom components for DTDS, see "Creating the Module Using a DTD," p. 266.

Overview of Schemas

Over the years document authors voiced many complaints about the nature and limitations of the document type definition as the basis of a markup language. Many people find the notation and formatting used to be overly formal and, primarily, too confusing for the non-expert to be able to readily grasp.

Additionally, document type definitions are limited in the constraints that can be placed on data content within elements, and the type of string data that can be found in attribute values.

EXAMPLE

For instance, documents that contain phone numbers could make use of a <telephone> element. Nothing other than the number (and its dividing dashes) should be present:

```
<telephone>941-555-1234</telephone>
```

Using a document type definition, the element content can only be restricted to PCDATA, or *parsed character data*. This means that I could write the following element, and still be valid:

```
<telephone>I shouldn't be writing text here, but the DTD cannot prohibit
➥it.</telephone>
```

Obviously that's not what we want to see in a telephone element. In other computing disciplines, especially in the world of database management, we've been able to constrain data to specific string types or even patterns.

In 1998, the W3C began work on creating a new way of defining markup languages that offered these additional constraints. The effort became known as XML Schemas. Experts from a wide range of disciplines were brought together: those who helped draft the XML Recommendations, database experts, SGML experts, and other information architects. At the time this book was printed, the XML Schema documents were nearing the end of their working draft phase, and were about to move into the final review process. You'll walk through a very basic primer on XML Schemas in Chapter 15.

NOTE

Any material changes in this book dealing with the schema drafts that occurs after publication will be updated on the book's supporting Web site.

The hope stored in much of this effort is that schemas will be more user-friendly. Additionally, they should offer sufficient facets for constraining information so that document authors will be able to move easily between a document-based information storage system and a data-driven system (and of course other scenarios we probably haven't thought of yet). To address the "user-friendly" aspect, XML Schemas are written in an XML-style format instead of the more formal (and cryptic) notation used in document type definitions.

What's Next

In this chapter you have learned how XML can provide document authors with the freedom to give meaning to their document structures by giving them names that correspond to their purpose or contents. A parser or other user agent won't know what these mean or even particularly "care" about them, but data management systems can manage content much more easily searching for <foo>, rather than a generic <p> structure that has the text string "foo" inside of it.

We've also taken a close look at the definition of well-formedness, both from an XML viewpoint and specifically the requirements for XHTML. Conformance to a language can go further than well-formedness, by validating against a DTD or a schema.

Next in Chapter 11, "Using Cascading Style Sheets with XHTML," we'll take an in-depth look at XHTML 1.1, a version that takes a closer step toward XML by removing deprecated elements and syntactical conventions.

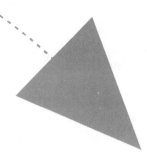

11

Using Cascading Style Sheets with XHTML

The last chapter introduced you to XHTML 1.1, where all presentational elements and attributes have been removed from the language. Of course this doesn't mean that Web pages created using XHTML 1.1 will be dry, text-only documents. Instead, it means that presentation and style must be applied to the document in some manner other than with XHTML. That job now falls to a document known as a *style sheet*.

Style sheets can be written in a number of languages. In this chapter, we'll review one that might be familiar to you: Cascading Style Sheets (CSS). CSS first became popular as an adjunct to HTML. Today, it can still be used with XHTML and has the benefit of familiarity among many Web developers. This chapter is not intended as a comprehensive tutorial on developing style sheets. Such an endeavor could fill at least one book all by itself. Instead, you will review the syntax used to create style rules, review the different selectors available to bind styles to elements or instances of elements, and take a quick tour through some commonly used style properties.

This chapter teaches you:

- The syntax of a basic style rule
- How to create non-element selectors (class and ID)
- How to use text styles
- How to apply style within blocks

Style in the XHTML World

It is possible, using XHTML 1.0, to create an internal style sheet within a document using the `style` element. XHTML 1.1 also allows that, if you use the stylesheet module. XML depends on external style sheets, so though you can use internal style sheets at this point with XHTML, I'd encourage you to get comfortable in using external style sheets, especially if you haven't done so before. Additionally, external style sheets can reduce time needed for maintenance. Therefore the examples in this chapter, and moving forward in the book, will all use external style sheets.

Writing the external style sheet itself is as simple as ever. Just open a blank document in your text editor and write your style rules. It can be as simple as a single rule for text in a paragraph:

```
p {text-decoration: underline;}
```

The file is then saved using the `.css` file extension. The style sheet is then *linked* to the document using the `link` element inside the `head` element.

EXAMPLE

The XHTML document begins as it normally would:

```
<?xml version="1.0" encoding="UTF-8"?>
<!DOCTYPE html PUBLIC "-//W3C//DTD XHTML 1.1//EN"
    "http://www.w3.org/TR/xhtml11/DTD/xhtml11.dtd">
<html xmlns="http://www.w3.org/1999/xhtml" xml:lang="en" >
<head>
<title>Meeting Data</title>
```

Before the `head` element is closed, the new `link` element will be inserted. This element takes a minimum of two attributes: `rel` and `href`. The `rel` attribute describes the relationship between the current document and the document being linked. The `href` attribute works as it does with an anchor (a) element; it provides the URI of the linked document. Our `link` element, then, is written as follows:

```
<link rel="stylesheet" href="calendar.css" />
```

The `head` element can be closed after this, and the remainder of the document put in place:

```
</head>
<body>
<h1>Scheduled Meeting</h1>
<p><b>With:</b> Shane McCarron<br />
<b>From:</b> ApTest<br />
<b>Time:</b> 10:00 am</p>
<h2>Details</h2>
<p>Discuss parameters of test suite for conformance of Widgets 1.0 to the W3C
standards.</p>
</body>
</html>
```

The results are shown in Figure 11.1, where you'll find underlined text within the paragraphs.

OUTPUT

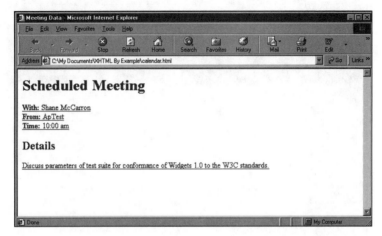

Figure 11.1: *This XHTML page was created using an external style sheet.*

NOTE

The bold portions of the text in Figure 11.1 also are underlined. This is because the bold element *inherited* the underlining from the paragraph element. Inheritance is one of the main features of working with CSS, in that an element contained within another element inherits the properties of its parent element. For example, the bold element is contained within the paragraph element, sometimes referred to as child (bold) and parent (paragraph).

The possibilities available to designers working with style sheets are quite complex, allowing for some very stunning results. One of my favorite implementations, even if it does seem a bit biased, is the HTML Writers Guild site (see Figure 11.2).

For example, take a look at the navigation bar down the left side of the screen in Figure 11.2. The links look like graphical buttons; they're raised, with beveled edges. The larger blocks of color, across the top and behind the "Recent Announcements" section, are set using a CSS rule, as are the colored borders around text in the main (white) portion of the page.

To generate looks like this, the Webmaster made extensive use of classes, grouping similar selectors together to write a single rule.

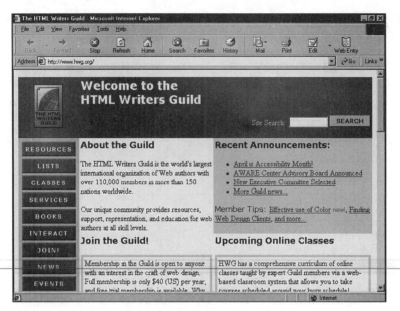

Figure 11.2: *Complex visual design is possible using CSS.*

Identifying Selectors

A *selector* is the element, or group of elements, to which a style will be applied. Selectors can be individual elements, lists of like elements, or specific instances of elements identified by class or ID attributes. In this next section, we'll look at selectors of each type.

Elements as Selectors

Using an element as a selector is pretty straightforward. The style rule is written by giving the element (selector), followed by the property or properties and values bound within braces:

```
selector {property: value}
```

Multiple elements that will have the same properties can be grouped to save redundancy in the style sheet document. For instance, you might want all headings to be colored red. Instead of writing

```
h1 {color:red}
h2 {color:red}
h3 {color:red}
h4 {color:red}
h5 {color:red}
h6 {color:red}
```

the selector can be written as a comma-delimited list of elements with the single property definition:

```
h1, h2, h3, h4, h5, h6 {color:red}
```

Elements don't have to be related to be grouped as a selector. That is, you aren't limited to "headings only" as in the previous example. If you wanted, you could create a selector out of h1, p, li, and div, and the rule would function the same way: Each element would be colored red:

```
h1, p, li, div {color:red}
```

There will inevitably be times, however, when you'll want the majority of instances of a given element to be treated in one manner, but one or more instances need to be given a different look. To handle this a new type of selector, one not based on element names, needs to be used. These selectors are known as *classes*.

Creating Classes

The syntax within the style sheet using a class as a selector is nearly identical to that used when the element is the selector. The only difference is that classes use other-than-element names and begin with the period character; for example

```
.myclass {text-align:right; color:blue}
```

Applying a class-based style works a little differently, because the class name doesn't appear natively in the XHTML document. To invoke the style, the class attribute is added to the element where the style is desired.

Listing 11.1 has three small paragraphs. The designer wants to apply a different set of style properties to the middle paragraph than are found on the first and third paragraphs. This can be done by creating a style class.

EXAMPLE   **Listing 11.1:** class.html

```
<!DOCTYPE html PUBLIC "-//W3C//DTD XHTML 1.0 Strict//EN"
  "http://www.w3.org/TR/xhtml1/DTD/xhtml1-strict.dtd">
<html xmlns="http://www.w3.org/1999/xhtml" xml:lang="en" >
<head>
<title>The fox and the dog</titles>
<link rel="stylesheet" href="class.css" />
</head>
<body>
<p>The quick brown fox jumped over the lazy dog.</p>
<p>The quick brown fox is lucky that it wasn't a dog that would chase him!</p>
<p>The quick brown fox jumped over the lazy dog.</p>
</body>
</html>
```

The style sheet has only two rules:

```
p {text-align:left; color:black}
.newp {text-align:right; color:blue}
```

The <p> tag on the second paragraph needs to be adjusted to take the new class assignment:

```
<p class="newp">
```

Note that the `class` attribute value is the name of the class *without* the . character. Figure 12.3 shows the results; quite a difference between them, isn't there?

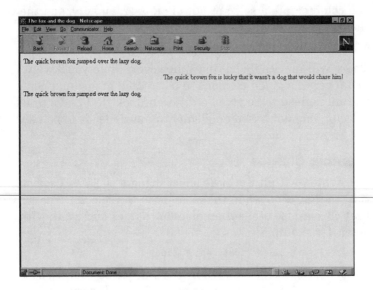

Figure 11.3: *Three* p *elements, one is modified using a class selector.*

NOTE

Although our example had a base style rule for the p element, it is not necessary for there to be an existing style rule before a class rule can be applied.

Single-Occurrence Style Rules

Taking advantage of the structural nature of XHTML, individual elements can be given a label that is unique within a document using the `id` attribute. If the designer wants to create a style rule for that specific element, it could be done using a style class as discussed in the previous section. However, the unique label provided by the `id` attribute has already provided the hook necessary to bind a rule to the element instance: the `id` attribute itself. The selector is written as follows:

`#idvalue {property:value}`

The selector name is the value of the `id` attribute, prepended with the hash character (#). A rule created for the element

`<h1 id="a1">Generic Heading</h1>`

would be written as

`#a1 {property:rule}`

In most design cases, class selectors will be used rather than ID selectors, unless you're fitting an existing document with the specialized ID structure already in place.

NOTE

The style attribute, to be used for inline styling in documents, is being deprecated. Deprectation, you'll recall, means that the W3C is indicating that the method may not appear in future versions of the language, and generally, an alternative method will be provided.

Applying Style

Now with the structure of style rules under your belt, let's take a quick tour of popular styles. The full spectrum of style rules and possible values can be found in the CSS recommendations on the W3C Web site. CSS Level 1, the first version of CSS, is located at http://www.w3.org/TR/REC-CSS1. CSS Level 2, which builds upon Level 1, is found at http://www.w3.org/TR/ REC-CSS2/. CSS1 covered the basics: fonts, list formatting, and box properties such as margins and padding. CSS2 continued the work by adding control of positioning, the ability to float boxes in a given area, and what's known as the *z-index*, for a psuedo-three-dimensional presentation.

At present not all browsers fully implement CSS1. CSS2 support in browsers is far from complete. Internet Explorer 5.5 and the previews of Netscape 6 come close to fully implementing CSS1.

Styles for Text

Most use of style in documents belongs to one of three types: fonts, colors, and alignment. Table 11.1 lists five properties for fonts and the type of values that might be assigned to them.

Table 11.1: Style Properties for Fonts

Style Property	Values
font-family	Font names, such as Arial, Times, Courier, or generic font types such as sans serif
font-style	normal, italic, oblique keyword (small, medium, large, and
font-size	so on), relative sizes (+2 for twice the size, -1 for half, and so on), or percentages (for example, 50% for half the base size)
font-variant	small-caps
font-weight	bold

Block Level Formatting

One way of describing the layout of HTML documents is called the *box model*. In this model, small boxes fit inside larger boxes, which all fit inside a single big box (see Figure 12.4).

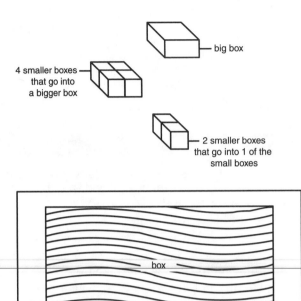

Figure 11.4: This shows how a document layout can be visualized as a set of nested boxes.

The large outer box is the html element, containing everything else in the document. The biggest box inside is the body element, smaller boxes in that are paragraphs, tables, lists, headings, and so on.

XHTML elements are easily divided up into block-level elements and the rest, which are known as *inline* elements. All block elements are rendered beginning on a new line in the browser. You'll have noticed that headings, paragraphs, and div behave in this manner. Inline elements, on the other hand, are "in the current line." Tags such as em, strong, span are inline elements.

CAUTION

It is possible to change the display model for elements using the CSS display property. However, unless there's a particularly compelling reason to do so (and I'm hard pressed to think of any), avoid changing these expected semantics. It's far better to find an element with the correct semantics and use that.

Block elements have three distinct areas of space surrounding them: the margin, the padding, and the border. Each of these areas is shown in the drawing in Figure 11.5.

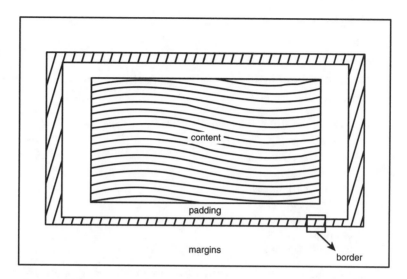

Figure 11.5: *This shows margin, padding, and border spaces surrounding a box.*

These spaces are typically modified in terms of width and height to provide visual white space between box elements and, when using the border space, to provide a colored or other distinctive frame.

EXAMPLE

The document in Listing 11.2 has a heading and two simple paragraphs. To demonstrate each of the box spacing properties, we've defined two style rules using the h1 and p selectors.

The heading is given borders 10 pixels wide on the top and bottom only, colored in green. The paragraphs have 2 pixel-wide borders on all sides, colored purple. Additionally, the paragraphs have a left margin of 4 em spaces and a padding of 1 em space. The style sheet is shown in Listing 11.3.

The listing in 11.2 is a simple XHTML document to which we will apply the box.css CSS style sheet.

Listing 11.2: A Simple XHTML Document Where You Can Apply the box.css CSS Style Sheet

```
<html>
<head>
<link rel="stylesheet" href="box.css">
</head>
<body>
<h1>Did you know?</h1>
<p>There's a special paragraph that contains every letter in
the English language. Students who have taken a typing class
will surely be familiar with it.</p>
<p>The quick brown fox jumped over the lazy dog.</p>
```

Listing 11.2: continued

```
</body>
</html>
```

Listing 11.3 applies box spacing properties to the XHTML document listed in Listing 11.2.

Listing 11.3: The XHTML Document After Applying Box Spacing Properties

```
h1 {border-top-width:10px;
    border-bottom-width:10px;
    border-style:solid;
    border-color:green}
p {border-width:2px;
   border-color:purple;
   padding:1em;
   margin-left:4em}
```

The resulting page (shown in Figure 11.6) clearly shows the results of the padding, with a four-sided gutter of space between the text and the purple border, as well as the deeper left-side margin for the paragraphs.

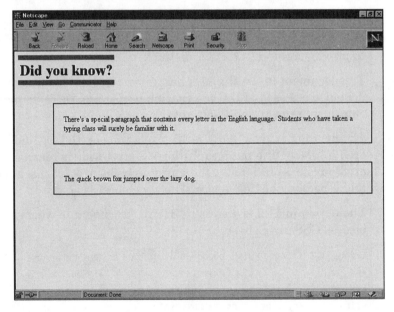

Figure 11.6: *This page shows the results of the padding.*

Spacing Within Blocks

Margins, borders, and padding all deal with spacing outside the actual text block. There are CSS properties available inside the text block as well. These features include alignment and indentation of text, line height, and word or letter spacing. These properties and their potential values are listed in Table 11.2.

Table 11.2: Intra-block Spacing Properties

Style Property	Potential Values
text-align	left, right, center, justify
text-indent	length, percentage
line-height	length, percentage
word-spacing	normal, length
letter-spacing	normal, length

TEXT ALIGNMENT

Aligning text is a process you're already familiar with using the align attribute. The property used in CSS is the "text-align" property. The default placement in XHTML is aligned to the left margin. Other possibilities are aligned to the center, to the right margin, or a *justified* alignment, where it appears that the text is aligned to *both* the left and right margins. Justification is actually achieved by stretching the spaces within the line to allow the ends to stay docked at the margin.

INDENTATION

For many years the ability, or perhaps better put the inability, to indent the beginning of paragraphs became a seemingly never-ending quest. Designers would try to force spaces using the   character entity, only to have a browser collapse the white space. They'd use small blank .gif images, yet struggle with the changes in font sizes and line height.

When CSS was developed, a new property was defined: text-indent. The value is a measure, expressed either in units such as pixels or em spaces, or as a percentage of the available space within the block. Using the standard three-em indent so long sought after, the rule is expressed like this:

```
p {text-indent:3em}
```

Provided your browser supports this property, the result would look like Figure 11.7.

LINE HEIGHT

Line height is a measurement from the baseline of one line of text to the baseline of the line above or below it. The baseline is the invisible line on which the bottoms of most letters rest (letters like g and q project below the baseline with their "tails"). Potential values for the line-height property include specific units (pixels, centimeters, and so on), and relative values. If a font size is set to 10 pt, a line-height value of 1.4 results in the same space allocated to a 14-pt font.

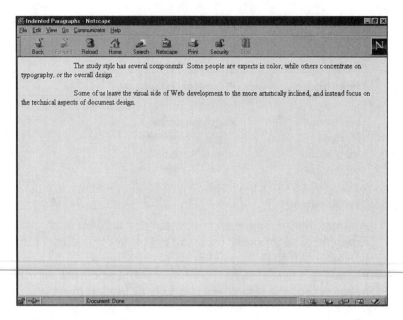

Figure 11.7: This page shows paragraphs with indented first lines, thanks to the text-indent CSS property.

TIP

When working with line heights, keep in mind that the excess space, known as the *leading* (that not occupied by the font in use) is equally divided above and below the space occupied by the font.

WORD AND LETTER SPACING

If you've used justified text alignment, you've already seen word spacing in action. The even margins are achieved by stretching the space between words to fill the available distance between the first and last word on the line.

You can change this distance manually using the word-spacing property. The default value of this property is "normal"—what the browser will choose based on the font designer's choices. Manual adjustments use a CSS length value (pixels, em spaces, and so on).

Although word spacing operates on the space between whole words, the letter-spacing property, also valued in CSS lengths, adjusts the space between individual letters.

Care should be taken when modifying this property for large blocks of text. Font designers have developed significant expertise in the readability of their fonts and provide default settings for the space between individual letter pairs. For instance, the space between a V and an A when next to each other, "VA," is often different from the space between a P and an O, "PO," because of how neatly the V and A letters fit together based on their complementary angles. Font designers have taken these issues into consideration when setting the defaults. Adjusting them can lead the reader to notice that something is slightly "off" in the presentation, though they'll often not be able to discern just what that is.

What's Next

In this chapter we've reviewed the basic syntax for creating and referencing external CSS style sheets. You've developed style rules based on single elements, groups of elements, classes, and `id` selectors.

Next up in Chapter 12, "XSL—Style the XML Way," we'll take a look at the XML-based style language XSL: the Extensible Style Sheet Language.

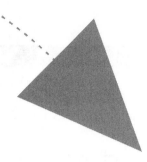

XSL—Style the XML Way

In the last chapter, you learned about the separation of structure and presentation in XHTML 1.1 and saw one way to apply style information to XHTML 1.1 pages using Cascading Style Sheets.

Such complete separation of structure (content) from presentation in XHTML 1.1 implements one of the basic principles of the Extensible Markup Language (XML).

XHTML, whether version 1.0 or 1.1, complies with the syntax requirements of XML 1.0, for example the need to have an end tag for each start tag. But XHTML 1.0 only went part way to making HTML fully XML compliant. XHTML 1.0 included many presentation elements within it, thus mixing content and presentation. To move XHTML closer to full compliance with XML principles, those presentation-related elements had to go. XHTML 1.1 removes the presentation elements (tags) from XHTML, bringing XHTML more fully into line with the requirements and principles of XML 1.0.

Cascading Style Sheets can be used with XML or XHTML, but CSS has limitations when applied to documents where there is no presentation information at all—for example, with respect to reordering elements in the output document. In this chapter you will learn about another solution to the need to apply style to XML documents, Extensible Stylesheet Language Transformations (XSLT), when content and presentation are completely separated. Because XHTML 1.1 documents are XML documents, the principles you learn will apply fully to XHTML documents, from XHTML 1.1 onwards.

This chapter teaches you:

- Extensible Stylesheet Language Transformations (XSLT)
- XML Path Language (XPath)
- Extensible Stylesheet Language Formatting Objects (XSL-FO)
- How to create an XSLT style sheet

Understanding XSLT

It's possible to use XHTML 1.0 pretty much as if it were simply HTML. But to obtain full benefit from XHTML's compliance with XML, you will need to begin learning about aspects of XML which have no direct equivalent in HTML or XHTML 1.0.

One of the most powerful technologies in the XML family is *Extensible Stylesheet Language Transformations*, usually abbreviated to XSLT.

XML 101

Before diving straight into XSLT, you will need to understand a few points about XML that are relevant to how XSLT works.

The XML family of technologies is very flexible, which can be very useful because there can be many ways of achieving much the same thing and many solutions that can be found. But flexibility, by giving various ways to achieve the same or similar output, also can be confusing until you get a clear picture about the advantages and disadvantages of different approaches.

The *element* is a foundational part of XML. Each element that has *content* has a *start tag* and an *end tag*.

For example, if you wanted to use a particular piece of text in an XSLT style sheet, you might use this element:

```
<xsl:text>To be or not to be?</xsl:text>
```

EXAMPLE The start-tag is `<xsl:text>`. The end-tag is `</xsl:text>`. And, not surprisingly the content is `To be or not to be?`

When a tag is nested within another tag, the outer tag is said to be the *parent* and the contained tag is said to be the *child*. For example, in this simple example XML document, the `<chapter>` element is the parent of the `<paragraph>` element:

```
<?xml version='1.0'?>
<chapter>
<paragraph>The paragraph element is a child of the chapter element.
</paragraph>
</chapter>
```

Each XML document is allowed to have only one *root element*—an element within which every other element in the document is properly nested. In the example, which you have just seen, the root element is the `<chapter>` element.

But the root element (or *element root*) is not the root of the whole document. Outside of the root element but still within the document is, for example, the prolog of the XML document, consisting of the XML declaration (where present), processing instructions, the DOCTYPE declaration (where present), and any comments you might choose to include.

All the content of an XML document is viewed, from the perspective of XML 1.0, as being contained within the *document entity*. The root element is a child of the document entity.

Sometimes the term *root* is used in an unqualified way to refer to either the document entity or the root element. Because, as you will see later in the chapter, it is important in navigating through XML documents to know exactly where you are, you need to be sure where any particular element is located relative to the document entity and the root element.

The prolog of an XML document precedes the root element but is contained within the document entity. The prolog might contain an XML declaration, processing instructions, comments, and the DOCTYPE declaration. It is in the prolog that you can use a processing instruction to attach an XSLT style sheet to an XML or XHTML document, as you will see later.

There is very much more to XML 1.0 than has been mentioned here, but this basic information is needed for you to understand the discussion of XSLT, Xpath, and XSL-FO which follows.

The full text of the Extensible Markup Language (XML) 1.0 Recommendation can be viewed at

`http://www.w3.org/TR/1998/REC-xml-19980210`

XSLT and Other Pieces of the Jigsaw

Originally, the concept for displaying XML documents was that the Extensible Stylesheet Language (XSL) would perform for XML documents a function similar to that which external Cascading Style Sheets performed for HTML pages. As the World Wide Web Consortium (W3C) worked through the details of possible style sheet languages, as they might apply to XML rather than HTML, it became clear that transformation of a source XML document was foundational to most presentations of XML content. There were perceived technical advantages at the time to separating work on transformations.

Thus, the W3C focussed on the transformational aspect of Extensible Stylesheet Language and was able to complete a solution and release it as the XSL Transformations (XSLT) Version 1.0 Recommendation on November 16, 1999.

If you want to see the full scope of XSLT, the text of the Recommendation is available at

`http://www.w3.org/TR/1999/REC-xslt-19991116`

Part of the work on XSL transformations took account of the fact that there was a need to navigate around XML documents, and it also was seen that another W3C activity (XPointer) had similar navigational needs. Rather than produce two standards, work on those navigational needs was focussed into an initiative from which emerged the XML Path Language as a W3C Recommendation on the same day that the XSLT was released.

The full XPath Recommendation, XML Path Language (XPath) Version 1.0, can be viewed at

`http://www.w3.org/TR/1999/REC-xpath-19991116`

XPath will be discussed in more detail later in this chapter.

What Is XSL?

It might seem pretty odd to ask what XSL is in a chapter like this, but different people have used and are using the term to refer to different things. If you are to avoid the possibility of getting very confused and wasting quite a bit of time trying to work out why you are having problems, you need to be aware of that difference in usage of the term *XSL*. The different types of XSL will work together in some circumstances but not in others. Knowing which meaning of XSL applies in a particular context therefore will help you to avoid problems, either in your thinking or, sometimes, when one version of XSL will simply not work at all or fails to work as you expect it to.

There are basically four different ways in which the term XSL is used:

- As a combination of XSLT and XSL-FO

- As XSL-FO without XSLT

- As Microsoft proprietary XSL, that is non–W3C-compliant XSL

- Ambiguously or indiscriminately to refer to any one or combination of the first three

Part of the potential for confusion arises from variations in terminology by the W3C over time. For example, one W3C document implies XSLT can be used separately from XSL, whereas others state that XSLT is part of XSL. Part of the problem in unambiguously describing this area arises because XSLT and XSL-FO will, when XSL-FO is finalized, operate very closely together.

To complicate things further, there are several versions of Microsoft XSL available currently, each with varying degrees of compliance with the W3C standards. The Microsoft XSL originally supplied with Internet Explorer 5.0 is now obsolete. At the time of this writing, the July 2000 Preview Release was current and was significantly closer to W3C standards than previous flavors of Microsoft XSL had been. Microsoft have stated that their XSL will be made fully compliant with W3C standards, but that has not yet been achieved.

In this chapter, the terms *XSLT* and *XSL-FO* are used to refer, respectively, to the standards expressed in the W3C Extensible Stylesheet Languages Transformations Recommendation and the Extensible Stylesheet Language Working Draft. XSLT transforms the source XML document into an output document (for example, in another dialect of XML, XTHML). XSL-FO applies the formatting information to the transformed document, controlling how it is displayed—whether in a desktop browser, in a mobile browser, or on paper.

Because of the ambiguity surrounding the term *XSL*, it won't be used (without explanation) in the remainder of this chapter.

What Does XSLT Do?

How does XSLT work? Put simply, an XSLT style sheet contains the instructions for an XSLT processor about how a new document should be constructed from the source XML document and the XSLT style sheet.

How do you know which XSLT style sheet will be applied to an XML document? Basically, there are two techniques. First, within an XML or XHTML document there might be a reference associating that document with an XSLT transformation sheet, also known as a style sheet. Another technique is to make the association between the XML document and the XSLT style sheet being applied to it from the command line. Instant Saxon, mentioned later, operates in the latter way.

As a result of processing by an XSLT processor, the content of the source XML document is manipulated ("transformed") by the XSLT processor so that the output document differs from the source document.

The transformation of the source document need not be combined with formatting for display, but in this chapter it is XSLT transformation as a prelude to display that will be explained. The transformation of XML documents into other documents is of great importance for ecommerce. XSLT can, for example, transform the XML used by one business into the format used by a customer or supplier, thus facilitating the electronic exchange of information. However, this will not be considered further in this chapter.

To better understand the process of transformation, it is necessary to take a closer look at how an XSLT processor works.

XSLT Processors

An XSLT processor is a piece of software that can transform an XML source document into a result or an output document. The result or output document can be another XML document (to which formatting objects might be applied, but need not be), an XHTML or HTML document, or a plain text document.

XSLT processors are routinely combined with an XML parser (sometimes called an XML processor), but increasingly XSLT processors also are combined with other software modules—for example, an XML editor in development environments that are more or less well integrated.

In some circumstances the result document might be saved to disc, such as when a static XHTML page is created from an XML source file. On other occasions the result document will be created dynamically and displayed to a user but never exist other than in memory and onscreen.

Several XSLT processors are freely available for download. If you are using a Windows 9x PC, an XSLT processor called Instant Saxon is particularly easy to download and install. A full Java-based version of Saxon that can be installed on most PC platforms also is available for download without charge.

Instant Saxon can be downloaded from

`http://users.iclway.co.uk/mhkay/saxon/instant.html`

To understand how an XSLT processor works, you need to understand a little about the XSLT Data Model and how an XSLT processor makes use of it.

All XML files are merely text files. One character simply follows another. But the strictly defined syntax of an XML document means that within the XML file there is a logical structure contained within that sequence of characters.

Among the character stream of an XML document, in the prolog of the document, will likely be a command that associates an XSLT transformation sheet with the source XML document.

EXAMPLE

XSLT processors differ in how they associate a style sheet with an XML file. One way is to include an `<?xml-stylesheet?>` processing instruction within the prolog of the XML document. If you do this using Internet Explorer 5.0, the style sheet will be associated with the XML document. In addition (assuming the style sheet is situated in the location indicated by the processing instruction and is a legitimate style sheet), the source XML document will be transformed according to the transformations contained within the style sheet. Early Preview Releases of Netscape 6 have not contained XSLT functionality.

To associate a CSS style sheet with an XML document, you might use a command something like

```
<?xml-stylesheet href="myfirst.css" type="text/css"?>
```

To associate an XSLT style sheet with an XML file, you would use a command something like this:

```
<?xml-stylesheet href="myfirst.xsl" type="text/xml"?>
```

NOTE

Further details of how to use the `<?xml-stylesheet?>` processing instruction are found in the W3C Recommendation titled "Associating Style Sheets with XML Documents Version 1.0," which can be accessed at

`http://www.w3.org/1999/06/REC-xml-stylesheet-19990629`

EXAMPLE

Other XSLT processors can associate a style sheet with an XML file from the command line. For example, using Instant Saxon to associate an XSLT style sheet `myfirst.xsl` with an XML document called `myfirst.xml` and produce an XHTML file called `myfirst.html`, you would issue the following command:

```
saxon myfirst.xml myfirst.xsl > myfirst.html
```

If you are using a different XSLT processor, the syntax might differ.

To extract or make use of the logical structure contained within a well-formed or valid XML document, it is necessary for the XSLT processor, which will typically include an XML parser, to create a tree-like structure of nodes in memory which captures the logical content of the XML document. Remember that the XSL style sheet is itself an XML document so it, too, is transformed into a hierarchical tree-like structure in memory.

CAUTION

If you are familiar with the Document Object Model, you might notice that the XSLT object model is very similar. However, you should be aware that the DOM and XSLT data models are not identical. Detailed consideration of the differences is beyond the scope of this chapter.

Further information on the DOM Level 1 can be viewed at `http://www.w3.org/TR/1998/REC-DOM-Level-1-19981001`.

DOM Level 2 is currently being drafted by the W3C. Further details can be found at `http://www.w3.org/TR/2000/CR-DOM-Level-2-20000510`.

The XML parser creates from the stream of characters in each XML document (the source XML document and the XSLT style sheet) a tree-like structure in memory. The tree-like branching structure contains a hierarchical, branching structure consisting of several types of node, which will be discussed in more detail later.

In fact, when an XSLT processor is processing an XML or XHTML document, there are typically three trees in memory at the same time:

- The source tree, which is usually an XML (or XHTML) document
- The tree representing the XSLT style sheet document (itself an XML document)
- The result tree, which is the document in a new form ready for display whether it be an XML document, an XHTML document, or HTML document or text

Once the result tree is created, if it is an XHTML document, it can be displayed directly in a Web browser or saved to disk. Optionally, a Cascading Style Sheet can be applied to it to improve or create the presentation of the output tree. Simple examples of both will be shown toward the end of this chapter.

Many XSLT transformations will take place in the setting of complex ecommerce systems. In such circumstances it is quite possible that there might be multiple XML source documents processed by one style sheet; the style sheet itself might consist of modules, and a result tree might not be displayed or saved to disk but might act as the source XML document for a further transformation. Detailed consideration of such systems is beyond the scope of this chapter.

CAUTION

XML documents include *white space*—space characters, tabs, new lines, and carriage returns. There are many subtle issues related to processing and outputting white space characters. To avoid frustration you will need to read and understand the issues relating to white space in the XML 1.0 and XSLT 1.0 Recommendations.

Namespaces in XML

Increasingly, the XML family of technologies are interdependent and work together. One of the necessary technologies to make XSLT work involves using XML namespaces. We need to take a quick look at what namespaces are and how they work.

One of the innovations in XHTML 1.1 is the use of modules of elements and the ability to create new elements for use in XHTML documents. You will learn more about this in Chapters 14 through 16. This creates the potential for confusion if two providers of modules happen to use the same element name.

XML, and therefore XHTML, solves this problem by the use of namespaces. Perhaps the easiest way to think of this is to think how human beings solve a similar problem.

Depending where you live in the world, you might know several people named Andrew. In most Western countries the way to distinguish one Andrew from another is very simple—you can use the surname to distinguish Andrew Smith from Andrew Patterson from Andrew Watt. For most practical day-to-day purposes that removes the likelihood of confusing one person named Andrew with another.

XML uses a similar mechanism to solve the problem of potentially confusing one XHTML or XML element with another similarly named element coming from different modules but which are used within the same XML or XHTML document.

EXAMPLE

So if we want to distinguish two elements called `<text>` from each other, we could give one its full name, `<xsl:text>`. An `<xsl:text>` element is part of the XSLT specification, as it happens. There are so many other possible prefixes of the other `<text>` element that confusion is unlikely to occur.

Just as humans list other people with surname often coming first so XML gives the namespace prefix first (in this case `xsl`), follows that by a colon, and then what is called the *local part* (in this case `text`).

Returning to the example of surnames, for everyday use surnames are fine. However, if we want to look into family trees then we need to have more detail like date and place of birth to identify an individual uniquely.

XML namespaces also have a need to identify each namespace uniquely. The namespace declaration associates the namespace prefix, `xsl`, with a Uniform Resource Identifier (URI). For most practical purposes, at present a URI can be thought of as synonymous with a URL (Uniform Resource Locator).

Strangely, perhaps, the URI which identifies an XML namespace doesn't actually need to contain anything at all. It is the string of characters in the URI which are (hoped to be) unique. The prefix is really an alias for the text string of the much longer (but unwieldy) URI. The chances of two URIs being identical is tiny, but it is recommended that you use only a URI that refers to a domain name that you control.

EXAMPLE

XSLT style sheets typically declare the XSL namespace as an attribute of the opening `<xsl:stylesheet>` element like this:

```
<xsl:stylesheet
    xmlns:xsl="http://www.w3.org/1999/XSL/Transform"
    version="1.0">
```

This has exactly the same meaning as

```
<xsl:transform
    xmlns:xsl="http://www.w3.org/1999/XSL/Transform"
    version="1.0">
```

In other words, the `<xsl:stylesheet>` and `<xsl:transform>` elements in an XSLT style sheet (or transformation sheet) are identical in meaning. Just as I use the terms style sheet and transformation sheet interchangeably, so the XSLT Recommendation provides two elements with identical meaning.

XML namespaces are used to identify unambiguously the XSLT elements, such as `<xsl:stylesheet>`, `<xsl:template>`, and so on.

XML namespaces also have importance within the tree of nodes, but detailed consideration of those issues is beyond the scope of this chapter. Further information is contained in the XSLT 1.0 and XPath Recommendations.

XPath—XML Path Language

To be able to do anything useful with XSLT, as well as knowing a little about XML namespaces, you need to understand at least the basics of the XML Path Language, which is usually called XPath.

If you look at XSLT as the way to describe how the XSLT processor is to alter a node in the source XSLT tree during processing and XPath as the way to tell the XSLT processor which node or nodes that transformation is to be applied to, you have begun to grasp how XSLT and XPath work together.

How Does XPath Work?

The first time you come across XPath it can seem pretty intimidating. There is certainly quite a bit of jargon associated with it and XPath *expressions*, after you get beyond basic ones, can be pretty complex. But the principle behind XPath is very simple. If you think of XPath expressions as the XML equivalent to giving someone street directions then you have gone a long way to understanding what XPath is about.

If you are asking for street directions, you might be told to go back one block and then do something. XPath allows us to find a parent node in the tree of nodes. In the street, exactly where you end up depends on where you started from. Similarly, in XPath the node you arrive at is determined by the node you start at, the *context node*.

If you find the right street, you might be told to go along the street until you find a building with a particular number. XPath allows you to choose a particular element (or an attribute of a particular element) within the tree of nodes to apply the desired transformation to.

When you get street directions the way they are expressed varies depending on where you are starting from. XPath works just the same way. For the XSLT processor to be able to know where to apply a transformation, it needs to know where you are starting from. The XPath term for your current location is called the context node. This simply refers to the node in the XSLT tree where you can think of the XSLT processor as focussing on at present.

Before looking in more detail at what in XPath jargon are called *location paths*, you need to know a little about XPath nodes.

XPath Nodes

As mentioned in the discussion earlier in this chapter, an XML document is converted when loaded into memory and parsed into a tree-like structure of nodes.

XPath allows for seven different types of node within a tree:

- **Root nodes**—There is only one of these in an individual document, which corresponds to the document entity of the XML 1.0 specification. A root node can have as its children element nodes, processing instruction nodes, and comment nodes.

- **Element nodes**—There is an element node for each element in the source XML document. One element node, the element root, is a child of the root node in a well-formed XML document.

- **Text nodes**—Character data is grouped into text nodes. As much character data as possible is grouped into each text node.

- **Attribute nodes**—Each element node has an associated set of attribute nodes; the element is the parent of each of these attribute nodes. However, an attribute node is not a child of its parent element.

- **Namespace nodes**—This can be envisaged as a representation of the Namespace Declaration. An element node will have a namespace node for each namespace declaration which is in scope.

- **Processing instruction nodes**—There is a processing instruction node for every processing instruction in a source document, except for those processing instructions which may be contained in a document type declaration.

- **Comment nodes**—There is a comment node for each comment in the source XML document, except for those comments occurring within the document type declaration:

```
<?xml version="1.0"?>
<!-- This is a comment -->
<chapter>Chapter 12</chapter>
```

When processed in memory, this very simple XML document would have a root node (representing the invisible document entity), which would have two child nodes: a comment node representing the comment that forms the second line of the code and an element node representing the <chapter> element. In addition, a text node representing the content of the <chapter> element would be present as a child of the element node, which represents the <chapter> element.

Location Paths

The XPath term for the equivalent of street directions is *location path*. A location path can be of one of two forms—an absolute location path, which takes its starting point as the root node of the tree or a relative location path, which takes the context node as its starting point. These will be compared in more detail a little later in this chapter.

A location path consists of one or more *location steps* separated by a slash (/). A location step has three parts:

- **An axis**—Specifies the tree relationship between the nodes selected by the location step and the context node. Example axes are parent and child.

- **A node test**—Specifies the node type and expanded-name of the nodes selected by the location step.

- **Zero or more predicates**—Use arbitrary expressions to further refine the set of nodes selected by the location step.

A location path returns the node set selected by the location path (a location path is a special type of XPath expression). Location paths also can return Boolean values, numbers, or strings in some circumstances.

Detailed consideration of location steps, XPath functions, and so on is beyond the scope of this chapter.

Abbreviated and Unabbreviated Syntax

Like many things related to XML, there is more than one way to achieve the same thing.

XPath provides for two types of syntax to describe the location path of an object. The abbreviated syntax, not surprisingly, provides a shorter way to express XPath expressions.

EXAMPLE

Let's compare some XPath expressions in the unabbreviated and abbreviated syntax for a simple XML document:

```
<?xml version='1.0'?>
<book title="XHTML By Example">
<!-- Some other chapters would be listed here -->

<chapter title="XSL: Style the XML Way">
<section title="XSLT - Transformation"></section>
<section title="XPath - XML Path Language"></section>
<section title="XSL-FO - XSL Formatting Objects"></section>
<section title="Creating an XSL Stylesheet"></section>
</chapter>

<!-- Some more chapters would be listed here -->

</book>
```

If the current context node was <book> then to find a <chapter> element, which is a child of the <book> element, we could use the following XPath expression:

```
child::chapter
```

which is the unabbreviated syntax, or

```
chapter
```

which is the abbreviated syntax.

In this example, `child::` is the axis. It can be omitted in the abbreviated syntax, because `child::` is the default axis. The node test is `chapter`. There is no predicate in this XPath location path, either in the unabbreviated or abbreviated syntax.

An XSLT processor will process the unabbreviated and abbreviated syntax identically (assuming each has been written correctly). Which syntax you use is partly a matter of personal preference in some circumstances. The unabbreviated syntax is typically more explicit, whereas the abbreviated syntax is typically shorter. For some location paths, there is no abbreviated equivalent, so the unabbreviated syntax must be used.

Because in our simplified document all children of the <book> element are, in fact, <chapter> elements, if the context node was the node corresponding to the <book> element, we could achieve the same thing by writing

```
child::*
```

in unabbreviated syntax, or

```
*
```

in abbreviated syntax. Yes, that's right; a simple asterisk will choose all direct children of the context node. Note that the * does not select the children of such child nodes.

Similar to the XPath expressions for selecting elements, there are corresponding expressions to select attributes, which will not be detailed here.

Relative and Absolute Location Paths

EXAMPLE

So far in this chapter you have seen relative location paths, that is, relative to a context node. However, XPath expressions also allow for absolute addressing. Another way to look at absolute location paths is that they, too, are relative—but relative to the root node of the XSLT/XPath tree. You will see some examples of XPath expressions that use absolute location paths using the previous example:

```
<?xml version='1.0'?>
<book title="XHTML By Example">
<!-- Some other chapters would be listed here -->

<chapter title="XSL: Style the XML Way">
<section title="XSLT - Transformation"></section>
<section title="XPath - XML Path Language"></section>
<section title="XSL-FO - XSL Formatting Objects"></section>
<section title="Creating an XSL Stylesheet"></section>
</chapter>

<!-- Some more chapters would be listed here -->

</book>
```

To select a <chapter> element we can use the absolute location path

```
/book/chapter
```

because the / at the beginning of the XPath expression indicates that it begins with the root node of the XML document. The only child of the root node is the element root, which in this document is the <book> element. The XPath expression also can be expressed in unabbreviated syntax:

```
/child::book/child::chapter
```

To select <section> elements using an absolute location path, we could use the following XPath expressions, respectively abbreviated or unabbreviated:

```
/book/chapter/section
```

or

```
/child::book/child::chapter/child::section
```

Both the abbreviated and unabbreviated syntax would select all four of the <section> elements that are present in our document.

To make a more precise selection of just one of the <section> elements, we could use an XPath expression to make a selection by specifying the title attribute of a particular <section> element:

```
/book/chapter/section[title="XPath - XML Path Language"]
```

or

```
/child::book/child::chapter/child::section[attribute::title="XPath - XML Path Language"]
```

Note that selecting an element on the basis of the value of one of its attributes is not the same as selecting the attribute.

Some straightforward usage of XPath will be illustrated later in the chapter when you see some example XSLT style sheets.

XSL-FO—Formatting Objects

The Extensible Stylesheet Language Transformations Recommendation was issued by W3C in November 1999. Currently, W3C is working on an Extensible Stylesheet Language Working Draft, which focuses largely on XSL Formatting Objects (XSL-FO).

The W3C work on XSL-FO aims to capture all the functionality of Cascading Style Sheets for use with XML documents on the Web but also intends to add many layout facilities to allow use of XML documents not only on the Web but also in print. By separating content from presentation this becomes possible.

When an XSLT processor is applied, with an appropriate XSLT style sheet, to an XML document a transformation of the source document occurs, producing an output or result tree.

That same process is carried out when using XSL Formatting Objects by including such formatting objects in the tree output by the XSL Transformation.

A second step then takes place called *formatting* which, not surprisingly, is carried out by an XSL *formatter*. In this context XSL refers to a combination of XSLT and XSL-FO included in the output tree.

The most recent W3C Working Draft summarizes the process as follows:

> "Formatting is enabled by including formatting semantics in the result tree. Formatting semantics are expressed in terms of a catalog of classes of formatting objects. The nodes of the result tree are formatting objects. The classes of formatting objects denote typographic abstractions such as page, paragraph, table, and so forth. Finer control over the presentation of these abstractions is provided by a set of formatting properties, such as those controlling indents, word- and letter-spacing, and widow, orphan, and hyphenation control. In XSL, the classes of formatting objects and formatting properties provide the vocabulary for expressing presentation intent."

What that means is that a formatter will obtain information from nodes in the result tree that are formatting objects to provide the framework for the presentation of the output XML document and that smaller scale, fine control of detail in the output document is provided by formatting properties.

In principle, a formatter will be able to create output for traditional desktop Web browsers, mobile browsers, and output on paper.

Typically, many of the nodes in the result tree will be in the formatting object's namespace.

Each formatting object represents part of the specification of the output, for example, layout and style.

The Working Draft summarizes the formatting process as follows:

> "Formatting consists of the generation of a tree of geometric areas, called the area tree. The geometric areas are positioned on a sequence of one or more pages (a browser typically uses a single page). Each geometric area has a position on the page, a specification of what to display in that area and may have a background, padding, and borders. For example, formatting a single character generates an area sufficiently large enough to hold the glyph that is used to present the character visually and the glyph is what is displayed in this area. These areas may be nested. For example, the glyph may be positioned within a line, within a block, within a page."

If you had difficulty understanding the ideas involved in an XSLT output tree of nodes, you might find the idea of a tree of geometric areas a little overwhelming. Broadly, it is helpful to visualize the geometric areas' nodes as reserved areas on the output page that are set aside for particular parts of the output tree to be displayed.

The current Working Draft describing XSL-FO is many times larger than, for example, the XSLT 1.0 Recommendation, and detailed consideration of its contents is beyond the scope of this chapter. I estimate that the current Working Draft is equivalent to a printed document of perhaps 500 pages! Thus, you will realize that this section is a very compressed account of a topic that would require a substantial book simply to describe it.

If you want to explore some of the detail of the current Working Draft, you can find it at

```
http://www.w3.org/TR/2000/WD-xsl-20000327/
```

At the present time Web browsers do not support XSL-FO, and are unlikely to do so for some time after the XSL-FO Recommendation is finalized.

Creating an XSL Style Sheet

So, now that you have looked at some of the XML technologies relevant to XSL Transformations, how does it all work in practice?

In this section you will see two examples of using XSLT style sheets (also known as transformation sheets).

After the XSL-FO part of the Extensible Stylesheet Language is released as a W3C Recommendation, you can expect to be able to use XSL style sheets to combine transformation (XSLT) and the inclusion of formatting objects (XSL-FO) in the result tree.

Basic Style Sheet Concepts

An XSLT style sheet is an XML document. Therefore, although it is not compulsory, it is useful to include an XML declaration as the first line of your XSLT style sheet.

The simplest form of XML declaration is

```
<?xml version='1.0'?>
```

All XSLT style sheets must have either an `<xsl:transform>` or an `<xsl: stylesheet>` element as the root element. The `<xsl:transform>` and `<xsl:stylesheet>` elements mean exactly the same thing.

CAUTION

Remember that the element root—either `<xsl:transform>` or `<xsl:stylesheet>`—is the outermost element *within* a document. The document entity itself is the root node in the XSLT tree, and the element root is a child of the document entity. If, for example, you mix up the two concepts, you may find that your XPath location paths fail to select the nodes you want to choose.

The `<xsl:stylesheet>` element typically will have a namespace declaration and version number as attributes contained within it, like this:

```
<xsl:stylesheet
    xmlns:xsl="http://www.w3.org/1999/XSL/Transform"
    version="1.0">
```

CAUTION

If you find an XSL style sheet that includes the text `"xmlns:xsl="http://www.w3.org/TR/WD-xsl"` in the namespace declaration attribute of an `<xsl:stylesheet>` or `<xsl:transform>` element, the style sheet is using an outdated proprietary form of Microsoft XSL, which deviates from the W3C standard. Updates to a more conformant version of MSXML can be downloaded from the `www.microsoft.com` Web site.

The current form of the namespace declaration is

`"xmlns:xsl="http://www.w3.org/1999/XSL/Transform"`

So, the basic skeleton of an XSLT style sheet looks like this:

```
<?xml version="1.0" ?>
<xsl:stylesheet
    xmlns:xsl="http://www.w3.org/1999/XSL/Transform"
    version="1.0">
<!-- The "meat" of the stylesheet will go here -->
</xsl:stylesheet>
```

This style sheet is well-formed XML. Unfortunately, it does absolutely nothing. But the positive side of that is that it produces no errors either. So, now you can give thought to putting useful content into your first style sheet.

EXAMPLE

A Simple Example Style Sheet

It is traditional in many programming languages to include a self-contained program as the first example of a "real" program. So, because XSLT is in many senses very much a programming language, we will produce a short example, using the famous quote cited earlier in this chapter.

The source XML document looks like this:

```
<?xml version='1.0'?>
<famous_quote>To be or not to be?</famous_quote>
```

If we try to view that XML file just as it is in Microsoft Internet Explorer 5.0, it doesn't look very impressive.

Figure 12.1: *The XML document viewed in Internet Explorer 5.0 before any transformation (other than IE 5.0's default style sheet).*

Nor do we really want to see the start- and end-tags of the `<famous_quote>` element.

Instead of simply allowing Internet Explorer to display an XML file, we will be able to produce a neater output by using an XSL Transformation to create an XHTML file that Internet Explorer can display.

We want the output file to look something like this:

```
<html>
<head>
<title>
Shakespeare Quotation
</title>
</head>
<body>
<h1>To be or not to be?</h1>
</body>
</html>
```

NOTE

The output file might appear without any whitespace and so be considerably less readable than the XHTML that is shown here. To avoid the complexities involved in handling whitespace, no attempt will be made here to control whitespace either in the style sheet or the output document.

When viewed in Internet Explorer 5.0 the output, although still very simple, is a little tidier with a title in the browser window and a little basic layout.

Figure 12.2: *The XHTML output in Internet Explorer following transformation of the XML source document.*

Here is the XSLT style sheet which produced that output:

```
<?xml version="1.0" ?>
<xsl:stylesheet
    xmlns:xsl="http://www.w3.org/1999/XSL/Transform"
    version="1.0">
<xsl:template match="/">
<html>
<head>
<title>
Shakespeare Quotation
</title>
</head>
<body>
<xsl:apply-templates/>
</body>
</html>
</xsl:template>
<xsl:template match="famous_quote">
<h1><xsl:value-of select="."/></h1>
</xsl:template>
</xsl:stylesheet>
```

To help you understand the style sheet and how it works, we will go through key parts of it line by line.

```
<?xml version="1.0" ?>
```

This is the XML declaration which is advisable in XSL transformation sheets but not compulsory.

```
<xsl:stylesheet
    xmlns:xsl="http://www.w3.org/1999/XSL/Transform"
    version="1.0">
```

The start tag of the `<xsl:stylesheet>` element declares the XSL namespace using the official W3C URI for XSLT.

```
<xsl:template match="/">
```

The `<xsl:template>` element is key to the operation of many XSLT transformation sheets. The `/` is an XPath expression which matches the document root. Because our source XML document, in common with all source trees, has a document root this XSLT template is applied. Most of what the `<xsl:template>` does is to output a series of lines that form an XHTML file.

```
<html>
<head>
<title>
Shakespeare Quotation
</title>
</head>
<body>
```

This completes the initial series of lines of XHTML that are output as literal text.

```
<xsl:apply-templates/>
```

The `<xsl:apply-templates>` element is another commonly used and important XSLT element. Essentially, what it means here is to look for all elements in the source XML document and apply any template that matches relevant element nodes within the source document.

```
</body>
</html>
```

The closing `</body>` and `</html>` tags are output "after" the `<xsl:apply-templates>` element is processed.

NOTE

Strictly speaking, many operations carried out by XSLT processors need not be in strict order. However, it is useful when attempting to grasp how an XSLT transformation sheet works to think of these processes as being sequential. Discussion of when it is significant and when it is immaterial what order processing is carried out in is beyond the scope of this chapter.

The literal output stops here, and you see a second `<xsl:template>` element, which will be applied as a result of being called by the `<xsl:apply-templates>` element you saw a little earlier.

```
</xsl:template>
<xsl:template match="famous_quote">
<h1><xsl:value-of select="."/></h1>
```

Here we find an `<xsl:template>` element that matches the `<famous_quote>` element in the source XML document. Therefore, the template is applied to the `<famous_quote>` element. In this case an `<h1>` tag is created in the output tree. Then, an `<xsl:value-of>` element is applied to the content of the element which matches the XPath expression ., which means the current context element—the content of the `<famous_quote>` element. The value of that content, the text string `To be or not to be?` is added to the output tree at the point indicated by the `<xsl:apply-templates>` element earlier in the XSLT code.

```
</xsl:template>
</xsl:stylesheet>
```

These are simply closing tags for the `<xsl:template>` element (in this case the one which matches the XPath expression .—the `<famous_quote>` element) and for the `<xsl:stylesheet>` element.

Combining a CSS Style Sheet with XSLT

It is straightforward to attach a CSS style sheet to your HTML/XHTML output file. You can simply add a `<link>` tag referring to the appropriate CSS style sheet to the output file.

Here is the XSLT document with the link to the Cascading Style Sheet added:

```
<?xml version="1.0" ?>
<xsl:stylesheet
    xmlns:xsl="http://www.w3.org/1999/XSL/Transform"
    version="1.0">
<xsl:template match="/">
<html>
<link rel="stylesheet" href="quotestyle.css" type="text/css"/>
<head>
<title>
Shakespeare Quotation
</title>
</head>
<body>
<xsl:apply-templates/>
</body>
</html>
</xsl:template>
<xsl:template match="famous_quote">
<h1><xsl:value-of select="."/></h1>
</xsl:template>
</xsl:stylesheet>
```

The Cascading Style Sheet file is very simple:

```
h1 {color: red;
    text-align: right;
    text-decoration: underline;
    }
```

All it does is to make the color of the output text in <h1> elements red, to align it to the right, and to underline the text.

As you can see from Figure 12.3, the Cascading Style Sheet was successfully applied.

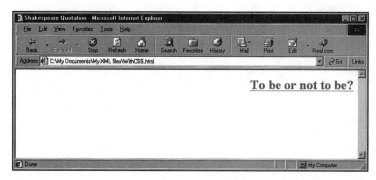

Figure 12.3: *The Shakespeare quotation following the application of the XSLT transformation sheet and the CSS style sheet shown earlier. Note that the text is now aligned right and is underlined, demonstrating the application of the CSS style sheet.*

In these examples you have seen straightforward use of the <xsl:stylesheet>, <xsl:template>, <xsl:apply-templates>, and <xsl:value-of> elements. These are commonly used in XSLT style sheets.

There are, of course, many other elements in the XSLT armory, which are described in the XSLT 1.0 Recommendation.

The full power of XSLT and XSL-FO will not be demonstrable until the XSL-FO component of the Extensible Style Sheet Language has been finalized.

Effective use of these powerful and flexible tools will demand a detailed grasp of XPath, XSLT, and XSL-FO individually; how the XML 1.0 Recommendation applies to this context; and how XPath and the two parts of the Extensible Style Sheet Language interact.

What's Next

In this chapter we've looked at some of the basic concepts that you need to understand to use XSLT, and you have seen some simple examples of putting those concepts into practice.

Next up in Chapter 13 we'll take a look at Document Type Definitions, which define what is allowable content for XHTML documents.

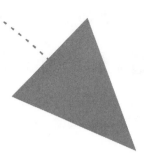

Document Type Definitions—The Syntax Rulebook

Every markup language has a set of rules that must be followed for a document to conform to the language. The XHTML language is defined in a set of three documents known as *Document Type Definitions*, or DTDs. You've used DTDs already by incorporating the document type declaration in your XHTML pages, and you've checked your authoring work against the DTD using the validation service.

As XHTML begins to incorporate advanced features such as Modularization, Web authors will hold an advantage if they are comfortable working with DTDs. At a minimum, you should be able to read a DTD, if not actually author your own.

This chapter teaches you:

- The syntax used to write DTDs
- How to declare an element
- How to create an attribute-list declaration
- Using Parameter Entities
- How to resolve parameter entities to fully understand an element and attribute-list declaration

Building Blocks of a Basic DTD

A DTD can be as simple as a single element declaration, provided, of course, that you're satisfied writing a document using just a single element! Before we can begin building or reading DTDs, you must understand the notation used.

EBNF: The Syntax of DTDs

DTDs are primarily intended for machine consumption, not human. When working with machines, success often depends on being extremely concise. In the earlier days of computing, 1960 to be specific, two computer scientists devised a formal notation that described the syntax of the ALGOL60 computer language. The notation was named after the pair, and became known as *Backus Naur Form*.

Over the years as the complexity of computer languages increased, the notation also became more complex. In its current state, it's called *Extended Backus Naur Form*, or simply *EBNF*.

EXAMPLE

Each syntax description is presented in the same basic form:

```
symbol ::= expression
```

The characters ::= should be read *is defined as*. A common example used to demonstrate this is the set of letters known as vowels:

```
vowels ::= [aeiou]
```

This rule would be read as "The symbol vowels is defined as the lowercase letters a, e, i, o, and u." If you didn't care which case was used, both versions are included in the expression:

```
vowels ::= [aeiouAEIOU]
```

Expressions aren't limited to lists as we've written here. Ranges of values also can be used. For instance, the first ten letters of the alphabet, in lowercase, might be described as:

```
FirstTen ::= [a-j]
```

GROUPING ITEMS WITHIN EXPRESSIONS

To be useful, descriptions must be able to handle far more than sequential characters and numbers. To accomplish this, we must be able to give instructions such as "and," "or," and "one but not the other." I'll call these constructions *complex expressions*.

EXAMPLE

The first complex expression we'll look at is "or." Consider that the symbol "Today" can be defined as "Monday," "Tuesday," "Wednesday," "Thursday," "Friday," "Saturday," or "Sunday," depending on the day of the week. To write that in EBNF, we'd say:

```
Today ::= (Monday | Tuesday | Wednesday | Thursday | Friday | Saturday | Sunday)
```

This would be read as "Today" is defined as Monday, Tuesday, Wednesday, Thursday, Friday, Saturday, or Sunday.

An instance you might be more likely to see in a DTD is the definition of *white space*. White space in XML applications (which includes XHTML) is defined as a space, a tab, a newline character, or a linefeed character. If S were the symbol for white space, the notation would be written as follows:

```
S ::= (#x20 | #x9 | #xD | #xA )+
```

The values shown are the hexadecimal numbers representing the characters place in the ASCII charts (hex being a popular machine-read representation). The + character outside the parentheses indicates *one or more of the enclosed values*. You would read this notation as follows:

"White space is defined as one or more space, tab, newline, or linefeed characters."

There will certainly be times when it's more succinct to define a symbol by what it doesn't contain than by what it does. For instance, "Weekdays" is defined in a less verbose fashion by saying "All days except Saturday and Sunday" instead of "Monday, Tuesday, Wednesday, Thursday, Friday." EBNF provides for these exceptions using an *exclusion set*. The weekdays example would be written as follows:

```
weekdays ::= ( [^Saturday Sunday] | Week)
```

The exclusion set is bound by the bracket characters [and], and the caret indicates the beginning of the set. The entire expression is predicated on the subject (Week) having been previously defined.

Finally, we can express constraints such as "one, but not the other" and "either/or."

Defining Elements

Elements are the basic building blocks of the document. Before an element can be used in a markup language, it must be declared (defined) in the DTD. The basic syntax for the declaration looks like this:

```
<!ELEMENT name ContentModel>
```

Name, in this expression, is the name of the element being defined. The content model is an expression of what the element can contain. With your knowledge of HTML, and the XHTML you've learned so far, you know that some elements can contain other elements, whereas others can contain just text, and some can't contain anything at all. These constraints on content are known as *content models*, and every element has one.

XML, and therefore XHTML, has four basic content model types, shown here in Table 13.1.

Table 13.1: Content Models Found in XHTML

Content Model	Allowable Content
Empty	No content is allowed (for example, img, hr, br)
Any	Any type of content is permitted (not found in XHTML 1.0, rarely used)
Element	Only other elements are permitted (for example, ul only allows li elements)
Mixed	Elements and data can be present (for example, p can contain em and strong, but also text)

The Empty content model says that no content is allowed in the element. Probably the most familiar example is the img element. It's also the easiest content model to declare. The actual img element declaration in the XHTML 1.0 DTDs looks like this:

```
<!ELEMENT img EMPTY>
```

This one was pretty easy to read, although I will say they can get a little more complex. Let's look at an element that has been given the Element content model: the unordered list element (ul).

```
<!ELEMENT ul (li)+>
```

The content model expression should be familiar to you from our previous discussion of EBNF. This declaration says that the element ul must contain one or more instances of the li element.

The + symbol used in the ul element declaration is known as an *occurrence indicator*. There are three indicators commonly used in DTDs, as seen in Table 13.2.

Table 13.2: Occurence Indicators Used in DTDs

Occurrence Indicator	Definition
?	Element is optional (zero or one occurrence)
*	Element is optional, AND can be repeated (zero or more occurrences)
+	Element is required, and might be repeated (one or more occurrences)

More than one element can be found in an Element-type content model. For instance, the table row element, tr, can contain one or more of the th and td elements. The element declaration for tr then, would be written as follows:

```
<!ELEMENT tr (th|td)+>
```

The vertical bar character between the two elements indicates that the document author has a choice of which to use, and the + occurrence indicator says that at least one of the elements must occur, though you can have more.

NOTE

The occurrence indicator operates on the whole of the expression bound by the parentheses. So when evaluating (th|td)+, it can be easier to work from the outside in. We could read that the tr element must contain one or more elements, and those elements might be th or td.

EXAMPLE

Content models can contain more than one of the indicators found in Table 13.2 when the mix of elements becomes more complex. Consider the XHTML 1.0 Transitional declaration for the table element:

```
<!ELEMENT table
    (caption?, (col*|colgroup*), thead?, tfoot?, (tbody+|tr+))>
```

There's quite a lot going on here, but we can take it apart piece by piece to fully understand the expression.

First, the comma-delimited list of elements is known as a *sequence*. Each of the elements in the sequence must appear within the element being defined (except when modified by an occurrence indicator with a zero option).

Reading left to right, the content model for table becomes:

> An optional caption element, one or more of the col or colgroup elements if so desired, a thead element if desired, a tfoot element if desired, and finally at least one tbody element or at least one tr element.

Looking closely, the only required elements here are a single tbody or tr element; all others are optional.

CAUTION

Before worrying about where the td elements are in this expression, think about what we're defining: the elements that might be or are required to be contained within the table element. The td element isn't contained within the table element itself; instead, it's contained within the tr element (which is the element contained within table). Because td is contained in something else, it's not mentioned here. Only the first level sub-elements are defined.

Creating Attributes

Elements alone aren't expressive enough to fill the needs of document authors. A secondary data structure, the attribute, is used to provide additional information about the individual element instance. A common attribute used in XHTML is the `align` attribute found in the Transitional version of the language.

Attributes are defined in an *attribute-list declaration* (sometimes shortened to "att-list"), which in this instance appears immediately after the element declaration in the DTD.

NOTE

Attribute-list declarations can occur anywhere within the DTD. In simple instances, declaring them immediately after the element makes for easier reading of the finished DTD. However, in more complex or larger DTDs many designers find it advantageous to declare commonly used attribute-lists early on, and re-use them throughout.

EXAMPLE

A food-related DTD might have an element "soup." An attribute could be used to provide the type (for example, chicken noodle, or split pea), whether it's served hot or cold, and any other desired facets. The element is defined first:

```
<!ELEMENT soup EMPTY>
```

Then the attribute-list is declared:

```
<!ATTLIST soup type CDATA #REQUIRED
            temp (hot | cold) #REQUIRED>
```

After the declaration begins (with the `<!ATTLIST` string), the element where the attributes will be used is noted, followed by the attribute name, the attribute value type, and then any necessary keywords. We'll take this apart piece by piece.

Attributes, like elements, each have a content model, although in this case they're known as *attribute value types*. There are four major types used in XHTML, which we'll define next (see Table 13.3).

Table 13.3: Major Attribute Value Types in XHTML

Attribute Value Type	Sample
String Types	A string of characters
Tokenized Types	NMTOKEN, ID, or IDREF
Enumerated Types	A list of fixed values
Entities	An entity defined elsewhere (for example, a URI)

STRING DATA TYPES

String types are pretty simple; the value can be just about any string of characters. A word is allowed, such as "dog," or a nonsensical string such as "wett123iqwre." The string data type is expressed using the keyword CDATA, which means character data, or simply a string.

TOKENIZED TYPES

A token is another name for a label. In XHTML, instances of certain elements need to be identified, so a label is required. Consider the input elements in forms.

NMTOKEN

The name attribute is used to identify and bind the value of the input into a name=value pair for processing by the CGI script. The value of the name attribute is a label, or token. When used in this manner, the attribute value is referred to as an NMTOKEN, or *name token*.

The strings that make up a name token are restricted by three rules:

1. It must begin with a letter.

2. Only letters, digits, and the characters - (dash), _ (underscore), : (colon), and . (period) can be used.

3. The first three characters cannot be the series xml, in any case variant (for example, not xml, XML, xMl, and so on).

ID AND IDREF

There are two additional tokenized types, which can identify individual elements or work in concert with each other: ID and IDREF. Whereas the NMTOKEN type can provide a name for an element, there is no requirement that the name be unique. Uniqueness isn't desirable when you're trying to match up a set of check boxes on that form.

When you do need a unique identifier, the ID attribute can provide that. The naming rules are the same as for NMTOKEN, with the added constraint that the name must be unique *within the document*.

The ID and IDREF types can be used together to provide a logical connection to two portions of a document. In a report, if you were to provide footnotes or bibliographic references at the end of the document, on paper you'd simply use a superscript number at the point of reference, and then the number again when writing out the note. If you were to create your own elements for this, you might choose an "info" element and corresponding note element. Attributes for each would need to hold the unique identifier. The markup might look like this:

EXAMPLE

```
<p>In this paragraph, we'll have a reference to  further information <info
↪reference="1" />.</p>
...additional content...
<note item="1">This is the additional information referenced previously in the
↪main text.</note>
```

The DTD segment pertaining to these elements and attributes would be written as follows:

```
<!ELEMENT info EMPTY>
    <!ATTLIST info reference ID #IMPLIED>
<!ELEMENT note (#PCDATA)>
    <!ATTLIST note item IDREF #REQUIRED>
```

Although in this example I've chosen to use a number for the value of the reference attribute, the attribute is defined as type ID, so any legal ID string would be possible there.

NOTE

You might have noticed that the attributes that hold the ID and IDREF values have different names; that's okay! What's important is the matching of the attribute values when the first has the type ID and the second IDREF.

ENUMERATED DATA TYPES

The enumerated data type doesn't restrict values to numbers, as you might infer from the name, but instead provides a specific list of potential values. The align attribute, found many places in XHTML, is given an enumerated data type. If this attribute were defined for the p element, ATTLIST could look like this:

```
<!ATTLIST p align (left | center | right)>
```

ENTITIES

We'll talk about entities in more detail later in this chapter (see "Parameter Entities" and "Planning for Global Entities and Attributes"). At this point, you need to know that general entities represent additional content or objects. For instance, a URI is an entity, so the src attribute on the img element is an entity attribute type.

Reading the XHTML DTDs

The best way to learn how to write DTDs is to study existing documents. Because we'll be working with the DTDs for XHTML beginning in Chapter 16, "Combining Custom Modules with XHTML," going through them now is a good learning exercise. The XHTML 1.0 Strict DTD is the smallest of the three and can be found online at http://www.w3.org/TR/xhtml1/DTD/ xhtml1-strict.dtd.

EXAMPLE

The beginning of the DTD has some informational comments, including copyright information, revision dates, and public and system identifiers. After the revision date, a large set of entities are defined. These deal with character mnemonics, names imported from various RFCs, generic attributes, and entities created to represent groups of element names. The element and attribute declarations begin in the section commented as Document Structure (see Figure 13.1).

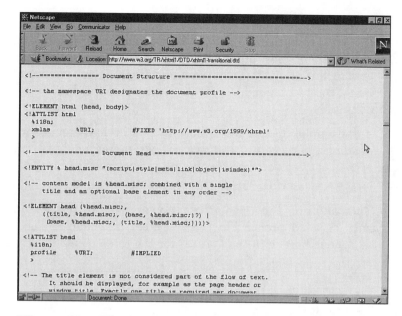

Figure 13.1: *The first elements and attributes defined are for major structural components.*

The root element for XHTML is defined thusly:

```
<!ELEMENT html (head, body)>
<!ATTLIST html
  %i18n;
  xmlns        %URI;          #FIXED 'http://www.w3.org/1999/xhtml'
  >
```

The html element must contain a single head element and a body element. It can take attributes defined by the i18n entity (i18n stands for "internationalization," an i with 18 additional letters before the final n), and the xmlns attribute.

Each additional section is well commented, both with dividing comments blocking out related sections (as seen in Figure 13.1), and with additional explanation or rationale provided to aid the human readability of the DTD document.

Entities, as used in the declarations shown here, are an important part of large DTDs. They deserve close inspection, and we'll walk through the resolution of an entire set of entities used in defining an element and attribute list in this next section.

Parameter Entities

Parameter entities are entities that are used only within the DTD that defines them. Most often, they're used as a form of shorthand. Instead of writing out attribute definitions repeatedly in the various elements that might contain them, a parameter entity is defined and then used for those definitions.

EXAMPLE

For example, the `align` attribute is used in many text-containing elements: headings, paragraphs, and so on. A parameter entity "TextAlign" is defined, acting as a replacement for the full att-list declaration:

```
<!ENTITY % TextAlign "align (left|center|right) #IMPLIED">
```

Then any time the `align` attribute is needed (for text alignment issues), the entity is used, prefaced by the % symbol, instead of the actual declaration, as is done here with the `ATTLIST` for the `h1` element:

```
<!ELEMENT h1 %Inline;>
<!ATTLIST h1
  %attrs;
  %TextAlign;
  >
```

As you can see, there are two other parameter entities in use in this element and att-list declaration: `Inline` and `attrs`. Parameter entities are used throughout XHTML to improve the readability of the DTD. At the same time, however, you need to understand all that the PEs represent when they're used in this manner. Let's expand each of the entities to see what the declarations would have looked like without them.

The first entity is `Inline`, which represents the content model for the `h1` element. `Inline` was defined as follows:

```
<!ENTITY % Inline "(#PCDATA | %inline; | %misc;)*">
```

The `Inline` entity provides a content model only, a choice between zero or more of #PCDATA, or the models represented by the `Inline` or `misc` entities. Replacing `Inline` with its expansion, the declaration for `h1` becomes

```
<!ELEMENT h1 (#PCDATA | %inline; | %misc;)*>
```

So next we need to look at the `Inline` entity:

```
<!ENTITY % inline "a | %special; | %fontstyle; | %phrase; | %inline.forms;">
```

This results in the following element declaration:

```
<!ELEMENT h1 (#PCDATA | a | %special; | %fontstyle; | %phrase; | %inline.forms;
➥| %misc;)>
```

Next to be expanded is the special entity:

```
<!ENTITY % special
    "br | span | bdo | object | applet | img | map | iframe">
```

No additional entities are contained here, so these elements represent the final resolution of the entities down this path. The h1 element declaration now looks like this:

```
<!ELEMENT h1 (#PCDATA | a | br | span | bdo | objects | applet | img | map |
➥iframe |
 %fontstyle; | %phrase; | %inline.forms; | %misc;)>
```

Next to be resolved is the fontstyle entity, which you'll find immediately below the special entity declaration in the XHTML DTD:

```
<!ENTITY % fontstyle "tt | i | b | big | small | u
                     | s | strike |font | basefont">
```

The phrase, inline.forms, and misc entities also are found in this location:

```
<!ENTITY % phrase "em | strong | dfn | code | q | sub | sup |
                   samp | kbd | var | cite | abbr | acronym">

<!ENTITY % inline.forms "input | select | textarea | label | button">
<!ENTITY % misc "ins | del | script | noscript">
```

The h1 element declaration now holds:

```
<!ELEMENT h1 (#PCDATA | a | br | span | bdo | objects | applet | img | map |
➥iframe |
 tt | i | b | big | small | u | s | strike | font | basefont | em | strong |
➥dfn | code |
 q | sub | sup | samp | kbd | var | cite | abbr | acronym | input | select |
➥textarea |
 label | button | ins | del | script | noscript )>
```

Next we can move on to the ATTLIST declaration for h1:

```
<!ATTLIST h1
  %attrs;
  %TextAlign;
  >
```

The attrs entity is defined as follows:

```
<!ENTITY % attrs "%coreattrs; %i18n; %events;">
expanding the att-list to:
<!ATTLIST h1
  %coreattrs;
  %i18n;
  %events;
  %TextAlign;
>
```

Going through the same exercise as with the element declaration, we'll expand each of these entities, beginning with coreattrs:

```
<!ENTITY % coreattrs
  "id          ID             #IMPLIED
   class       CDATA          #IMPLIED
```

```
    style       %StyleSheet;    #IMPLIED
    title       %Text;          #IMPLIED"
    >
```

Added to the existing ATTLIST, we get:

```
<!ATTLIST h1
    id          ID              #IMPLIED
    class       CDATA           #IMPLIED
    style       %Stylesheet;    #IMPLIED
    title       %Text;          #IMPLIED
    %i18n;
    %events;
    %TextAlign;
>
```

Delving deeper into coreattrs, we need to expand Stylesheet and Text:

```
<!ENTITY % StyleSheet "CDATA">
<!ENTITY % Text "CDATA">
which allows us to write:
<!ATTLIST h1
    id          ID              #IMPLIED
    class       CDATA           #IMPLIED
    style       CDATA           #IMPLIED
    title       CDATA           #IMPLIED
    %i18n;
    %events;
    %TextAlign;
>
```

Next we expand i18n:

```
<!ENTITY % i18n
 "lang         %LanguageCode; #IMPLIED
  xml:lang     %LanguageCode; #IMPLIED
  dir          (ltr|rtl)      #IMPLIED"
  >
```

Only the single entity LanguageCode needs to be resolved here:

```
<!ENTITY % LanguageCode "NMTOKEN">
```

TIP

Though DTDs don't have the power to constrain NMTOKEN any further than its initial naming rules, a comment in the DTD indicates that the token should conform to the list of language codes, which are defined in RFC1766.

At this point, the expanded ATTLIST looks like this:

```
<!ATTLIST h1
    id          ID              #IMPLIED
    class       CDATA           #IMPLIED
```

```
    style      CDATA          #IMPLIED
    title      CDATA          #IMPLIED
    lang       NMTOKEN           #IMPLIED
     xml:lang  NMTOKEN           #IMPLIED
     dir       (ltr|rtl)         #IMPLIED
    %events;
    %TextAlign;
>
```

The events entity is next:

```
<!ENTITY % events
  "onclick      %Script;        #IMPLIED
   ondblclick   %Script;        #IMPLIED
   onmousedown  %Script;        #IMPLIED
   onmouseup    %Script;        #IMPLIED
   onmouseover  %Script;        #IMPLIED
   onmousemove  %Script;        #IMPLIED
   onmouseout   %Script;        #IMPLIED
   onkeypress   %Script;        #IMPLIED
   onkeydown    %Script;        #IMPLIED
   onkeyup      %Script;        #IMPLIED"
   >
```

Only the `Script` entity needs further resolution:

```
<!ENTITY % Script "CDATA">
```

Folded into the previous `h1` ATTLIST, we now have

```
<!ATTLIST h1
    id          ID             #IMPLIED
    class       CDATA          #IMPLIED
    style       CDATA          #IMPLIED
    title       CDATA          #IMPLIED
    lang        NMTOKEN           #IMPLIED
     xml:lang   NMTOKEN           #IMPLIED
     dir        (ltr|rtl)         #IMPLIED
    onclick     CDATA          #IMPLIED
    ondblclick  CDATA          #IMPLIED
    onmousedown CDATA          #IMPLIED
    onmouseup   CDATA             #IMPLIED
    onmouseover CDATA          #IMPLIED
    onmousemove CDATA          #IMPLIED
    onmouseout  CDATA          #IMPLIED
    onkeypress  CDATA          #IMPLIED
    onkeydown   CDATA             #IMPLIED
    onkeyup     CDATA          #IMPLIED
    %TextAlign;
>
```

Finally, the TextAlign attribute is resolved and then incorporated into the ATTLIST declaration:

```
<!ENTITY % TextAlign "align (left|center|right) #IMPLIED">
```

The final, fully resolved element and ATTLIST declaration for the h1 element become

```
<!ELEMENT h1 (#PCDATA | a | br | span | bdo | objects | applet | img | map |
  iframe | tt | i | b | big | small | u | s | strike | font | basefont | em |
  strong | dfn | code | q | sub | sup | samp | kbd | var | cite | abbr | acronym |
  input | select | textarea | label | button | ins | del | script | noscript )>
<!ATTLIST h1
      id          ID              #IMPLIED
      class       CDATA           #IMPLIED
      style       CDATA           #IMPLIED
      title       CDATA           #IMPLIED
      lang        NMTOKEN         #IMPLIED
      xml:lang    NMTOKEN         #IMPLIED
      dir         (ltr|rtl)       #IMPLIED
      onclick     CDATA           #IMPLIED
      ondblclick  CDATA           #IMPLIED
      onmousedown PCDATA          #IMPLIED
      onmouseup   CDATA           #IMPLIED
      onmouseover CDATA           #IMPLIED
      onmousemove CDATA           #IMPLIED
      onmouseout  CDATA           #IMPLIED
      onkeypress  CDATA           #IMPLIED
      onkeydown   CDATA           #IMPLIED
      onkeyup     CDATA           #IMPLIED
      align       (left|center|right) #IMPLIED
   >
```

The parameterized version, shown again here, is certainly easier to read, isn't it?

```
<!ELEMENT h1   %Inline;>
<!ATTLIST h1
  %attrs;
  %TextAlign;
   >
```

The same process that we've stepped through here with the h1 element can be undertaken for any element or attribute list found in the XHTML DTDs, or any DTD for that matter.

Planning for Global Entities and Attributes

Whereas XHTML makes *extensive* use of parameter entities in its DTDs, doing so is not required or even necessarily desired for less complicated undertakings.

When looking at the finished DTD, the entities are, by necessity, all declared at the beginning of the document, because they must be defined before being used elsewhere. This doesn't mean, however, that the author of the DTD sat down and began by defining several dozen complex entities before declaring a single element or attribute list.

Instead, as a DTD author finds herself repeating the same expressions time and again, she should consider using an entity to save space and time and improve the readability of the document. Once the need for the entity is realized, going back to the top of the document and declaring it is easy.

What's Next

In this chapter you have learned how to read DTDs that use the Extended Backus Naur Form notation. You know how to write declarations for both elements and attribute lists. Entities are used as a powerful means to organize and shorten element and attribute declarations.

Next, in Chapter 14, "XHTML Modularization," we'll take a look at another means of expressing a language's rules: XML schemas.

Part III

Modularization

XHTML Modularization

There's no doubt that HTML has been embraced as a powerful means of producing documents for the World Wide Web. Its success was fed by the myriad of new features introduced over each successive version. Even so, it was still very much limited by the elements and attributes defined in the HTML Recommendations. Web authors clearly saw the need for more freedom in defining structures and behaviors for those structures beyond the bounds of HTML.

This chapter teaches you:

- How modularization works

- How to group elements into abstract modules

- How to understand the DTD implementation of an abstract module

- How to combine predefined modules into a new DTD

How Modularization Works

XML provides the flexibility desired by many, but brings its own challenges in having to define every piece of the document puzzle on your own. The promise of XHTML is retaining the semantics of HTML while adding the extensibility and flexibility of XML. To achieve this, Web authors needed a means to add and subtract feature sets without having to reinvent the wheel each time. The mechanism for doing so is referred to as XHTML Modularization. *XHTML Modularization* provides a set of building blocks that can be combined to produce a host of new languages.

Abstract Module Definitions

The first step taken when breaking down the XHTML 1.0 Recommendation was to divide elements into logical groups. Each of these groups contains elements that are both semantically similar, and as a group, distinct from all the others. These groups are called *abstract* modules because their definitions do not include the machine processing information. Instead, they're described in basic prose, much as we're describing the process here. Additionally, specific syntactic conventions are followed to convey the content model of elements and the presence and requirements of attributes.

NOTE

The expressions used for modeling XHTML abstract modules are not intended as a formal grammar for XHTML. However, they are sufficiently similar to the conventions used for writing XML DTDs that XML authors should find them familiar and easy to read.

TIP

A module is not required to have an abstract definition to conform to the XHTML Modularization Recommendation. However, module authors are strongly encouraged to provide one to lower the learning curve required to adopt the module and to provide a quick reference for document authors who don't need to delve into the DTD or schema definition of the module.

To fully understand how an abstract module definition is put together, we'll look at the List Module as it is defined in the XHTML Modularization Recommendation (section 5.2.4):

As its name suggests, the List Module provides list-oriented elements. Specifically, the List Module supports the following elements and attributes:

Elements	Attributes	Minimal Content Model
dl	Common	(dt|dd)+
dt	Common	(PCDATA|Inline)*
dd	Common	(PCDATA|Inline)*
ol	Common	li+
ul	Common	li+
li	Common	(PCDATA|Inline)*

This module also defines the content set list with the minimal content model (dl|ol|ul)+ and adds this set to the Flow content set of the Text Module.

The prose at the beginning of this abstract is very clear: The module contains the elements in XHTML used to create lists, including definition, ordered, and unordered lists. The table contains each of the element members of the module, the attributes allowed on each, and the minimal content model for the element.

READING THE ALLOWABLE ATTRIBUTES LIST

Rather than listing each potential attribute for an element, XHTML Modularization relies on attribute collections. The collections are defined elsewhere in the XHTML Modularization Recommendation. Before reviewing the attributes contained within each set, you need to understand the types of attributes allowed. Eight data types defined in the XML 1.0 Recommendation form the basis of the types allowed in XHTML. These include

- CDATA—Character data. Any arbitrary characters can be found in a CDATA section with a single exception: the < character.

- ID—A unique identifier for a given instance of an element. Only one attribute on an element can have the ID data type. The value of this attribute also must be unique within the document.

- IDREF—A reference to an element instance that has an attribute with the specified ID.

- IDREFS—A list of ID references, separated only by commas.

- NAME—A name, similar to the ID datatype, without the requirement of uniqueness.

- NMTOKEN—A name token, which is a name composed only of alphanumeric characters and optionally the characters ., ,, -, _, and : (period, comma, hyphen, underscore, and colon).

- NMTOKENS—A list of NMTOKEN names separated by white space.

- PCDATA—Processed character data. Character data with any incorporated entities having been processed.

NOTE

It should be noted that the requirement in the NMTOKEN datatype of alphanumeric characters doesn't limit an author's choices to the English alphabet or any specific language. Any glyph that is a part of the alphabet in any language around the world is considered part of the alphanumeric character set.

XHTML Modularization defines a host of new datatypes, 19 to be exact, that expand on the predefined list provided by XML (see Table 14.1). Many definitions refer to RFC documents. An *RFC* is a document published by the IETF (Internet Engineering Task Force) that discusses standard conventions or technical details about the Internet. RFC documents can be accessed from a number of sites; a full listing of all documents is available via FTP at ftp://ftp.isi.edu/in-notes/rfc-index.txt.

Table 14.1: Datatypes Defined by XML

Datatype	Description
Character	A single character (from any alphabet).
Charset	A character encoding defined in RFC2045 (for example, US-ASCII, ISO-8859-1).
Charsets	A space-delimited list of character encodings as defined by Charset.
Color	Any valid hexadecimal color value preceded by the hash character (for example, #000000), or one of 16 named colors (see Appendix A, "XHTML Abstract Module Definitions," for the full list).
ContentType	A media type as defined by RFC2045.
ContentTypes	A comma-delimited list of media types defined in ContentType.
Datetime	Date and time information.

Datatype	Description
FrameTarget	A name of an XHTML Frame, used as the destination for loading a document or other actions to be performed within that frame.
LanguageCode	A code representing a language, as defined in RFC1766 (for example, 'en' for English, 'fr' for French).
Length	A measure, either in pixels or a percentage of available space.
LinkTypes	One of, or a list of, names from a defined set of link types. See Appendix A for the complete list and their conventional meanings.
MediaDesc	A comma-delimited list of media descriptors (see Appendix A for the list of recognized descriptors).
MultiLength	A length as previously defined, or a relative length. Relative lengths are expressed as "i*", where "i" is an integer and the "*" character allocates an amount of space proportional to "i" when evaluated against the other integers present. For example, 1*, 3* sets up a 1 to 3 ratio of space.
Number	One or more digits.
Pixels	A numeric value representing a number of pixels.
Script	Data that must be passed on to a script engine and not parsed as XHTML.
Text	Any text-based data.
URI	A Uniform Resource Identifier as defined in RFC1738.
URIs	A space-delimited list of Uniform Resource Identifiers as defined previously.

Looking back at the List Module definition, you'll notice that each of the allowable attribute entries references an attribute collection: Common. Common is actually a collection of collections, comprised of the Core, Events, I18N, and Style collections. These four collections are defined, along with their data types, in Table 14.2.

Table 14.2: The Attribute Collections That Make Up the Common Collection

Collection	Attributes
Core	class (NMTOKEN), id (ID), title (CDATA)
I18N	xml:lang (NMTOKEN)
Events	onclick (Script), ondblclick (Script), onmousedown (Script), onmouseup (Script), onmouseover (Script), onmousemove (Script), onmouseout (Script), onkeypress (Script), onkeydown (Script), onkeyup (Script)
Style	style (CDATA)

THE MINIMAL CONTENT MODEL

A content model is a definition of what elements or data are allowed to be present within another element. This section of an abstract module definition is the one that follows XML DTD-like syntax.

✔ For a complete review of DTD syntax, see "EBNF: The Syntax of DTDs," p. 226.

Taking the first element of the List Module, dl, the minimal content model is defined as (dt|dd)+. This says that the dl element is required to contain at least a dt element and/or a dd element.

The + occurrence indicator shows that one or more sets of dt and dd elements might be contained within dl.

Minimal content models also might reference collections of elements known as *content sets,* just as the set of allowable attributes is often defined by a collection. The minimal dt element in the List Module uses just such a collection when it is defined as (PCDATA|Inline)*. This model says that the dt element can contain processed character data and any elements contained within the Inline content set, either of which might be found zero or more times within the dt element.

The Inline content set is defined in the prose of the Text Module as the following elements: abbr, acronym, br, cite, code, dfn, em, kbd, q, samp, span, strong, and var (see Appendix A or http://www.w3.org/TR/xhtml1/xhtml-modularization-20000705.html#s_textmodule).

A link to the DTD implementation of each abstract module is found at the end of the prose description. We'll continue to explore the List Module by reviewing its implementation DTD.

Module DTDs or Schemas

The implementation of an abstract module is written as a fragment of a DTD. The DTD fragment from each abstract module that will be a part of the new document type is assembled into a single definitive DTD for the new XHTML Family Member document type. This resulting document type is as complete as any other document type, and can be used to validate documents written to conform to it, either through a validating parser or a tool such as the W3C Validation Service.

✔ For a review of using the W3C Validation Service, see "Using the W3C Validator," p. 145.

NOTE

It is the intention of the W3C to explore defining modules in XML Schema, but until that work has reached Recommendation status, the XHTML Modularization documents are written using DTDs.

The actual modularization of the DTD relies heavily on parameter entities. Six categories of entities are used to represent the abstract partitions of each module. Each category follows a specific naming convention using suffixes, as follows:

- .mod—Parameter entities representing a DTD module use the .mod suffix. Modules can be stored in separate file entities, which are then also named using the .mod suffix.

- .module—DTD modules can be switched on or off in a larger DTD using conditional sections. The keywords INCLUDE and IGNORE regulate the inclusion of the module, represented by the parameter entity with this suffix.

- .content—The content model of element types is parameterized using entities with this suffix.

- .class—Elements of the same class are represented using .class suffixed parameter entities.

- .mix—As the suffix implies, elements from different classes can be represented by a single parameter entity using the .mix suffix.

- .attrib—A group of name tokens that represent one or more complete attribute specifications within an ATTLIST declaration might be represented by this category of parameter entities.

We'll use most of these parameter entities later in Chapter 16, "Combining Custom Modules with XHTML," when we define a new module from scratch. As we step through one of the predefined modules, the XHTML List Module, you'll see several of them in use.

TAKING APART THE LIST MODULE

The W3C-defined modules all begin with commented information outlining the informal title of the module, the filename, a copyright statement, and revision data:

```
<!-- ........................................................... -->
<!-- XHTML Lists Module  ...................................... -->
<!-- file: xhtml-list-1.mod

     This is XHTML, a reformulation of HTML as a modular XML application.
     Copyright 1998-2000 W3C (MIT, INRIA, Keio), All Rights Reserved.
     Revision: $Id: xhtml-modularization-20000705.html,v 1.7 2000/07/03 13:46:01
     ➥shane Exp $ SMI
```

Next are the PUBLIC and SYSTEM identifiers used for the module, along with any revisions to those identifiers:

```
This DTD module is identified by the PUBLIC and SYSTEM identifiers:

    PUBLIC "-//W3C//ELEMENTS XHTML Lists 1.0//EN"
    SYSTEM "xhtml-list-1.mod"

Revisions:
(none)
................................................................ -->
```

A commented prose section briefly describes the purpose of the module:

```
<!-- Lists

        dl, dt, dd, ol, ul, li

    This module declares the list-oriented element types
    and their attributes.
-->
```

Next, the qualified names for each element presented in the module are defined in a parameter entity named after the element name suffixed by .qname, for example, dl.qname for the parameter entity representing the element name dl:

```
<!ENTITY % dl.qname   "dl" >
<!ENTITY % dt.qname   "dt" >
<!ENTITY % dd.qname   "dd" >
<!ENTITY % ol.qname   "ol" >
<!ENTITY % ul.qname   "ul" >
<!ENTITY % li.qname   "li" >
```

The next section reduces the declaration for the dl element to a single-parameter entity:

```
<!-- dl: Definition List ............................. -->

<!ENTITY % dl.element   "INCLUDE" >
<![%dl.element;[
<!ENTITY % dl.content   "( %dt.qname; | %dd.qname; )+" >
<!ELEMENT %dl.qname;   %dl.content; >
<!-- end of dl.element -->]]>
```

These entities can be read fairly easily if you approach them much like an algebra problem and work your way out from the inside. First, consider the dl.content parameter entity. Its definition holds two .qname parameter entities, for the dt and dd elements. The syntax surrounding those entities should be familiar to you. If expanded, it reads:

```
<!ENTITY % dl.content "(dt|dd)+" >
```

The element declaration immediately below the dl.content entity defines the element itself. Expanded, it reads:

```
<!ELEMENT dl (dt|dd)+>
```

Moving back up the section, the parameter entity dl.element is defined to include both the dl.content parameter entity declaration and the element declaration, reducing this passage to the single entity. When invoked in the module as

```
<!ENTITY % dl.element "INCLUDE" >
```

the dl element is included in the module, with the remaining information available for expansion as necessary by the parser.

The attribute list for the dl element is handled much in the same manner. A parameter entity is defined for the entire attlist, and incorporated using the INCLUDE keyword. The Common attribute collection, defined elsewhere in the final DTD, is references using an .attrib suffixed parameter entity:

```
<!ENTITY % dl.attlist   "INCLUDE" >
<![%dl.attlist;[
<!ATTLIST %dl.qname;
      %Common.attrib;
>
<!-- end of dl.attlist -->]]>
```

The same process of parameterizing the element and attribute declarations is carried out for the remaining elements in the module. The entire module can be seen in Listing 14.1.

Listing 14.1: xhtml-list-1.mod, the XHTML List Module

```
<!-- ........................................................... -->
<!-- XHTML Lists Module  ................................... -->
<!-- file: xhtml-list-1.mod

     This is XHTML, a reformulation of HTML as a modular XML application.
     Copyright 1998-2000 W3C (MIT, INRIA, Keio), All Rights Reserved.
     Revision: $Id: xhtml-modularization-20000705.html,v 1.7 2000/07/03 13:46:01
     ➥shane Exp $ SMI

     This DTD module is identified by the PUBLIC and SYSTEM identifiers:

       PUBLIC "-//W3C//ELEMENTS XHTML Lists 1.0//EN"
       SYSTEM "xhtml-list-1.mod"

     Revisions:
     (none)
     ............................................................ -->
```

Listing 14.1: continued

```
<!-- Lists
        dl, dt, dd, ol, ul, li
     This module declares the list-oriented element types
     and their attributes.
-->
<!ENTITY % dl.qname   "dl" >
<!ENTITY % dt.qname   "dt" >
<!ENTITY % dd.qname   "dd" >
<!ENTITY % ol.qname   "ol" >
<!ENTITY % ul.qname   "ul" >
<!ENTITY % li.qname   "li" >
<!-- dl: Definition List ............................ -->
<!ENTITY % dl.element   "INCLUDE" >
<![%dl.element;[
<!ENTITY % dl.content   "( %dt.qname; | %dd.qname; )+" >
<!ELEMENT %dl.qname;   %dl.content; >
<!-- end of dl.element -->]]>
<!ENTITY % dl.attlist   "INCLUDE" >
<![%dl.attlist;[
<!ATTLIST %dl.qname;
      %Common.attrib;
>
<!-- end of dl.attlist -->]]>
<!-- dt: Definition Term ............................ -->
<!ENTITY % dt.element   "INCLUDE" >
<![%dt.element;[
<!ENTITY % dt.content
     "( #PCDATA | %Inline.mix; )*"
>
<!ELEMENT %dt.qname;   %dt.content; >
<!-- end of dt.element -->]]>
<!ENTITY % dt.attlist   "INCLUDE" >
<![%dt.attlist;[
<!ATTLIST %dt.qname;
      %Common.attrib;
>
<!-- end of dt.attlist -->]]>
<!-- dd: Definition Description ...................... -->
<!ENTITY % dd.element   "INCLUDE" >
<![%dd.element;[
<!ENTITY % dd.content
     "( #PCDATA | %Flow.mix; )*"
>
<!ELEMENT %dd.qname;   %dd.content; >
<!-- end of dd.element -->]]>
```

Listing 14.1: continued

```
<!ENTITY % dd.attlist  "INCLUDE" >
<![%dd.attlist;[
<!ATTLIST %dd.qname;
      %Common.attrib;
>
<!-- end of dd.attlist -->]]>
<!-- ol: Ordered List (numbered styles) ................ -->
<!ENTITY % ol.element  "INCLUDE" >
<![%ol.element;[
<!ENTITY % ol.content  "( %li.qname; )+" >
<!ELEMENT %ol.qname;  %ol.content; >
<!-- end of ol.element -->]]>
<!ENTITY % ol.attlist  "INCLUDE" >
<![%ol.attlist;[
<!ATTLIST %ol.qname;
      %Common.attrib;
>
<!-- end of ol.attlist -->]]>
<!-- ul: Unordered List (bullet styles) ................ -->
<!ENTITY % ul.element  "INCLUDE" >
<![%ul.element;[
<!ENTITY % ul.content  "( %li.qname; )+" >
<!ELEMENT %ul.qname;  %ul.content; >
<!-- end of ul.element -->]]>
<!ENTITY % ul.attlist  "INCLUDE" >
<![%ul.attlist;[
<!ATTLIST %ul.qname;
      %Common.attrib;
>
<!-- end of ul.attlist -->]]>
<!-- li: List Item .................................... -->
<!ENTITY % li.element  "INCLUDE" >
<![%li.element;[
<!ENTITY % li.content
     "( #PCDATA | %Flow.mix; )*"
>
<!ELEMENT %li.qname;  %li.content; >
<!-- end of li.element -->]]>
<!ENTITY % li.attlist  "INCLUDE" >
<![%li.attlist;[
<!ATTLIST %li.qname;
      %Common.attrib;
>
<!-- end of li.attlist -->]]>
<!-- end of xhtml-list-1.mod -->
```

Combining Predefined Modules

EXAMPLE

The strength of XHTML Modularization lies in the relative ease in which modules can be combined into any number of new languages. I say relative ease, in that the process isn't exactly "plug and play." The creation of new modules is something that the designers of XHTML Modularization don't expect the average Web author to do very frequently, if at all. However, you are much more likely to want to take DTDs and add or subtract predefined modules to match the needs of your current client or project. Luckily, that portion of the process is one of the easiest if you follow the steps outlined here.

✔ For a full walk-through of combining modules to form a new DTD, see "Integrating the New Module," p. 279.

DTD Drivers: The Glue That Holds Modules Together

The W3C has provided the skeleton for a new DTD based on XHTML Modularization. It can be found online at `http://www.w3.org/TR/2000/WD-xhtml-building-20000105/template.dtd`, and is reproduced here in its entirety (see Listing 14.2).

Listing 14.2: `TEMPLATE.dtd`

```
<!-- ............................................................... -->
<!-- SKELETAL DTD ...................................................... -->
<!-- file: TEMPLATE.dtd
-->
<!-- SKELETAL DTD
-->
<!-- This is a skeletal driver file. Modify it however you want, paying
     careful attention to the embedded comments about order.

     Please use this formal public identifier to identify it:

         "-//W3C//DTD XHTML-MYDTD//EN"
-->
<!ENTITY % XHTML.version  "-//W3C//DTD XHTML-MYDTD//EN" >

<!-- Reserved for use with the XLink namespace:
-->
<!ENTITY % XLINK.ns "" >
<!ENTITY % XLinkns.attrib "" >


<!-- reserved for future use with document profiles -->
<!ENTITY % XHTML.profile  "" >
```

Listing 14.2: continued

```
<!-- Internationalization features
     This feature-test entity is used to declare elements
     and attributes used for internationalization support. Set it to INCLUDE
        or IGNORE as appropriate for your markup language.
-->
<!ENTITY % XHTML.I18n                "IGNORE" >


<!-- :::::::::::::::::::::::::::::::::::::::::::::::::::::::::::::::::::::::: -->


<!-- Define the Content Model
     Remember that you can modify this content model or replace it simply by
        changing the following ENTITY declaration.
-->
<!ENTITY % xhtml-model.mod
     PUBLIC "-//W3C//ENTITIES XHTML 1.1 Document Model 1.0//EN"
     SYSTEM "http://www.w3.org/TR/xhtml11/DTD/xhtml11-model-1.mod" >


<!-- Pre-Framework Redeclaration placeholder  ................... -->
<!-- this serves as a location to insert markup declarations
        into the DTD prior to the framework declarations.
-->
<!ENTITY % xhtml-prefw-redecl.module "IGNORE" >
<![%xhtml-prefw-redecl.module;[
%xhtml-prefw-redecl.mod;
<!-- end of xhtml-prefw-redecl.module -->]]>


<!-- The events module should be included here if you need it. In this
     skeleton it is IGNOREd.
-->
<!ENTITY % xhtml-events.module "IGNORE" >


<!-- Modular Framework Module  ................................. -->
<!ENTITY % xhtml-framework.module "INCLUDE" >
<![%xhtml-framework.module;[
<!ENTITY % xhtml-framework.mod
     PUBLIC "-//W3C//ENTITIES XHTML 1.1 Modular Framework 1.0//EN"
            "xhtml11-framework-1.mod" >
%xhtml-framework.mod;]]>


<!-- Post-Framework Redeclaration placeholder  ................. -->
<!-- this serves as a location to insert markup declarations
     into the DTD following the framework declarations.
-->
<!ENTITY % xhtml-postfw-redecl.module "IGNORE" >
<![%xhtml-postfw-redecl.module;[
%xhtml-postfw-redecl.mod;
```

Listing 14.2: continued

```
<!-- end of xhtml-postfw-redecl.module -->]]>


<!-- Basic Text Module (Required)  .............................. -->
<!ENTITY % xhtml-text.module "INCLUDE" >
<![%xhtml-text.module;[
<!ENTITY % xhtml-text.mod
     PUBLIC "-//W3C//ELEMENTS XHTML 1.1 Basic Text 1.0//EN"
             "xhtml11-text-1.mod" >
%xhtml-text.mod;]]>


<!-- Hypertext Module (required) ................................ -->
<!ENTITY % xhtml-hypertext.module "INCLUDE" >
<![%xhtml-hypertext.module;[
<!ENTITY % xhtml-hypertext.mod
     PUBLIC "-//W3C//ELEMENTS XHTML 1.1 Hypertext 1.0//EN"
             "xhtml11-hypertext-1.mod" >
%xhtml-hypertext.mod;]]>


<!-- Lists Module (required)  ................................... -->
<!ENTITY % xhtml-list.module "INCLUDE" >
<![%xhtml-list.module;[
<!ENTITY % xhtml-list.mod
     PUBLIC "-//W3C//ELEMENTS XHTML 1.1 Lists 1.0//EN"
             "xhtml11-list-1.mod" >
%xhtml-list.mod;]]>


<!-- Your modules can be included here.  Use the basic form defined above, and
     be sure to include the public FPI definition in your catalog file for
     each module that you define. You may also include W3C-defined modules at
     this point.
-->


<!-- Document Structure Module (required)  ...................... -->
<!ENTITY % xhtml-struct.module "INCLUDE" >
<![%xhtml-struct.module;[
<!ENTITY % xhtml-struct.mod
     PUBLIC "-//W3C//ELEMENTS XHTML 1.1 Document Structure 1.0//EN"
             "xhtml11-struct-1.mod" >
%xhtml-struct.mod;]]>


<!-- end of SKELETAL DTD ................................................ -->
<!-- ................................................................... -->
```

By taking this skeletal DTD file apart, we can explore how this driver file glues together the various module implementations to create the new

XHTML Family Markup Language. We'll take the core modules required of all XHTML Host Languages, and add the W3C-defined Basic Tables Module to come up with the Tables Markup Language.

The first edits to be made include the name of the file, the formal public identifier used to identify your new language, and the namespace that corresponds to it:

```
<!-- ............................................................ -->
<!-- SKELETAL DTD .................................................. -->
<!-- file: TableML.dtd
-->

<!-- SKELETAL DTD
-->
<!-- This is a skeletal driver file. Modify it however you want, paying
     careful attention to the embedded comments about order.

     Please use this formal public identifier to identify it:

         "-//WEBGEEK//DTD XHTML-TABLEML//EN"
-->
<!ENTITY % XHTML.version  "-//WEBGEEK//DTD XHTML-TABLEML//EN" >
```

We're not going to be defining any new modules in this markup language, so the section on modifying the document model can just be left alone.

Finally, it's time to add the Basic Tables module into the DTD. We do so just after the comment that says "Your modules can be included here":

```
<!-- Your modules can be included here.  Use the basic form defined above, and
     be sure to include the public FPI definition in your catalog file for
     each module that you define. You may also include W3C-defined modules at
     this point.
-->
```

The entry for the Basic Tables module follows the same form as the others. The pertinent details can be found in the implementation of that module, which is found in the Modularization document at http://www.w3.org/TR/2000/PR-xhtml-modularization-20000705/ dtd_module_defs.html#sec_F.3.5:

```
<!-- Basic Tables Module  ........................................ -->
<!ENTITY % xhtml-basic-table-1.module "INCLUDE" >
<![ %xhtml-basic-table-1.module;[
<!ENTITY % xhtml-basic-table-1.mod
     PUBLIC "-//W3C/ELEMENTS XHTML Basic Tables 1.0//EN"
              "xhtml-basic-table-1.mod"
%xhtml-basic-table-1.mod;]]>
```

The finished DTD can now be seen in Listing 14.3.

Listing 14.3: TableML.DTD

```
<!-- ....................................................... -->
<!-- Table Markup Language DTD  ............................. -->
<!-- file: TableML.dtd
-->


<!-- SKELETAL DTD
-->
<!-- This is a skeletal driver file. Modify it however you want, paying
     careful attention to the embedded comments about order.

     Please use this formal public identifier to identify it:

         "-//WEBGEEK//DTD XHTML-TABLEML 1.0//EN"
-->
<!ENTITY % XHTML.version  "-//WEBGEEK//DTD XHTML-TABLEML 1.0//EN" >

<!-- Reserved for use with the XLink namespace:
-->
<!ENTITY % XLINK.ns "" >
<!ENTITY % XLinkns.attrib "" >



<!-- reserved for future use with document profiles -->
<!ENTITY % XHTML.profile  "" >

<!-- Internationalization features
     This feature-test entity is used to declare elements
     and attributes used for internationalization support. Set it to INCLUDE
         or IGNORE as appropriate for your markup language.
-->
<!ENTITY % XHTML.I18n            "IGNORE" >

<!-- ::::::::::::::::::::::::::::::::::::::::::::::::::::::::::::::: -->

<!-- Define the Content Model
     Remember that you can modify this content model or replace it simply by
         changing the following ENTITY declaration.
-->
<!ENTITY % xhtml-model.mod
     PUBLIC "-//W3C//ENTITIES XHTML 1.1 Document Model 1.0//EN"
     SYSTEM "http://www.w3.org/TR/xhtml11/DTD/xhtml11-model-1.mod" >

<!-- Pre-Framework Redeclaration placeholder  .................... -->
<!-- this serves as a location to insert markup declarations
         into the DTD prior to the framework declarations.
```

Listing 14.3: continued

```
-->
<!ENTITY % xhtml-prefw-redecl.module "IGNORE" >
<![%xhtml-prefw-redecl.module;[
%xhtml-prefw-redecl.mod;
<!-- end of xhtml-prefw-redecl.module -->]]>


<!-- The events module should be included here if you need it. In this
     skeleton it is IGNOREd.
-->
<!ENTITY % xhtml-events.module "IGNORE" >


<!-- Modular Framework Module  .................................. -->
<!ENTITY % xhtml-framework.module "INCLUDE" >
<![%xhtml-framework.module;[
<!ENTITY % xhtml-framework.mod
     PUBLIC "-//W3C//ENTITIES XHTML 1.1 Modular Framework 1.0//EN"
            "xhtml11-framework-1.mod" >
%xhtml-framework.mod;]]>


<!-- Post-Framework Redeclaration placeholder  ................... -->
<!-- this serves as a location to insert markup declarations
     into the DTD following the framework declarations.
-->
<!ENTITY % xhtml-postfw-redecl.module "IGNORE" >
<![%xhtml-postfw-redecl.module;[
%xhtml-postfw-redecl.mod;
<!-- end of xhtml-postfw-redecl.module -->]]>


<!-- Basic Text Module (Required)  ............................. -->
<!ENTITY % xhtml-text.module "INCLUDE" >
<![%xhtml-text.module;[
<!ENTITY % xhtml-text.mod
     PUBLIC "-//W3C//ELEMENTS XHTML 1.1 Basic Text 1.0//EN"
            "xhtml11-text-1.mod" >
%xhtml-text.mod;]]>


<!-- Hypertext Module (required) ............................... -->
<!ENTITY % xhtml-hypertext.module "INCLUDE" >
<![%xhtml-hypertext.module;[
<!ENTITY % xhtml-hypertext.mod
     PUBLIC "-//W3C//ELEMENTS XHTML 1.1 Hypertext 1.0//EN"
            "xhtml11-hypertext-1.mod" >
%xhtml-hypertext.mod;]]>


<!-- Lists Module (required)  .................................... -->
<!ENTITY % xhtml-list.module "INCLUDE" >
```

Listing 14.3: continued

```
<![%xhtml-list.module;[
<!ENTITY % xhtml-list.mod
        PUBLIC "-//W3C//ELEMENTS XHTML 1.1 Lists 1.0//EN"
                "xhtml11-list-1.mod" >
%xhtml-list.mod;]]>

<!-- Your modules can be included here.  Use the basic form defined above, and
        be sure to include the public FPI definition in your catalog file for
        each module that you define. You may also include W3C-defined modules at
        this point.
-->

<!-- Basic Tables Module  ......................................... -->
<!ENTITY % xhtml-basic-table-1.module "INCLUDE" >
<![ %xhtml-basic-table-1.module;[
<!ENTITY % xhtml-basic-table-1.mod
        PUBLIC "-//W3C/ELEMENTS XHTML Basic Tables 1.0//EN"
                "xhtml-basic-table-1.mod"
%xhtml-basic-table-1.mod;]]>

<!-- Document Structure Module (required)  ...................... -->
<!ENTITY % xhtml-struct.module "INCLUDE" >
<![%xhtml-struct.module;[
<!ENTITY % xhtml-struct.mod
        PUBLIC "-//W3C//ELEMENTS XHTML 1.1 Document Structure 1.0//EN"
                "xhtml11-struct-1.mod" >
%xhtml-struct.mod;]]>

<!-- end of Table Markup Language DTD ..................................... -->
<!-- ...................................................................... -->
```

EXAMPLE

Using a Modularized DTD on the Web

After the DTD is complete, using it in your Web documents is as easy as using any other DTD. Simply reference it in your DOCTYPE declaration with the proper formal public identifier and SYSTEM identifier. A document created with our sample Table Markup Language would begin like this:

```
<!DOCTYPE html PUBLIC "-//WEBGEEK//DTD XHTML-TABLEML 1.0//EN"
            "http://www.webgeek.com/DTDs/TableML.dtd">
<html xmlns:tml="http://www.webgeek.com/DTDs/TableML1.dtd">
```

Because we haven't used any modules, elements, or attributes that aren't defined in the XHTML Modularization documents, existing HTML user agents won't have any difficulty processing documents written in this language. If we had included new features, we'd need to use a browser with an XML parser built in, such as Internet Explorer 5 for the PC, which could render the new elements, provided a style sheet was developed for them.

✔ To learn more about applying style sheets to XHTML, see "Creating an XSL Style Sheet," p. 215.

What's Next

In this chapter you have learned how the features of XHTML were divided into logical groups of elements that shared the same semantics. Each atomic group forms an abstract module, defined by a brief prose section outlining its use, and a table of elements, their allowable attributes, and minimal content models. Each abstract module has a corresponding DTD implementation, which is combined with other module DTDs to create the final DTD used to represent the new language.

Next, in Chapter 15, "Creating a Custom HTML Module," you'll dive deeper into the world of Modularization and create your own abstract module and its corresponding DTD implementation. You will plan the content model, define qnames, parameter entities, and the element and attribute-list declarations.

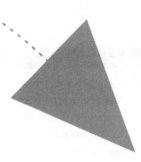

Creating a Custom XHTML Module

The power of the Extensible Hypertext Markup Language certainly lies in its extensibility. XML offers document authors the ultimate extensibility in allowing them to create entirely new markup languages using whichever design principles they find the most compelling. For those of us who just need to get some work done, however, re-inventing the wheel—even if it meant doing so in a way that we liked better than how the originators did it—uses an awful lot of time and energy.

So, we'll use the power of extensibility and the comfort of HTML to create new document types for our own purposes. An online recipe archive presents just this sort of challenge. HTML provides the basic text features we'll want to use, yet we need the additional structure of XML for segments of the recipes themselves to allow for easy searching, storage, and other data management activities that might be performed on a large archive. To handle this, we'll spend this chapter creating a customized recipe module that will be combined with a basic set of XHTML features to create a new DTD.

This chapter teaches you:

- How to organize your data storage needs

- How to write an abstract module definition

- How to use parameter entities to manage namespaces

- How to define elements and attributes in a Declaration sub-module

Planning the Content Model

Before you begin writing even the abstract module definition for your new module, it's always a good idea to sit down with pen and paper and map out all the components that need to be addressed. When developing new elements it's not always readily apparent what information should be stored in attributes, sub-elements, or even as PCDATA. Having a visual model of your data can help sort the information into the proper structures.

To create the model, three major questions need to be answered:

1. What data needs to be stored?

2. How is the data used?

3. What constraints, if any, need to be placed on the data?

To illustrate the process we'll create a new abstract module and its corresponding DTD implementation for presenting recipes on the Web.

What Data Needs to Be Stored?

A recipe has two major sections: a list of ingredients, and then instructions for preparation. Within the ingredients list there are, at a minimum, three different data points to consider: quantity, unit of measure, and the actual ingredient. Figure 15.1 shows these pieces arranged in a basic organizational chart.

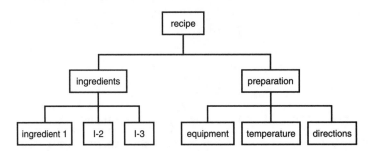

Figure 15.1: *The components of a recipe can be arranged as an organizational chart.*

At this stage don't discount any aspect of the data that might be important. In the organizational chart you can see we've listed cooking methods (baking, frying, sautéing), temperatures, and equipment. This information might end up simply being presented in prose within an element's content (PCDATA), but we might choose to create another element or attribute to store it. Early assumptions about how you'll handle data can result in needing to rework your content model and/or DTD much later in the game when it's more difficult to do so.

How Will the Data Be Used?

In the basic organization chart, we see a list of ingredients. Each ingredient line, however, holds multiple pieces of data. Consider the following typical presentation:

```
2 cups  all-purpose flour
```

The ingredient can be divided into three parts: quantity (2), a unit of measure (cups), and the item itself. All three of these pieces will need to be recorded in a potential `ingredient` element.

The next major segment of a recipe is the preparation instructions. What kind of information might appear there? Certainly you'll have text, so we'll need to allow for paragraphs, perhaps lists, and other text structures. This suggests we'd want to allow Block XHTML elements to appear within a `prep` element.

The Abstract Module Definition

Now that we've thought through the data that needs to be stored in the structures belonging to this module, and how they'd best be used, we're ready to write the abstract module definition. Begin as always with a simple prose description of the module's purpose:

```
The XHTML Recipe Module defines markup used when documenting the
ingredients and methods used when preparing a given recipe. The elements
and attributes defined in this module are
```

Next comes the table of elements, attributes, and minimal content models:

Element	Attributes	Minimal Content Model
recipe	Common, (CDATA), title, category	ingredients, prep
ingredients	Common	ingredient+
ingredient	Common, quantity, unit, item	EMPTY
prep	Common	(PCDATA|Flow)+

When this module is selected, it adds the recipe element to the Block content set, and it defines the content set Recipe with a minimal content model of ingredients, prep, and adds it to the Inline content set as these are defined in the Text Module.

Creating the Module Using a DTD

The DTD implementation of a module actually consists of two smaller module parts referred to as sub-modules: a QName module and a Declaration module. We'll take a look at both in this section.

Working with QNames

QNames is an XML term for qualified names. Qualified names are constructed when XML Namespaces are used to differentiate elements from more than one markup language. For instance, XHTML has a `title` element that's used to give a title to the document. Some other language might use a `title` element to refer to a person's rank or other salutary title such as Doctor, Reverend, or even Her Royal Highness.

XML Namespaces identify which language a given element belongs to through the use of a prefix appended to the element. The XHTML `title` element, when written using its fully *qualified* name would be written as `xhtml:title`.

The QName module contains parameter entities (PEs) that are used to store the QNames of the elements to be defined in the Declaration module for those times in which the elements must be presented in their qualified form.

NOTE

For more on XML Namespaces see `http://www.w3.org/TR/REC-xml-names/` or *XML by Example*, also published by Que.

The QName sub-module begins with a commented section that details the module name, its filename, the public and system identifiers used to reference it, and the namespace declaration. Putting each of these in place, our QName sub-module begins like this:

```
<!-- ........................................................... -->
<!--Recipe Qname Module        ........................................ -->
<!-- file: recipe-qname-1.mod

    PUBLIC "-//WebGeek//ELEMENTS XHTML Recipe Qnames 1.0//"
    SYSTEM "http://www.webgeek.com/DTDs/recipe-qname-1.mod"

    xmlns:recipe="http://www.webgeek.com/xmlns/recipe"
    ............................................................ -->
```

Several conventions have been used in this section. First, the sub-module file is named with the suffix `.mod`, which will correlate to the parameter entity suffix used to identify it later when pulling the module components together. Next, the Formal Public Identifier (FPI) must take a specific form.

The string will always begin with the -// characters. The next portion identifies the company or individual that owns the module—in this case, my company WebGeek, Inc. Another set of // characters follow, then the word ELEMENTS in capital letters, followed by the title and version of the module. A final set of // characters close out the string, for a complete FPI of

```
"-//WebGeek/ELEMENTS XHTML Recipe Qnames 1.0//"
```

The system identifier is a URI where the file entity for the module might be found. It might be expressed in fully qualified form, or as a relative URI when working locally. In this case, we've chosen the former:

```
SYSTEM "http://www.webgeek.com/DTDs/recipe-qname-1.mod"
```

Finally, the XML Namespace is always declared in two parts: the xmlns: prefix followed by a short string that will be used throughout as a token representing the full URI given in the second part of the declaration, for example:

```
xmlns:recipe="http://www.webgeek.com/xmlns/recipe"
```

The URI used to represent a namespace doesn't necessarily have anything to be found if you attempt to access it as a URL on the Web. It is used only as a name.

Next we begin defining the parameter entities that will be used by the XHTML Framework module to help construct the final DTD. The first sets whether or not the elements in the new module will use their namespace-qualified names. By default, this option is set to "IGNORE".

```
<!ENTITY % NS.prefixed "IGNORE" >
```

This entity has a corresponding PE identified for this specific module:

```
<!ENTITY % Recipe.prefixed "%NS.prefixed;" >
```

This prefixed parameter entity is created to allow an override, forcing a document instance to prefix all elements with their namespaces.

The actual namespace of the module is declared next. Namespaces are probably the most difficult concept to get your thoughts around when working with Modularization. I'll try and simply explain the purpose of this namespace-qualification work coming up.

XHTML Modularization goes to great lengths to define an environment in which traditional XML DTDs can be used with or without support for XML Namespaces. The mechanism used for this is informally called the "namespace hack."

That mechanism defines series of steps, described in this and the next chapter, that permit the development of document types that adhere to the requirements of XML Namespaces if a document author wants to use Namespaces. It also permits the document author to ignore XML

Namespaces and still have confidence that his document is valid. The way the namespace hack accomplishes these two tasks is complicated. A simple explanation of it is

- Each element in a module has a name that is defined symbolically.

- If the document type author or the document author chooses, the element names can be prefixed with their namespace identifier.

- This namespace identifier can be set to any value. It is mapped to the namespace's URI—a world-unique identifier.

- Whether or not a document author chooses to use namespaces, if the document has the correct structure, it is a valid XHTML family document.

XML Namespaces are a somewhat futuristic application within XML—they are not in wide use in the Web document authoring community. However, as more and more collections of elements are developed into XHTML Modules, these modules will need to rely upon XML Namespaces to a) help imply the semantics associated with an element or attribute and b) help ensure that there are no name collisions.

So to get back to our module, you'll remember that this information noted at the beginning of the sub-module file was in comments, meant for human consumption, not machine. This entity takes the following form:

```
<!ENTITY % Recipe.xmlns "http://www.webgeek.com/xmlns/recipe" >
```

The prefix to be used when the namespace-qualified names are used must be declared in its own PE, identified by the `.prefix` suffix in the PE name:

```
<!ENTITY %Recipe.prefix "recipe" >
<![ %Recipe.prefixed;[
<!ENTITY % Recipe.pfx "%Recipe.prefix;:" >
<!ENTITY % Recipe.xmlns.extra.attrib
        "xmlns:%Recipe.prefix;   %URI.datatype;   #FIXED  '%Recipe.xmlns;'" >
]]>
<!ENTITY % Recipe.pfx "" >
<!ENTITY % Recipe.xmlns.extra.attrib "">
```

Now, each of the elements that will be defined in the module need to have a parameter entity that represents their qualified names. These PEs are always named with the `.qname` suffix. The value of these entities is always `%Module.pfx;name`—where the identifying string for the module is substituted for `Module`, and `name` holds the place of the element name—for example, `%Recipe.pfx;ingredient`:

```
<!ENTITY % Recipe.recipe.qname "%Recipe.pfx;recipe" >
<!ENTITY % Recipe.ingredients.qname "%Recipe.pfx;ingredients" >
<!ENTITY % Recipe.ingredient.qname "%Recipe.pfx;ingredient" >
<!ENTITY % Recipe.prep.qname "%Recipe.pfx;prep" >
```

The QNames sub-module is now complete. It can be seen in it's entirety in Listing 15.1.

EXAMPLE

Listing 15.1: `recipe-qname-1.mod`, the QNames Sub-module for Our New XHTML Module

```
<!-- ................................................................ -->
<!--Recipe Qname Module        ............................................. -->
<!-- file: recipe-qname-1.mod

        PUBLIC "-//WebGeek//ELEMENTS XHTML Recipe Qnames 1.0//"
        SYSTEM "http://www.webgeek.com/DTDs/recipe-qname-1.mod"

        xmlns:recipe="http://www.webgeek.com/xmlns/recipe"
        .............................................................. -->
<!ENTITY % NS.prefixed "IGNORE" >
<!ENTITY % Recipe.prefixed "%NS.prefixed;" >
<!ENTITY % Recipe.xmlns "http://www.webgeek.com/xmlns/recipe" >
<!ENTITY %Recipe.prefix "recipe" >
<![ %Recipe.prefixed;[
<!ENTITY % Recipe.pfx "%Recipe.prefix;:" >
<!ENTITY % Recipe.xmlns.extra.attrib
   "xmlns:%Recipe.prefix;      %URI.datatype;      #FIXED      '%Recipe.xmlns;'" >
]]>
<!ENTITY % Recipe.pfx "" >
<!ENTITY % Recipe.xmlns.extra.attrib "">
<!ENTITY % Recipe.recipe.qname "%Recipe.pfx;recipe" >
<!ENTITY % Recipe.ingredients.qname "%Recipe.pfx;ingredients" >
<!ENTITY % Recipe.ingredient.qname "%Recipe.pfx;ingredient" >
<!ENTITY % Recipe.prep.qname "%Recipe.pfx;prep" >
```

Now it's time to actually declare the elements and attributes that make up this module using the Declaration sub-module.

The sub-module begins with the same type of commented section as the QName sub-module. Appropriate public and system identifiers are declared, and the same namespace URI is given:

```
<!-- ................................................................ -->
<!-- WebGeek Recipe Module      ............................................. -->
<!-- file: recipe-elements-1.mod
    PUBLIC "-//WEBGEEK//ELEMENTS XHTML-WebGeek Recipe 1.0//EN"
        SYSTEM "http://www.webgeek.com/DTDs/recipe-1.mod"
    xmlns:recipe="http://www.webgeek.com/xmlns/recipe"
        .............................................................. -->
```

Next is another commented section that names the module, lists the elements to be declared, and provides a basic description of the module's purpose:

```
<!-- WebGeek Recipe Module

        recipe:recipe
        recipe:ingredients
        recipe:ingredient
        recipe:prep

        This module defines structural components of a cooking recipe.
-->
```

The first declarative section invokes and defines a parameter entity that is used within the ATTLIST of each element being declared. Its purpose is to manage the prefixing of the attributes when the module is used to create a standalone DTD. When combined with the XHTML Framework Module, the value of these PEs are overridden by the global NS.attrib:

```
<![ %Recipe.prefixed;[
<!ENTITY % Recipe.xmlns.attrib
    "NS.prefixed.attrib;"
>
]]>
<!ENTITY % REcipe.xmlns.attrib
    "NS.prefixed.attrib;
    xmlns %URI.datatype;     #FIXED     '%Recipe.xmlns;'"
>
```

Now, each element is defined using the parameter entities created in the QNames sub-module, along with any ATTLIST definitions required:

```
<!ELEMENT %Recipe.recipe.qname;
    (%Recipe.ingredients.qname;, %Recipe.prep.qname;) >
<!ATTLIST %Recipe.recipe.qname;
    %Common;
    title      CDATA     #REQUIRED
    category CDATA     #IMPLIED
    %Recipe.ns.attrib;
>

<!ELEMENT %Recipe.ingredients.qname;
    (%Recipe.ingredient.qname;)+ >
<!ATTLIST %Recipe.ingredients.qname;
    %Common;
    %Recipe.ns.attrib;
>

<!ELEMENT %Recipe.ingredient.qname; EMPTY >
```

```
<!ATTLIST %Recipe.ingredient.qname;
    %Common;
    quantity    CDATA      #REQUIRED
    unit        CDATA      #REQUIRED
    item        CDATA      #REQUIRED
    %Recipe.ns.attrib;
>


<!ELEMENT %Recipe.prep.qname;
    (PCDATA| %Flow;)+ >
<!ATTLIST %Recipe.prep.qname;
    %Common;
    %Recipe.ns.attrib;
>
```

The completed Declaration sub-module can now be put together in Listing 15.2.

Listing 15.2: A Complete Declaration Sub-module

```
<!-- ............................................................ -->
<!-- WebGeek Recipe Module     ............................................ -->
<!-- file: recipe-1.mod
     PUBLIC "-//WEBGEEK//ELEMENTS XHTML-WebGeek Recipe 1.0//EN"
         SYSTEM "http://www.webgeek.com/DTDs/recipe-1.mod"
     xmlns:recipe="http://www.webgeek.com/xmlns/recipe"
         ............................................................ -->

<!-- WebGeek Recipe Module


        recipe:recipe
        recipe:ingredients
        recipe:ingredient
        recipe:prep


        This module defines structural components of a cooking recipe.
-->
<![ %Recipe.prefixed;[
<!ENTITY % Recipe.xmlns.attrib
    "NS.prefixed.attrib;"
>
]]>
<!ENTITY % Recipe.xmlns.attrib
    "NS.prefixed.attrib;
    xmlns %URI.datatype;      #FIXED      '%Recipe.xmlns;'"
>

<!ELEMENT %Recipe.recipe.qname;
```

Listing 15.2: continued

```
    (%Recipe.ingredients.qname;, %Recipe.prep.qname;) >
<!ATTLIST %Recipe.recipe.qname;
    %Common;
    title    CDATA     #REQUIRED
    category CDATA     #IMPLIED
    %Recipe.ns.attrib;
>


<!ELEMENT %Recipe.ingredients.qname;
    (%Recipe.ingredient.qname;)+ >
<!ATTLIST %Recipe.ingredients.qname;
    %Common;
    %Recipe.ns.attrib;
>


<!ELEMENT %Recipe.ingredient.qname; EMPTY >
<!ATTLIST %Recipe.ingredient.qname;
    %Common;
    quantity    CDATA     #REQUIRED
    unit        CDATA     #REQUIRED
    item        CDATA     #REQUIRED
    %Recipe.ns.attrib;
>


<!ELEMENT %Recipe.prep.qname;
    (PCDATA| %Flow;)+ >
<!ATTLIST %Recipe.prep.qname;
    %Common;
    %Recipe.ns.attrib;
>
<!-- end of recipe-1.mod -->
```

What's Next

In this chapter we've completed the process of gathering the type of information we need to store in new elements, determining how that information will be used within the document, and planning the content model of elements that should be created. We then took that abstract definition and constructed both a QNames and a Declaration sub-module that parameterize and define elements and attributes to be used to hold this data.

Next, in Chapter 16, "Combining Custom Modules with XHTML," we'll take the QNames and Declaration sub-modules we created here and incorporate them into a larger DTD that governs a new XHTML Family Language. Using that DTD, we'll create new Web pages that are fully interoperable on today's Web.

Combining Custom Modules with XHTML

So far in your studies of XHTML Modularization, you've seen how the Modularization process is designed, how abstract modules are written, and how content models are defined. You've also stepped through the process of creating a customized module to be combined with existing W3C-provided modules to create a new XHTML-based markup language.

The final step in the process of creating such a language is the creation of the final DTD. This is where each of the modules defined are brought together in a single document, the language's DTD against which all documents will be authored.

This chapter teaches you:

- How the Modular Framework Module incorporates necessary basic structures
- How to plug your custom module into the Modularized DTD template
- How to edit the template as necessary based on your design decisions
- How to create a new document based on your completed DTD

A Look at the XHTML Modular Framework Module

Authors who want to make highly customized XHTML-based markup languages will soon become very familiar with the XHTML Modular Framework Module. This module provides the structure for the basic components that need to be "plugged in" to make the modularized scheme of XHTML work. The module can be found in its entirety in Listing 16.1, and we'll step through it piece by piece in this section.

EXAMPLE

Listing 16.1: The XHTML Modular Framework Module

```
<!-- ................................................................. -->
        <!-- XHTML Modular Framework Module  .............................. -->
        <!-- file: xhtml-framework-1.mod

            This is XHTML, a reformulation of HTML as a modular XML
    ➥application.
            Copyright 1998-2000 W3C (MIT, INRIA, Keio), All Rights Reserved.
            Revision: $Id: dtd_module_defs.html,v 1.7 2000/07/03 13:45:27 shane
    ➥Exp $ SMI

            This DTD module is identified by the PUBLIC and SYSTEM identifiers:

                PUBLIC "-//W3C//ENTITIES XHTML Modular Framework 1.0//EN"
                SYSTEM "xhtml-framework-1.mod"

            Revisions:
            (none)
            ...................................................... -->

    <!-- Modular Framework

            This required module instantiates the modules needed
            to support the XHTML modularization model, including:

                +  notations
                +  datatypes
                +  namespace-qualified names
                +  common attributes
                +  document model
                +  character entities

            The Intrinsic Events module is ignored by default but
            occurs in this module because it must be instantiated
            prior to Attributes but after Datatypes.
    -->

        <!ENTITY % xhtml-arch.module "INCLUDE" >
```

Listing 16.1: continued

```
<![%xhtml-arch.module;[
        <!ENTITY % xhtml-arch.mod
                PUBLIC "-//W3C//ELEMENTS XHTML Base Architecture 1.0//EN"
                        "xhtml-arch-1.mod" >
        %xhtml-arch.mod;]]>

        <!ENTITY % xhtml-notations.module "INCLUDE" >
        <![%xhtml-notations.module;[
        <!ENTITY % xhtml-notations.mod
                PUBLIC "-//W3C//NOTATIONS XHTML Notations 1.0//EN"
                        "xhtml-notations-1.mod" >
        %xhtml-notations.mod;]]>

        <!ENTITY % xhtml-datatypes.module "INCLUDE" >
        <![%xhtml-datatypes.module;[
        <!ENTITY % xhtml-datatypes.mod
                PUBLIC "-//W3C//ENTITIES XHTML Datatypes 1.0//EN"
                        "xhtml-datatypes-1.mod" >
        %xhtml-datatypes.mod;]]>

        <!ENTITY % xhtml-qname.module "INCLUDE" >
        <![%xhtml-qname.module;[
        <!ENTITY % xhtml-qname.mod
                PUBLIC "-//W3C//ENTITIES XHTML Qualified Names 1.0//EN"
                        "xhtml-qname-1.mod" >
        %xhtml-qname.mod;]]>

        <!ENTITY % xhtml-events.module "IGNORE" >
        <![%xhtml-events.module;[
        <!ENTITY % xhtml-events.mod
                PUBLIC "-//W3C//ENTITIES XHTML Intrinsic Events 1.0//EN"
                        "xhtml-events-1.mod" >
        %xhtml-events.mod;]]>

        <!ENTITY % xhtml-attribs.module "INCLUDE" >
        <![%xhtml-attribs.module;[
        <!ENTITY % xhtml-attribs.mod
                PUBLIC "-//W3C//ENTITIES XHTML Common Attributes 1.0//EN"
                        "xhtml-attribs-1.mod" >
        %xhtml-attribs.mod;]]>

        <!-- placeholder for content model redeclarations -->
        <!ENTITY % xhtml-model.redecl "" >
        %xhtml-model.redecl;

        <!ENTITY % xhtml-model.module "INCLUDE" >
        <![%xhtml-model.module;[
```

Listing 16.1: continued

```
<!-- instantiate the Document Model module declared in the DTD driver
-->
%xhtml-model.mod;]]>

<!ENTITY % xhtml-charent.module "INCLUDE" >
<![%xhtml-charent.module;[
<!ENTITY % xhtml-charent.mod
        PUBLIC "-//W3C//ENTITIES XHTML Character Entities 1.0//EN"
                "xhtml-charent-1.mod" >
%xhtml-charent.mod;]]>

<!-- end of xhtml-framework-1.mod -->
```

The first segment contains the standard description filenames, copyright statement, and notes on which public and system identifiers will be used, namely:

```
PUBLIC "-//W3C//ENTITIES XHTML Modular Framework 1.0//EN"
                SYSTEM "xhtml-framework-1.mod"
```

Next is the description of the module's purpose, namely to provide the DTD components that will be required in all XHTML compliant languages:

- Notations—Conventions used in other languages and some defined in XHTML, including CDATA, FPI, and others.

- Data types—Definitions of terms such as length, number, pixels, and so on.

- Namespace-qualified names—Add the ability to use namespaces to qualify names for differentiation between XHTML names and names from other markup languages.

- Common attributes—Define the attribute sets referenced by existing and extended XHTML modules.

- The document model—Instantiated by the Document Model module declared by the DTD driver.

- Character entities—Provide the ability to include the Latin 1, Symbol, and Special Character collections in your documents.

- Support for intrinsic events—Turned off by default.

It's not necessary to edit any of these components, and it's not even really necessary to understand how they work. Just know that this Modular Framework Module provides the basic components required for a complete markup language in the XHTML Family.

Now that you know where each piece of the DTD puzzle is coming from, it's time to create a DTD for our new language.

Integrating the New Module

You'll remember that for a language to conform as an XHTML Host Language, five specific conditions need to be met:

1. The document type must be implemented using W3C defined techniques (currently DTDs).

2. It must conform to the stated naming rules when choosing its unique identifier.

3. The language must contain at least the Structure, Hypertext, Basic Text, and List modules.

4. None of the W3C-defined modules can be reduced or subsetted. All defined elements, attributes, and required minimal content models must be included.

5. Any new elements and attributes are defined in their own namespaces.

To aid language designers, the W3C has provided a DTD template that can be used as a guide to creating conformate DTDs. It can be found online at `http://www.w3.org/TR/xhtml-modularization/DTD/templates/template.dtd` and is reproduced here in Listing 16.2. We'll edit each segment along the way to create the DTD for our new language.

EXAMPLE

Listing 16.2: The New DTD Template

```
<!-- .............................................................. -->
<!-- SKELETAL DTD ................................................... -->
<!-- file: TEMPLATE.dtd
-->

<!-- SKELETAL DTD
-->
<!-- This is a skeletal driver file. Modify it however you want, paying
     careful attention to the embedded comments about order.

     Please use this formal public identifier to identify it:

         "-//W3C//DTD XHTML MYDTD//EN"
-->
<!ENTITY % XHTML.version  "-//W3C//DTD XHTML MYDTD//EN" >

<!-- Bring in any qualified name modules outside of XHTML -->
<!ENTITY % MODULE-qname.mod "">
%MODULE-qname.mod;

<!-- Define any extra prefixed namespaces that this DTD relies upon -->
```

Listing 16.2: continued

```
<!ENTITY NS.prefixed.extras.attrib "" >

<!-- Define the Content Model file for the framework to use -->
<!ENTITY % xhtml-model.mod "MYMODEL">

<!-- reserved for future use with document profiles -->
<!ENTITY % XHTML.profile  "" >

<!-- Bi-directional text support
     This feature-test entity is used to declare elements
     and attributes used for internationalization support. Set it to INCLUDE
          or IGNORE as appropriate for your markup language.
-->
<!ENTITY % XHTML.bidi              "IGNORE" >
```

```
<!-- :::::::::::::::::::::::::::::::::::::::::::::::::::::::::::::::::::::::::: -->


<!-- Pre-Framework Redeclaration placeholder  .................... -->
<!-- This serves as a location to insert markup declarations
     into the DTD prior to the framework declarations.
-->
<!ENTITY % xhtml-prefw-redecl.module "IGNORE" >
<![%xhtml-prefw-redecl.module;[
%xhtml-prefw-redecl.mod;
<!-- end of xhtml-prefw-redecl.module -->]]>

<!-- The events module should be included here if you need it. In this
     skeleton it is IGNOREd.
-->
<!ENTITY % xhtml-events.module "IGNORE" >

<!-- Modular Framework Module  .................................. -->
<!ENTITY % xhtml-framework.module "INCLUDE" >
<![%xhtml-framework.module;[
<!ENTITY % xhtml-framework.mod
     PUBLIC "-//W3C//ENTITIES XHTML 1.1 Modular Framework 1.0//EN"
            "xhtml11-framework-1.mod" >
%xhtml-framework.mod;]]>

<!-- Post-Framework Redeclaration placeholder  .................. -->
<!-- This serves as a location to insert markup declarations
     into the DTD following the framework declarations.
-->
<!ENTITY % xhtml-postfw-redecl.module "IGNORE" >
<![%xhtml-postfw-redecl.module;[
%xhtml-postfw-redecl.mod;
```

Listing 16.2: continued

```
<!-- end of xhtml-postfw-redecl.module -->]]>


<!-- Text Module (required)  ............................. -->
<!ENTITY % xhtml-text.module "INCLUDE" >
<![%xhtml-text.module;[
<!ENTITY % xhtml-text.mod
     PUBLIC "-//W3C//ELEMENTS XHTML 1.1 Text 1.0//EN"
            "xhtml11-text-1.mod" >
%xhtml-text.mod;]]>


<!-- Hypertext Module (required) ............................. -->
<!ENTITY % xhtml-hypertext.module "INCLUDE" >
<![%xhtml-hypertext.module;[
<!ENTITY % xhtml-hypertext.mod
     PUBLIC "-//W3C//ELEMENTS XHTML 1.1 Hypertext 1.0//EN"
            "xhtml11-hypertext-1.mod" >
%xhtml-hypertext.mod;]]>


<!-- Lists Module (required)  ................................. -->
<!ENTITY % xhtml-list.module "INCLUDE" >
<![%xhtml-list.module;[
<!ENTITY % xhtml-list.mod
     PUBLIC "-//W3C//ELEMENTS XHTML 1.1 Lists 1.0//EN"
            "xhtml11-list-1.mod" >
%xhtml-list.mod;]]>


<!-- Your modules can be included here.  Use the basic form defined above, and
     be sure to include the public FPI definition in your catalog file for
         each module that you define. You may also include W3C-defined modules
         at this point.
-->


<!-- Document Structure Module (required)  ..................... -->
<!ENTITY % xhtml-struct.module "INCLUDE" >
<![%xhtml-struct.module;[
<!ENTITY % xhtml-struct.mod
     PUBLIC "-//W3C//ELEMENTS XHTML 1.1 Document Structure 1.0//EN"
            "xhtml11-struct-1.mod" >
%xhtml-struct.mod;]]>


<!-- end of SKELETAL DTD ............................................. -->
<!-- ............................................................... -->
```

As always, the first segment is a large comment providing filename and identifier information:

```
<!-- ............................................................... -->
<!-- Recipe DTD ..................................................... -->
```

Listing 16.2: continued

```
<!-- file: recipe-1_0.dtd
-->


<!-- This is the DTD driver for Recipe 1.0.

    Please use this formal public identifier to identify it:

        "-//WebGeek//DTD XHTML Recipe 1.0//EN"
    And this namespace for recipe-unique elements:
       xmlns:recipe="http://www.webgeek.com/xmlns/recipe"
-->
```

The first entity defined is that of our formal public identifier:

```
<!ENTITY % XHTML.version "-//WebGeek//DTD XHTML Recipe 1.0//EN" >
```

Here we define an entity and bring in the qualified names sub-module we defined in Chapter 15, "Creating a Custom XHTML Module":

```
<!ENTITY % Recipe-qname.mod
        SYSTEM "recipe-qname-1.mod" >
%Recipe-qname.mod;
```

No additional namespaces are necessary, so we can leave this next entity as it is:

```
<!-- no new namespaces needed -->
<!ENTITY NS.prefixed.extras.attrib "" >

<!-- Define the Content Model file for the framework to use -->
<!ENTITY % xhtml-model-1.mod "recipe-model-1.mod">
```

This entity references a content model definition module, which now needs to be prepared. The content model defined here for our recipe module is fairly generic. It is the DTD representation of the minimal content models described in the abstract module definitions, plus our extensions needed to incorporate the recipe root element as its appropriate content type.

As the recipe element is intended to act as an addition to the block element set, its Qname needs to be added to the %Block.extra parameter entity definition:

```
<!ENTITY % Block.extra
    "| %Recipe.recipe.qname; " >
```

Other than this, the only changes that need to be made in this generic content model module are the public and system identifiers, the filename, and the namespace, as is always done in the first section of the .mod file (see Listing 16.3).

Listing 16.3: The Completed Recipe Content Model Module

```
<!-- ............................................................... -->
<!-- Recipe Content Model Module  ...................................... -->
<!-- file: recipe-model-1.mod

          PUBLIC "-//WebGeek//ELEMENTS XHTML Recipe Model 1.0//"
          SYSTEM "http://www.webgeek.com/DTDs/recipe-model-1.mod"

          xmlns:recipe="http://www.webgeek.com/xmlns/recipe"


     ............................................................... -->
<!-- Define the content model for Misc.extra -->
<!ENTITY % Misc.class
     "| %script.qname; | %noscript.qname; ">
<!-- ................... Inline Elements ..................... -->
<!ENTITY % Head-opts.mix
     "( %style.qname; | %meta.qname; )*" >
<!ENTITY % I18n.class "" >
<!ENTITY % Inlstruct.class "%br.qname; | %span.qname;" >
<!ENTITY % Inlphras.class
     "| %em.qname; | %strong.qname; | %dfn.qname; | %code.qname;
      | %samp.qname; | %kbd.qname; | %var.qname; | %cite.qname;
      | %abbr.qname; | %acronym.qname; | %q.qname;" >
<!ENTITY % Inlpres.class
     "| %tt.qname; | %i.qname; | %b.qname; | %big.qname;
      | %small.qname; | %sub.qname; | %sup.qname;" >
<!ENTITY % Anchor.class "| %a.qname;" >
<!ENTITY % Inlspecial.class "| %img.qname; " >
<!ENTITY % Inline.extra "" >
<!-- %Inline.class; includes all inline elements,
     used as a component in mixes
-->
<!ENTITY % Inline.class
     "%Inlstruct.class;
      %Inlphras.class;
      %Inlpres.class;
      %Anchor.class;
      %Inlspecial.class;"
>
<!-- %Inline-noA.class; includes all non-anchor inlines,
     used as a component in mixes
-->
<!ENTITY % Inline-noA.class
     "%Inlstruct.class;
      %Inlphras.class;
      %Inlpres.class;
      %Inlspecial.class;"
```

Listing 16.3: continued

```
>
<!-- %Inline-noA.mix; includes all non-anchor inlines
-->
<!ENTITY % Inline-noA.mix
     "%Inline-noA.class;
      %Misc.class;"
>
<!-- %Inline.mix; includes all inline elements, including %Misc.class;
-->
<!ENTITY % Inline.mix
     "%Inline.class;
      %Misc.class;"
>
<!-- .................... Block Elements ..................... -->
<!ENTITY % Heading.class
      "%H1.qname; | %H2.qname; | %H3.qname;
       | %H4.qname; | %H5.qname; | %H6.qname;" >
<!ENTITY % List.class "%Ul.qname; | %Ol.qname; | %Dl.qname;" >
<!ENTITY % Blkstruct.class "%P.qname; | %Div.qname;" >
<!ENTITY % Blkphras.class
      "| %Pre.qname; | %Blockquote.qname; | %Address.qname;" >
<!ENTITY % Blkpres.class "| %Hr.qname;" >
<!ENTITY % Block.extra
      "| %Recipe.recipe.qname; " >

<!-- %Block.class; includes all block elements,
     used as an component in mixes
-->
<!ENTITY % Block.class
     "%Blkstruct.class;
      %Blkphras.class;
      %Blkpres.class;
      %Block.extra;"
>
<!-- %Block.mix; includes all block elements plus %Misc.class;
-->
<!ENTITY % Block.mix
     "%Heading.class;
      | %List.class;
      | %Block.class;
      %Misc.class;"
>
<!-- ............... All Content Elements ................. -->

<!-- %Flow.mix; includes all text content, block and inline
-->
```

Listing 16.3: continued

```
<!ENTITY % Flow.mix
      "%Heading.class;
        | %List.class;
        | %Block.class;
        | %Inline.class;
        %Misc.class;"
>
<!-- end of recipe-model-1.mod -->
```

Turning our attention back to the Recipe DTD itself, the next item to be addressed is document profiles. We aren't working with document profiles at this stage, so the entity for that remains empty:

```
<!-- reserved for future use with document profiles -->
<!ENTITY % XHTML.profile  "" >
```

For simplicity's sake, we'll disable bi-directional support in this language:

```
<!-- Bi-directional text support is not included here
-->
<!ENTITY % XHTML.bidi              "IGNORE" >
```

Neither will we need to do any pre-framework redeclarations, nor will we support events. The pre-framework placeholder information can simply be deleted (the area bound by our delete comments), and the events module remains IGNOREd:

```
<!-- this part can be deleted -->
<!-- Pre-Framework Redeclaration placeholder  .................... -->
<!-- This serves as a location to insert markup declarations
       into the DTD prior to the framework declarations.
-->
<!ENTITY % xhtml-prefw-redecl.module "IGNORE" >
<![%xhtml-prefw-redecl.module;[
%xhtml-prefw-redecl.mod;
<!-- end of xhtml-prefw-redecl.module -->]]>
<!-- end of section to be deleted -->
<!-- The events module should be included here if you need it. In this
       skeleton it is IGNOREd.
-->
<!ENTITY % xhtml-events.module "IGNORE" >
```

Now the Framework and required modules are defined and brought into place. No post-framework redeclarations were needed, so that segment has been left out here. That is the only edit you need to make in this section:

```
<!-- Modular Framework Module  .................................... -->
<!ENTITY % xhtml-framework.module "INCLUDE" >
<![%xhtml-framework.module;[
<!ENTITY % xhtml-framework.mod
      PUBLIC "-//W3C//ENTITIES XHTML 1.1 Modular Framework 1.0//EN"
             "xhtml11-framework-1.mod" >
```

```
%xhtml-framework.mod;]]>
<!-- Text Module (required) ................................ -->
<!ENTITY % xhtml-text.module "INCLUDE" >
<![%xhtml-text.module;[
<!ENTITY % xhtml-text.mod
      PUBLIC "-//W3C//ELEMENTS XHTML 1.1 Text 1.0//EN"
             "xhtml11-text-1.mod" >
%xhtml-text.mod;]]>
<!-- Hypertext Module (required) ............................. -->
<!ENTITY % xhtml-hypertext.module "INCLUDE" >
<![%xhtml-hypertext.module;[
<!ENTITY % xhtml-hypertext.mod
      PUBLIC "-//W3C//ELEMENTS XHTML 1.1 Hypertext 1.0//EN"
             "xhtml11-hypertext-1.mod" >
%xhtml-hypertext.mod;]]>
<!-- Lists Module (required) ................................. -->
<!ENTITY % xhtml-list.module "INCLUDE" >
<![%xhtml-list.module;[
<!ENTITY % xhtml-list.mod
      PUBLIC "-//W3C//ELEMENTS XHTML 1.1 Lists 1.0//EN"
             "xhtml11-list-1.mod" >
%xhtml-list.mod;]]>
```

Now our elements are brought in to the DTD:

```
<!-- Recipe Module ........................................... -->
<!ENTITY % Recipe-elements.mod
        SYSTEM "recipe-elements-1.mod" >
%Recipe-elements.mod;
```

Finally, the required Structure module is incorporated:

```
<!-- Document Structure Module (required) ...................... -->
<!ENTITY % xhtml-struct.module "INCLUDE" >
<![%xhtml-struct.module;[
<!ENTITY % xhtml-struct.mod
      PUBLIC "-//W3C//ELEMENTS XHTML 1.1 Document Structure 1.0//EN"
             "xhtml11-struct-1.mod" >
%xhtml-struct.mod;]]>
```

If these were the only features we wanted to support, we'd be done!
However, a few extra modules will make a nicely rounded document. Let's
include the Images, Metainformation, and Stylesheet modules. These are
inserted before the final Structure module:

```
<!-- XHTML Images module ........................................ -->
<!ENTITY % xhtml-image.mod
      PUBLIC "-//W3C//ELEMENTS XHTML Images 1.0//EN"
             "http://www.w3.org/TR/xhtml-modularization/DTD/xhtml-image-1.mod" >
%xhtml-image.mod;
```

```
<!-- Document Metainformation Module ......................... -->
<!ENTITY % xhtml-meta.mod
    PUBLIC "-//W3C//ELEMENTS XHTML Metainformation 1.0//EN"
        "xhtml-meta-1.mod" >
%xhtml-meta.mod;


<!-- XHTML Stylesheet Module .................................... -->
<!ENTITY %xhtml-style.mod
    PUBLIC "-//W3C//ELEMENTS XHTML Stylesheets 1.0//EN"
        "http://www.w3.org/TR/xhtml-modularization/DTD/xhtml-style-1.mod" >
%xhtml-style.mod;


<!-- Document Structure Module (required)  ...................... -->
<!ENTITY % xhtml-struct.module "INCLUDE" >
<![%xhtml-struct.module;[
<!ENTITY % xhtml-struct.mod
      PUBLIC "-//W3C//ELEMENTS XHTML 1.1 Document Structure 1.0//EN"
             "xhtml11-struct-1.mod" >
%xhtml-struct.mod;]]>
```

The Finished DTD

The fruit of your hard labor throughout these three chapters on
Modularization can now be summed up in a single file, Listing 16.4, the
Recipe Markup Language DTD file.

Listing 16.4: The Recipe Markup Language DTD

```
<!-- ............................................................... -->
<!-- Recipe DTD  ..................................................... -->
<!-- file: recipe-1_0.dtd
-->


<!-- This is the DTD driver for Recipe 1.0.

      Please use this formal public identifier to identify it:

          "-//WebGeek//DTD XHTML Recipe 1.0//EN"
      And this namespace for recipe-unique elements:
      xmlns:recipe="http://www.webgeek.com/xmlns/recipe"
-->
<!ENTITY % XHTML.version "-//WebGeek//DTD XHTML Recipe 1.0//EN" >
<!ENTITY % Recipe-qname.mod
        SYSTEM "recipe-qname-1.mod" >
%Recipe-qname.mod;
<!-- no new namespaces needed -->
<!ENTITY NS.prefixed.extras.attrib "" >
<!-- Define the Content Model file for the framework to use -->
```

Listing 16.4: continued

```
<!ENTITY % xhtml-model-1.mod "recipe-model-1.mod">
<!-- reserved for future use with document profiles -->
<!ENTITY % XHTML.profile   "" >
<!-- Bi-directional text support is not included here
-->
<!ENTITY % XHTML.bidi            "IGNORE" >
<!-- The events module should be included here if you need it. In this
     skeleton it is IGNOREd.
-->
<!ENTITY % xhtml-events.module "IGNORE" >
<!-- Modular Framework Module  .................................. -->
<!ENTITY % xhtml-framework.module "INCLUDE" >
<![%xhtml-framework.module;[
<!ENTITY % xhtml-framework.mod
     PUBLIC "-//W3C//ENTITIES XHTML 1.1 Modular Framework 1.0//EN"
              "xhtml11-framework-1.mod" >
%xhtml-framework.mod;]]>
<!-- Text Module (required)  ........................... -->
<!ENTITY % xhtml-text.module "INCLUDE" >
<![%xhtml-text.module;[
<!ENTITY % xhtml-text.mod
     PUBLIC "-//W3C//ELEMENTS XHTML 1.1 Text 1.0//EN"
              "xhtml11-text-1.mod" >
%xhtml-text.mod;]]>
<!-- Hypertext Module (required) ............................. -->
<!ENTITY % xhtml-hypertext.module "INCLUDE" >
<![%xhtml-hypertext.module;[
<!ENTITY % xhtml-hypertext.mod
     PUBLIC "-//W3C//ELEMENTS XHTML 1.1 Hypertext 1.0//EN"
              "xhtml11-hypertext-1.mod" >
%xhtml-hypertext.mod;]]>
<!-- Lists Module (required)  ................................. -->
<!ENTITY % xhtml-list.module "INCLUDE" >
<![%xhtml-list.module;[
<!ENTITY % xhtml-list.mod
     PUBLIC "-//W3C//ELEMENTS XHTML 1.1 Lists 1.0//EN"
              "xhtml11-list-1.mod" >
%xhtml-list.mod;]]>
<!-- Recipe Module ........................................... -->
<!ENTITY % Recipe-elements.mod
     SYSTEM "recipe-elements-1.mod" >
%Recipe-elements.mod;
<!-- XHTML Images module ....................................... -->
<!ENTITY % xhtml-image.mod
     PUBLIC "-//W3C//ELEMENTS XHTML Images 1.0//EN"
         "http://www.w3.org/TR/xhtml-modularization/DTD/xhtml-image-1.mod" >
```

Listing 16.4: continued

```
%xhtml-image.mod;


<!-- Document Metainformation Module ........................... -->
<!ENTITY % xhtml-meta.mod
    PUBLIC "-//W3C//ELEMENTS XHTML Metainformation 1.0//EN"
        "xhtml-meta-1.mod" >
%xhtml-meta.mod;


<!-- XHTML Stylesheet Module .................................. -->
<!ENTITY %xhtml-style.mod
    PUBLIC "-//W3C//ELEMENTS XHTML Stylesheets 1.0//EN"
        "http://www.w3.org/TR/xhtml-modularization/DTD/xhtml-style-1.mod" >
%xhtml-style.mod;


<!-- Document Structure Module (required)  ..................... -->
<!ENTITY % xhtml-struct.module "INCLUDE" >
<![%xhtml-struct.module;[
<!ENTITY % xhtml-struct.mod
    PUBLIC "-//W3C//ELEMENTS XHTML 1.1 Document Structure 1.0//EN"
            "xhtml11-struct-1.mod" >
%xhtml-struct.mod;]]>
<!-- end of Recipe DTD  ............................................ -->
<!-- ............................................................... -->
```

Using the New Doctype

Using the DOCTYPE we just created is as simple as using any W3C-supplied DOCTYPE. Simply declare it at the beginning of your XHTML document as you would any other; for example:

```
<!DOCTYPE html SYSTEM "recipe-1_0.dtd" >
```

Listing 16.5 shows a complete recipe developed using this DTD.

Listing 16.5: recipe.html

```
<!DOCTYPE html SYSTEM "recipe-1_0.dtd">
<html>
<head>
<meta name="description" content="Recipe for Glazed Carrots from the
  Navarro Family Recipe Collection" />
<title>Navarro Family Recipe Collection: Glazed Carrots</title>
</head>
<body>
<h1>Glazed Carrots</h1>
<div>
<img src="carrots.jpg" alt="Glazed Carrots" width="150" height="150" />
</div>
<recipe title="Glazed Carrots">
```

Listing 16.5: continued

```
<ingredients>
<ingredient quantity="1" unit="pound" item="carrots" />
<ingredient quantity="1/4" unit="cup" item="orange juice" />
<ingredient quantity="2" unit="tablespoon" item="butter" />
<ingredient quantity="2" unit="tablespoon" item="brown sugar" />
</ingredients>
<prep>
<p>Trim carrots and cut into bite-size pieces as preferred (e.g. jullienned,
circles, etc). Steam or boil in unsalted water until tender. Drain in
collander. In the same pan, melt butter. Add sugar, stir quickly until
incorporated and sugar just begins to caramelize. Add orange juice, stir
until sugar is incorporated, reduce as necessary to achieve syrupy
consistency. Add carrots back into pan. Stir to coat.</p>
</prep>
</recipe>
</body>
</html>
```

Figure 16.1 shows this file when saved as recipe.xml and rendered by the Internet Explorer XML processor.

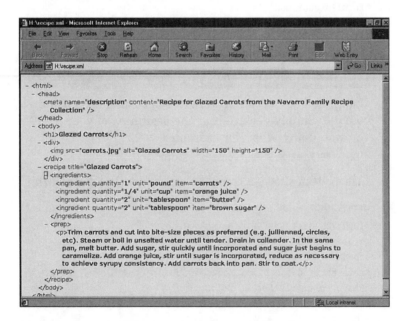

Figure 16.1: *Our Recipe Markup Language file as displayed by Internet Explorer in XML mode.*

To display the file fully in an HTML-based browser, we need some additional information by way of an XSL style sheet. Experiment with the techniques you learned in Chapter 12, "XSL—Style the XML Way," to see how you might style these new elements.

What's Next

In this chapter you've taken the custom XHTML module defined in Chapter 15 and incorporated it into a new markup language with its own DTD. We've also reviewed a document written using this markup language.

Next, in Chapter 17, "Subsetting XHTML: XHTML Basic," we'll take a look at additional applications of XHTML Modularization, specifically the idea of an XHTML subset for smaller devices in XHTML Basic.

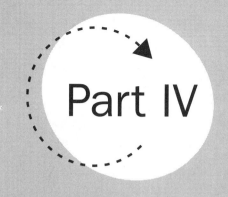

Part IV

The Future of XHTML

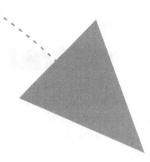

Subsetting XHTML: XHTML Basic

When people think about the flexibility that an extensible language like XHTML offers, it's easy to forget that you don't necessarily have to *add* to the language, that you can instead subtract from it, or make it more restrictive.

XHTML Basic is the first XHTML Family Member vocabulary to be published by the W3C that takes this approach. Its intent is to act as a basic platform for further development in vocabularies used on small footprint devices.

This chapter teaches you:

- How small footprint devices are being used to access the Internet
- What kinds of devices are gaining in popularity
- How to convert an existing HTML document to XHTML Basic
- How XHTML Basic compares to other XHTML document types

Using XHTML on Small-Footprint Devices

One of the most exciting, and perhaps sometimes frustrating, realities of living in an ultra-"wired" society is the realization of accessing digital information and the Internet from just about anywhere. We've seen live updates to Web sites from Mt. Everest and the middle of the world's oceans, and we can send email from the comfort of our airplane seat while cruising along at 35,000 feet.

In large part, this "access everywhere" lifestyle has been accomplished through desktop and laptop systems. With the advent of wireless connections for small devices, such as Palms and other PDAs, and even cellular telephones, the capabilities of the devices connecting to the Internet are changing at an incredibly rapid pace.

Miniature Computers

The form factor of many laptop and portable devices is certainly getting smaller by the year. However, the systems worthy of mention in this section aren't just smaller devices, but those that are both small and run on operating systems optimized to perform under the tight constraints present in these devices. 3Com and now Palm Computing offer the PalmOS found in the wildly popular Palm Pilot line of PDAs, and Microsoft has joined the fray with the Windows CE operating system. Both palm-sized devices operate primarily with a stylus, and miniature keyboard-based systems known as "hand-helds" can take advantage of WinCE.

These machines typically have just 2MB–16MB of memory in which to operate. That's not RAM, as in our desktop machines, but the entire storage system!

Understandably, the software used on these machines must have a significantly smaller footprint than those used on traditional computers. Because of the limited space for software to operate, the features available within programs can be limited. For instance, a Web browser might not have a Java Virtual Machine installed, or it might not have the capability to process scripts or style sheets. It's also unlikely that these browsers will have plug-ins available to support advanced Web features such as video, audio, or animations such as Shockwave and SMIL.

Nontraditional Appliances

A nontraditional appliance is one where, at least until very recently, you wouldn't normally think about a computer being present, let alone one with access to the Internet!

Wireless Access

Wireless access to the Internet is one of the fastest growing user segments. Cellular telephones are used by as much as 60%–70% of the population in Sweden and Finland, followed quite closely by the Japanese.

Limited Use Devices

A limited use device, as opposed to a nontraditional appliance, is one that generally looks and feels like a computer, but is decidedly limited in what applications it can run. WebTV falls into this category, as do the email-only and email-plus-Web appliances now being marketed as a "low barrier to entry" way to get online.

Exploring the XHTML Basic DTD

XHTML Basic is, as noted earlier, a host language implementation of XHTML Modularization. In Chapter 16, "Combining Custom Modules with XHTML," we defined a host language as a document type built using, at a minimum, the four required XHTML modules: the Structure Module, Text Module, Hypertext Module, and List Module. Table 17.1 lists the elements included in these modules.

Table 17.1: Required XHTML Modules Included in XHTML Basic

Module	Elements
Structure Module	html, head, title, body
Text Module	abbr, acronym, address, blockquote, br, cite, code, dfn, div, em, h1, h2, h3, h4, h5, h6, kbd, p, pre, q, samp, span, strong, var
Hypertext Module	a
List Module	ol, ul, li, dl, dt, dd

Developing to XHTML Basic

EXAMPLE

Let's take a look at an existing Web site and see what would need to be done if it were to be updated for XHTML Basic. Orion's Domain is the personal Web site of a good friend of mine, and he has graciously allowed me to use his pages here in this book (see Figure 17.1). Note that his home page is currently a valid HTML 4.0 Transitional document. The page source is found in Listing 17.1.

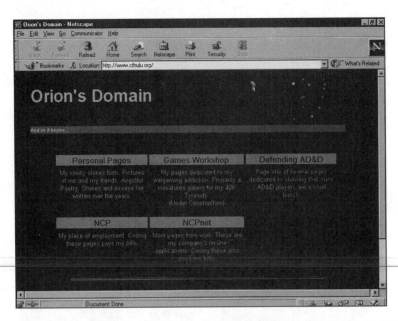

Figure 17.1: *Orion's Domain: a valid HTML 4.0 Transitional Web site that we'll transform to XHTML Basic.*

Listing 17.1: orion.html

```
<!DOCTYPE HTML PUBLIC "-//W3C//DTD HTML 4.0 Transitional//EN"
          "http://www.w3.org/TR/REC-html40/loose.dtd">
<HTML>
<HEAD>
    <TITLE>Orion's Domain</TITLE>
    <META NAME="description"
          CONTENT="Orion's pages. Warhammer. Apollo Smile. Angst.
          Street Fighter II.
          These are just a few of my favorite things.">
    <META NAME="keywords"
          CONTENT="orion, marshall, jansen, angst, poetry, anime, space,
          madness, deep, seas, dino, mush, mud, evil!, xibo, apollo, smile,
          warhammer, 40k, fantasy, tyranid, chaos, gw, eldar, miniatures,
          painting, conversion, crimson, fists, dark, eldar, elves, hello,
          kitty, slaanesh, tzeentch, khorne, nurgle">
    <LINK REL=STYLESHEET TYPE="text/css" HREF="styles/main.css">
</HEAD>
<BODY>
<TABLE WIDTH="90%">
  <TR>
    <TD><H1 CLASS="head">Orion's Domain</H1></TD>
    <TD ALIGN="RIGHT"><IMG SRC="pics/orion.jpg"
                      WIDTH=152
```

Listing 17.1: continued

```
HEIGHT=96

                               BORDER=0
                               ALT="Orion's Domain"></TD>
  </TR>
  <TR>
    <TD CLASS="back" COLSPAN=2><P CLASS="back">And so it begins...</P></TD>
  </TR>
</TABLE>
<BR><BR>
<TABLE ALIGN="CENTER" WIDTH="80%" CELLPADDING=2>
  <TR ALIGN="CENTER">
    <TD CLASS="jump" WIDTH="25%"><A HREF="welcome.html">Personal Pages</A></TD>
    <TD CLASS="jump" WIDTH="25%"><A HREF="gw/index.html">Games Workshop</A></TD>
    <TD CLASS="jump" WIDTH="25%"><A HREF="add.html">Defending AD&amp;D</A></TD>
  </TR>
  <TR ALIGN="CENTER">
    <TD CLASS="text" VALIGN="TOP">My vanity shines forth.
➡Pictures of me and my friends. Angstful Poetry.
➡Stories and essays I've written over the years.<BR><BR></TD>
    <TD CLASS="text" VALIGN="TOP">My pages dedicated to my wargaming addiction.
➡Primarily a miniatures gallery for my 40K Tyranids.<BR>(Under Construction)<BR>
➡<BR></TD>
    <TD CLASS="text" VALIGN="TOP">Page one of several pages dedicated to showing
➡that surly AD&amp;D players are a cruel bunch.<BR><BR></TD>
  </TR>
  <TR ALIGN="CENTER">
    <TD CLASS="jump" WIDTH="25%"><A HREF="http://www.ncprint.com/">NCP</A></TD>
    <TD CLASS="jump" WIDTH="25%"><A HREF="http://www.ncpnet.com/">NCPnet</A></TD>
    <TD WIDTH="25%"> </TD>
  </TR>
  <TR ALIGN="CENTER">
    <TD CLASS="text" VALIGN="TOP">My place of employment.
➡Coding these pages pays my bills.</TD>
    <TD CLASS="text" VALIGN="TOP">More pages from work.
➡These are my company's on-line applications.
➡Coding these also pays my bills.</TD>
    <TD VALIGN="TOP"> </TD>
  </TR>
</TABLE>
<BR>
<HR ALIGN="CENTER" WIDTH="75%" SIZE="3">
<BR>
<TABLE WIDTH="100%" CELLPADDING=4>
  <TR>
    <TD CLASS="hwg" ALIGN="CENTER">
```

Listing 17.1: continued

```
      The author is<BR>a member of<BR>
      <A HREF="http://www.hwg.org/"><IMG
      SRC="pics/lo-025.gif"
      WIDTH=64
      HEIGHT=90
      BORDER=0
      ALT="The HTML Writers Guild"></A>
      </TD>
      <TD>
      <DIV CLASS="address">
This page was last updated
<SCRIPT TYPE="text/javascript" LANGUAGE="JavaScript">
<!--
    document.write(" on  " + document.lastModified + " ");
// -->
</SCRIPT>
<BR>by Marshall Jansen, AKA Orion<BR>
<A HREF="mailto:webtyrant@cthulu.org">WebTyrant@cthulu.org</A><BR>
        </DIV>
      </TD>
      <TD>
       <A HREF="http://validator.w3.org/check/referer"><IMG
       SRC="pics/vh40.gif"
       HEIGHT=31
       WIDTH=88
       BORDER=0
       ALT="Valid HTML 4.0!"></A>
      </TD>
    </TR>
</TABLE>
</BODY>
</HTML>
```

A good start on our conversion is to bring the document into XHTML. To that end, I'll run it through TidyGUI, the graphical HTML Tidy utility introduced in Chapter 9, "Implementing XHTML Today."

✔ For more information on HTML Tidy, see "HTML Tidy," p. 167.

Tidy converts all the elements and attributes to lowercase for me, and adds the required slashes to empty elements (see Figure 17.2).

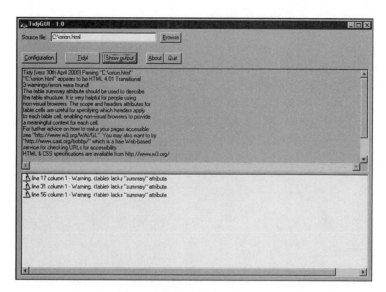

Figure 17.2: *Converting HTML 4.0 Transitional to XHTML 1.0 Transitional is a first step toward authoring in XHTML Basic.*

Next, we'll step through the document and make any necessary changes between XHTML 1.0 Transitional and XHTML Basic. Immediately, we need to change the DOCTYPE definition from

```
<!DOCTYPE html PUBLIC "-//W3C//DTD XHTML 1.0 Transitional//EN"
    "http://www.w3.org/TR/xhtml1/DTD/xhtml1-transitional.dtd">
```

to

```
<!DOCTYPE html PUBLIC "-//W3C//DTD XHTML Basic 1.0//EN"
    "http://www.w3.org/TR/2000/WD-xhtml-basic-20000210/xhtml-basic10.dtd">
```

The first trouble spot we run into is the width, alignment, and cellpadding attributes on each of the tables and table cells. As presentational attributes, they've been removed from the XHTML Basic DTD.

TIP

Remember, although these presentational attributes aren't supported in XHTML Basic, that doesn't mean the effect cannot be rendered in the document. CSS provides for table manipulation properties, allowing the same effect to be transferred from the XHTML source document to the style sheet. With the class identifiers already in place within the table, there's already a hook available.

Horizontal rules aren't supported, so the divider between the content of this page and the address and other information below the rule will need to be removed. Also, the JavaScript date insertion needs to be converted to plain text as seen here:

```
<table width="100%">
<tr>
```

```
<td class="hwg" >The author is<br />
a member of<br />
 <object data="lo-025.gif"
width="64" height="90"
title="The HTML Writers Guild">
<a href="http://www.hwg.org/">The HTML Writers Guild</a></object>
</td>
<td>
<div class="address">This page was last updated
on July 7, 2000
<br />
by Marshall Jansen, AKA Orion<br />
<a
href="mailto:webtyrant@cthulu.org">WebTyrant@cthulu.org</a><br />
</div>
</td>
<td><a href="http://validator.w3.org/check/referer">
<img src="http://www.webgeek.com/xhtml/orion/vh40.gif" height="61" width="108">
</a></td>
</tr>
</table>
```

Now the document is in order, and you can see the markup itself in Listing 17.2 and a view from a traditional browser in Figure 17.3.

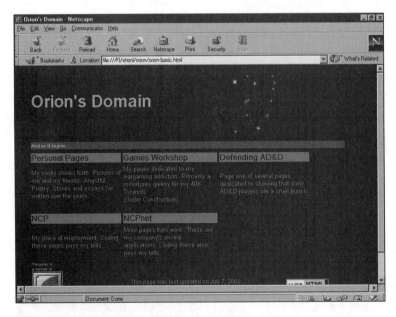

Figure 17.3: *The XHTML Basic version of Orion's Domain, with no additional changes to the style sheet.*

Listing 17.2: `orion-basic.html`, Orion's Domain Written in XHTML Basic

```
<!DOCTYPE html PUBLIC "-//W3C//DTD XHTML Basic 1.0//EN"
    "http://www.w3.org/TR/2000/WD-xhtml-basic-20000210/xhtml-basic10.dtd">
<html xmlns="http://www.w3.org/1999/xhtml">
<head>
<meta name="generator" content="HTML Tidy, see www.w3.org" />
<title>Orion's Domain</title>
<meta name="description"
content="Orion's pages. Warhammer. Apollo Smile. Angst. Street Fighter II.
These are just a few of my favorite things." />
<meta name="keywords"
content="orion, marshall, jansen, angst, poetry, anime, space, madness, deep,
seas, dino, mush, mud, evil!, xibo, apollo, smile, warhammer, 40k, fantasy,
tyranid, chaos, gw, eldar, miniatures, painting, conversion, crimson, fists,
dark, eldar, elves, hello, kitty, slaanesh, tzeentch, khorne, nurgle" />
<link rel="STYLESHEET" type="text/css" href="main.css" />
</head>
<body>
<table width="90%">
<tr>
<td>
<h1 class="head">Orion's Domain</h1>
</td>
<td><img src="http://www.webgeek.com/xhtml/orion/orion.jpg" width="192"
➥height="136" alt="Orion's Domain" />
</td>
</tr>
<tr>
<td class="back" colspan="2">
<p class="back">And so it begins...</p>
</td>
</tr>
</table>
<table width="80%">
<tr>
<td class="jump"><a href="welcome.html">Personal
Pages</a></td>
<td class="jump"><a href="gw/index.html">Games
Workshop</a></td>
<td class="jump"><a href="add.html">Defending
AD&amp;D</a></td>
</tr>
<tr>
<td class="text">My vanity shines forth. Pictures of
me and my friends. Angstful Poetry. Stories and essays I've written
over the years.<br />
<br />
```

Listing 17.2: continued

```
</td>
<td class="text">My pages dedicated to my wargaming
addiction. Primarily a miniatures gallery for my 40K
Tyranids.<br />
(Under Construction)<br />
<br />
</td>
<td class="text">Page one of several pages dedicated
to showing that surly AD&amp;D players are a cruel bunch.<br />
<br />
</td>
</tr>
<tr>
<td class="jump" ><a href="http://www.ncprint.com/">
NCP</a></td>
<td class="jump" ><a href="http://www.ncpnet.com/">
NCPnet</a></td>
<td > </td>
</tr>
<tr >
<td class="text" >My place of employment. Coding these
pages pays my bills.</td>
<td class="text" >More pages from work. These are my
company's on-line applications. Coding these also pays my
bills.</td>
<td > </td>
</tr>
</table>
<table width="100%">
<tr>
<td class="hwg" >The author is<br />
a member of<br />
 <a href="http://www.hwg.org/"><img src="lo-025.gif"
alt="The HTML Writers Guild" /></a>
</td>
<td>
<div class="address">This page was last updated
on July 7, 2000
<br />
by Marshall Jansen, AKA Orion<br />
<a
href="mailto:webtyrant@cthulu.org">WebTyrant@cthulu.org</a><br />
</div>
</td>
<td><a href="http://validator.w3.org/check/referer">
<img src="http://www.webgeek.com/xhtml/orion/vh40.gif" /></a><td>
```

```
</tr>
</table>
</body>
</html>
```

Evaluating the Results

An interesting exercise is to change the DOCTYPE declaration in orion.html to that used for XHTML 1.0 Strict and then revalidate. Getting a passing mark lets you know that XHTML Basic hasn't *included* anything that wouldn't otherwise pass validation for XHTML 1.0 Strict. In the same manner, it's possible to check documents developed to XHTML 1.0 Strict or XHTML 1.0 Transitional for compliance with XHTML Basic by simply changing the doctype and reviewing the results as we did moving from HTML 4.01 to XHTML with Orion's Domain.

What's Next

In this chapter, you have learned about the wide variety of computing devices that now have access to the Internet. You've become familiar with the unique requirements that many of these devices present, both in terms of the software they can run and the type of documents they are able to process.

You've gone through the steps of converting an existing HTML document over to XHTML Basic and compared the results to both the original presentation and XHTML 1.0 Strict.

Next, in Chapter 18, "XHTML Document Profiling," we'll take a look at how XHTML documents can be described and managed using document profiling techniques.

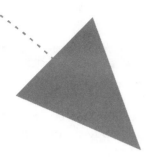

## 18

XHTML Document Profiling

Up until this point we've discussed the technologies behind creating XHTML documents, as well as defining and validating their grammars. The next step in managing a set of Web documents is to work with them as a collection. To manage, sort, or otherwise document the properties of a collection, you must first know what each individual member of that set represents. To that end, methods have been developed to describe and categorize documents as a larger part of information management systems.

XHTML has facilities for describing documents that are compatible with these efforts, and the future holds promise for several more techniques that will further enhance the abilities for XHTML.

This chapter teaches you:

- What metadata is

- How metadata is included in XHTML documents

- How to build descriptive meta elements

- How to use meta elements to suggest HTTP response headers

Meta Information

Before we can talk too much about what meta information provides for us, it's essential that you fully understand what metadata, as it has pertained to Web documents, actually is. The most simplistic definition of metadata is "data about data." Practically, that means descriptive information about a document or collection of data such as a database or other concentrated store of data. In XHTML, the meta element provides document authors with an opportunity to include this descriptive information.

What Current Techniques Tell Us

The intent of the XHTML meta element is to provide servers and clients a means of retrieving information about the document being served to index it, as in the case of search engines, and identify it or catalog it for other applications.

Let's take a close look at how the meta element is defined in XHTML 1.0 by reviewing the element and attribute-list declaration from the XHTML 1.0 Transitional DTD:

```
<!ELEMENT meta EMPTY>
<!ATTLIST meta
  %i18n;
  http-equiv  NMTOKEN #IMPLIED
  name        NMTOKEN #IMPLIED
  content     CDATA #REQUIRED
  scheme      CDATA #IMPLIED
>
```

The interesting parts of the meta element are the attributes, because meta is an empty element. The presence of the i18n parameter entity indicates that meta can take any of the attributes represented by i18n (to review what's provided in the internationalization attribute set, see Chapter 13, "Document Type Definitions—The Syntax Rulebook").

The two most common attributes used are name and content. The name attribute provides a label for the meta information being supplied in the element. The content attribute value holds the actual meta data. For example, to identify the author of this book, if it were written as an XHTML file, the meta element would appear as

```
<meta name="author" content="Ann Navarro" />
```

The http-equiv attribute is used in place of the name attribute when the information is intended for the benefit of http servers gathering information to produce compatible http-response headers. We'll come back to the http-equiv attribute later in this chapter.

Finally, the `scheme` attribute allows additional contextual information to be provided, giving semantic meaning to the data found in the `content` attribute. If I were to create a `meta` element designed to be a unique identifier for this book, I could use the book's ISBN number:

```
<meta scheme="ISBN" name="identifier" content="0789723859" />
```

In practice, the `scheme` attribute is rarely used. Instead, the name attribute would take `"ISBN"` and the context would be understood by any human readers.

NOTE

The collection of and processing of metadata is a science unto itself. The Dublin Core Metadata Initiative is one project that's specific to the world of electronic resources. Visit its Web site at `http://purl.org/DC/`.

Because metadata is flexible, there isn't a set of standard metadata names that should be used in `meta` elements and populated with content. This flexibility, however, can be confusing to many Web page authors looking for guidance in what to describe. The key is to think about how any descriptive information might be used by the document author, someone else in the organization, or by anyone else who might be reading the source document. Descriptive information can

- Identify the author of the document

- Issue a statement of copyright

- Provide a basic description of the document content

- Document the tools used to generate the page

- Record the date the document was last modified

Additionally, `meta` elements can be used to control how machines interact with the document. The `meta` element can provide

- Instructions for indexing robots

- Hints to the client about when to refresh the document in cache

- An expiration date for the document

- Keywords that could be used when searching for related data

The human-use information, as shown in the first list, can be as general or specific as you want to get. When I create Web documents, I usually include author information, the date the document was credited and/or edited, a simple copyright statement, and a description. Those `meta` elements might appear as

```
<meta name="author" content="Ann Navarro" />
<meta name="DateCreated" content="June 30, 2000" />
<meta name="LastModified" content="September 1, 2000" />
<meta name="Copyright" content="June, 2000, WebGeek, Inc." />
<meta name="description" content="A tutorial on the use of metadata in Web
documents." />
<meta http-equiv="Expires" content="Tue, 31 Oct 2000 00:00:01 GMT">
<meta http-equiv="PICS-Label" content='(PICS-1.1 "http://www.rsac.org/
ratingsv01.html"
 l gen false comment "RSACi North America Server" for
"http://www.webgeek.com/xhtml/index.html" on "2000.10.02T18:20-0800"
 r (n 0 s 0 v 0 l 0))'>
```

The remainder of the `meta` elements commonly used are for the benefit of search engines, browsers, or other automated systems, such as the last two elements seen in this example. The `http-equiv` attribute with the value "`Expires`" tells the browser when it should retrieve a fresh copy of the page from the server, rather than relying on a copy stored in cache. The last `meta` element seen is a content ratings system that can be used by proxies or other content-filtering systems to disallow access to objectionable material. The rating service used to develop this `meta` element was the Internet Content Rating Association, which can be found online at `http://www.rsac.org/`.

Using Metadata for Machine Instructions

The use of metadata for machine instructions falls into two basic camps: information for search engines, and directives for the client. The simplest of these `meta` elements uses the value `robots` in the `name` attribute:

```
<meta name="robots" content="noindex, nofollow" />
```

This element tells spidering agents, or *robots*, that they should not index a document when this metadata appears with the `noindex` instruction. Additionally, `nofollow` tells the spider not to look for or *follow* any links found within the document.

TIP

Not all search engine spiders recognize or obey the preferences stated in the `robots` `meta` element. However, many more follow the Robots Exclusion Protocol that was developed in 1994 as a cooperative project between the programmers of robots and spiders and site administrators. Information on using the Robots Exclusion Protocol and the resulting `robots.txt` file generated can be found at `http://info.webcrawler.com/mak/projects/robots/exclusion-admin.html`.

Most search engines determine when they'll return a given Web page by comparing the search term provided by the user with the information it has stored about a given site or page. Frequently that store of data is a list of keywords found in the document. Authors can provide keywords that *they* want the search engines to match by using the keywords meta element.

Just how many keywords can be read, or whether you need to use every form of a word pertaining to your site, has always been a hotly debated topic. The reality is there will never be one set answer for all purposes. Some search engines don't record your keywords and instead index the entire page, whereas others will read the keywords but limit themselves to the first few. Most sources suggest using no more than about 25 words, or perhaps 250 characters of keyword data, and ordering them by relevance. That is, the keywords that best describe your site should come first in the list.

Let's take a look at the use of keywords on a popular Web site. The Lycos Network has a site known as Gamesville, where visitors can play free games for the opportunity to win small, and many not so small, cash prizes (see Figure 18.1).

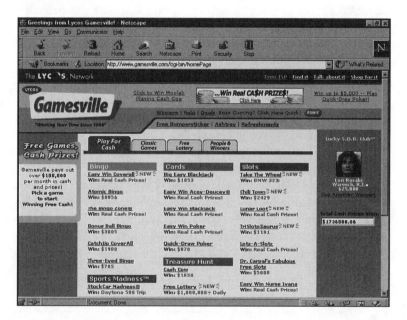

Figure 18.1: *We'll be looking at the* meta *elements for this popular site.*

The description meta element (edited here to conform to XHTML 1.0 requirements by making sure element and attribute names are in lowercase, and we have the closing / at the end that is now required of empty elements) is short and to the point:

```
<meta name="description" content="Play free games, win cash prizes!" />
```

The `keywords` meta element stays on focus as well:

```
<meta name="keywords" content="game, games, computer game, computer games,
online gaming, free
game, free games, gamesville, online game, online games, gamesville.com, card
game, card games,
bingo, www.gamesville.com, poker, slots, blackjack, free stuff, free, lottery,
sweepstake,
sweepstakes, trivia, free money, casino" />
```

At 26 keywords, this is about as large as you'd want this element's content to get.

TIP

Notice that the keywords listed in the Gamesville sample aren't all just a single "word." Short phrases also can be used as keywords. The commas in the list mark where one word ends and the next begins.

Considerable information on the behavior of search engine spiders and various features of search engines can be found at the Search Engine Watch site, located at `http://searchenginewatch.internet.com/webmasters/features.html` (this article is publicly available, though some articles on the site are only available via paid subscription).

Some machine-usable `meta` elements are written not by using the `name` attribute, but instead use the `http-equiv` attribute. If we can digress only for a moment, you know that Web pages are requested and delivered over the Internet using the Hypertext Transfer Protocol, or HTTP. The client that makes the request and the server that responds share additional information with each other by way of HTTP "headers," essentially extra bits of data pre-pended to the exchange. The property name used as the `http-equiv` attribute value in a `meta` element can be used to create a header in the HTTP response between the client and server. Table 21.1 outlines a number of popular `http-equiv`-based properties. Listing 21.1 puts them to use in the head of an XHTML document.

Table 21.1: Sample `http-equiv` Properties and Values

Property	Content Values	Usage
`expires`	Date/time stamp	Instructs a cache to retrieve a new copy of the document after the specified date/time
`Content-type`	Media type (and optional character set)	Allows pre-loading of plug-ins and/or character sets
`Content-Script-Type`	Scripting language identifier	Sets the base scripting language in use
`Content-Style-Type`	Style language identifier	Sets the base style language in use
`Pragma`	"nocache"	Controls caching in HTTP 1.0

Listing 21.1: A Sample Set of meta Elements

```
<head>
<title>Metadata Samples</title>
<meta name="author" content="Ann Navarro" />
<meta name="copyright" content="Copyright 2000, WebGeek, Inc. /">
<meta name="description" content="A document used to provide examples of meta
elements" />
<meta name="keywords" content="meta, metadata, descriptions" />
<meta http-equiv="Expires" content="Sun, 31 Dec 2000 23:59:59 GMT" />
<meta http-equiv="Content-Type" content="text/html" />
<meta http-equiv="Content-Script-Type" content="text/JavaScript" />
<meta http-equiv="Content-Style-Type" content="text/CSS" />
<meta http-equiv="Pragma" content="nocache" />
</head>
```

Tools for Developing meta Elements

Developing effective meta elements is often easier when you use tools developed for the process. Table 21.2 lists two sites for tools that I've found invaluable for understanding and developing metadata.

Table 21.2: Tools for Creating and Editing meta Elements

Site	Details
Meta Builder 2 http://vancouver-webpages.com/ META/mk-metas.html	Provides a form-based meta element generator for the most frequently used meta element. Also has an outstandingly complete dictionary of name and http-equiv attribute values and their uses.
Dublin Core Metadata Initiative Tools Page http://purl.org/DC/tools/index.htm	Comprehensive list of tools for the creation of or editing of metadata.

One of my favorite sites is the Reggie Metadata editor. This tool allows the user to select which metadata schema to use, and what syntax the output should be formatted with, such as HTML 4.0, RDF, or others. Once these options are selected, the user is prompted to fill in the details for commonly used metadata properties. Then the applet compiles the final markup for you (see Figure 21.2).

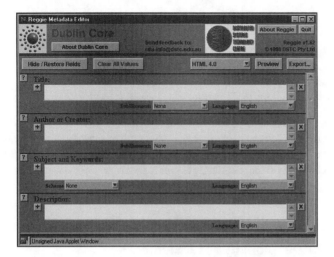

Figure 21.2: *The Reggie Metadata Editor in action.*

What's Missing?

So far we've explored ways to describe the contents of a document; to identify specific properties such as the author of the document, copyright statements, and creation or modification dates; as well as methods used to enhance the machine-processibility of the page. So what's missing?

A frequently heard complaint in some Web design circles is the inability to exert precise control over the presentation of their Web sites. These authors might not want a browser to attempt to render the document if it can't handle some portions of it, preferring to miss out on that visitor rather than change the display of the page content. Others might have preferences as to the path of substitution a browser takes if it can't render the document as first defined.

Today, XHMTL doesn't provide a mechanism for exerting that much control over the delivery of Web content. A request is made from the client, and the server happily pushes all that is there back out. It's the client's responsibility to determine how to display that content to the user, based on policies or decision trees set by the client's programmers.

Similarly, it's not possible for a device to let the server know that it can accept GIF images but not PNG, or that the browser in use doesn't understand JavaScript. Capabilities and preferences also don't necessarily have to be device or client related. A user with less-than-perfect eyesight might have chosen to increase the default font size of his display and would like that preference to carry over when his browsing software evaluates any font sizes set in a Web document. Many of these issues are being addressed in work getting underway at the W3C, as well as other standards and research bodies.

What's Next

In this chapter we've talked about systems for describing documents, including syntax for providing details for originator use such as creation and editing dates. The meta element can be used with the name attribute to provide any number of descriptive properties, and the http-equiv attribute is used to suggest http response headers.

Next, in Chapter 16, "Combining Custom Modules with XHTML," we'll take a look at several exciting "coming attractions" for XHTML. We've already touched briefly on the capabilities and profiling work to be done by CC/PP, and we'll take a closer look at the developments occurring in that field. Work is also underway in combining television and the Web, both from a "broadcast over the Internet" perspective as well as an "embedded Web documents in a TV broadcast" viewpoint. Finally, the ubiquitous form is in for an overhaul with extended capabilities being reviewed by the W3C XForms Working Group. We expect to see efforts to provide state management between form pages, databinding, and stronger form-field validation tools.

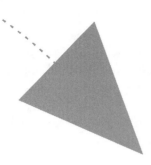

19

Next Steps for XHTML

In this chapter you will learn a little about some of the exciting likely future developments in Web standards that will impact XHTML or draw from recent or forthcoming XHTML standards.

The new possibilities being opened up are exciting, but you should be aware that *all* the material discussed in this chapter is at an early stage of development, and so is particularly liable to change. So please read this chapter with a view to grasping the big picture, the general concepts. By all means think about the preliminary detail provided but make sure to check the current versions of the documents cited to identify where major changes might have occurred.

It isn't possible to cover every emerging technology here, but the ones which are covered should give you a flavor of some of the substantial changes that are likely to further change the ways in which you can make use of the World Wide Web.

This chapter teaches you:

- A methodology that will permit Web servers to tailor output of documents to the type of browser that you choose to use at any one time. This embryonic technology goes by the name *Composite Capabilities / Preferences Profiles*, abbreviated to CC/PP.

- Possible ways in which television and the World Wide Web can benefit from the strengths of the partner technology.

- A new generation of XML-based Web forms, called XForms, which will improve on existing HTML/XHTML forms.

CC/PP—Composite Capabilities/Preferences Profiles

The advent of connection to the World Wide Web from mobile devices brings with it many possibilities and opportunities. Looking beyond the hype, of which there is an enormous amount at present, there also are genuinely exciting possibilities. In parallel with those opportunities, there also are significant technical issues yet to be solved.

One of those issues is how to ensure that the Web page (or "deck" on mobile browsers) sent by a Web server is appropriate to the browser to which it is sent.

The exchange of information between a browser and server, which will form an important mechanism underlying CC/PP, does not arise in a vacuum. Already it is possible to exchange information using the *header* of an HTTP message. There are already many ways to access such HTTP header information. In Figure 19.1, I show some information displayed by one of the currently available techniques—a simple JavaServer page—which can access information in an HTTP header.

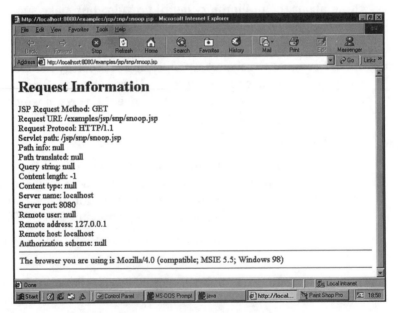

Figure 19.1: *This shows a simple JavaServer page, which displays some information extracted from an HTTP header. Note the information about the browser in the final line of the page.*

The existing information in an HTTP header provides information about the browser that's being used. CC/PP will provide further information to enable the server to serve an appropriately customized page.

CC/PP provides a composite view of the technical capabilities of a browser (the capabilities of CC/PP) and the personal preferences of the person using the browser regarding how they want the browser to behave (the preferences of CC/PP).

Most mobile browsers suffer from significant limitations when compared with a typical desktop PC-based browsing experience. The screen might be of the order of 100×100 pixels compared to perhaps 1,024×768 on the desktop. The screen might be monochrome compared to full color on the desktop. The keyboard of a mobile device is likely to be very limited compared to a standard or enhanced QWERTY keyboard. Bandwidth on wireless connections are, and for some time are likely to remain, significantly slower than on a wired connection. Most mobile devices will have markedly less memory than a typical desktop machine.

To attempt, say, to transmit a 500×500–pixel Flash movie to a typical mobile browser is hardly likely to be an experience to be enjoyed or to be repeated. Worse still, it is likely to communicate nothing to the user. A way is needed for users of mobile browsers to be able to access relevant content which the limitations of their mobile browser do not render incomprehensible, invisible, or a totally slow and frustrating ordeal.

If using mobile browsers is to be a productive activity, a way has to be found to match a browser with the material served to it. One answer is CC/PP. The purpose of the CC/PP initiative is to provide a way for mobile browsers particularly, but more generally to allow all browsers, to be served Web pages or other content that matches the capability of the browser in use at any point in time.

For this to work the browser must, in some way, be able to communicate directly or indirectly an indication of its capabilities. The Web server must be able to reliably identify a browser's capabilities and provide an appropriate Web page to that browser. This approach underlies much of CC/PP.

Another approach that might be applicable in some settings is to serve modularized data. A browser will only handle those parts that it understands. This might apply on a television-based browser that has no capability to express its preferences by sending capability information to the Web server.

Metadata and the Resource Description Framework

Metadata is data about the information contained within, for example, an XML document. It is *not* the information contained in the document but a description of one or more characteristics of it.

You might well be familiar with early attempts at providing metadata on the World Wide Web in the <META> tags of the head of HTML, and later XHTML, documents.

User agent (browser) profiles are expressed in terms of the Resource Description Framework (RDF). RDF is the foundation of much of the W3C's work on metadata. More specifically, RDF is the foundation for CC/PP.

RDF is a model for representing named properties and property values.

Everything described by RDF consists of *resources*. For example, such resources might include a Web page or a collection of Web pages.

A property is an aspect of a resource. A property will define its permitted values, the types of resources it can describe, and its relationship with other properties.

An RDF statement consists of a specific resource together with a named property and a value of that property.

The Resource Description Framework uses XML to exchange descriptions about the content of Web resources. Although XML is used within RDF, the content of the Web resources being described need not be in XML and can be in any format.

If you want to look at RDF in more detail, the current version is a Candidate Recommendation entitled "Resource Description Framework (RDF) Schema Specification 1.0," which is located at

`http://www.w3.org/TR/2000/CR-rdf-schema-20000327`

RDF is also the foundation of CC/PP, the semantics of which are overlaid on RDF.

CC/PP Terminology

For a Web server to be able to identify the nature and capabilities of the variety of browsers that might access it, new concepts are raised; not surprisingly, CC/PP involves quite a bit of new jargon.

Some terms might be familiar to you, but others are likely to be unfamiliar to at least some readers.

Not all the terminology relating to CC/PP is described here. Further details can be obtained by consulting the W3C documents listed later in this section.

Here are some of the terms that apply to the browser end of things:

- User Agent Profile—A description of the capabilities and preferences of a client device or user agent—in other words, a browser.

- Attributes—The characteristics or capabilities of a user agent that together constitute the user agent profile—for example, screen resolution.

- Hint—The expression of a preference. This will carry weight with the origin server (see the following) but is unlikely to be mandatory. For example, the browser might indicate that it prefers to be served XHTML rather than HTML.

At the Web server end, these terms are in use:

- Origin Server—A Web server that originates or supplies Web content to a user agent.

- Authentication—Confirmation of the identity of a user/browser.

- Content Selection—The selection of a document to serve that is appropriate to the CC/PP of the user agent.

Some terms involve both the client and browser:

- Capability—The attributes of, usually, the receiver of a message. It can, however, also apply to the capabilities of a server with regard to the types of messages it is capable of serving.

- Content Negotiation—A process that involves exchange of information between an origin server and a user agent allowing a user agent to make a choice about which of a range of available content formats is most acceptable.

A CC/PP profile describes client (or user agent) capabilities in terms of a number of CC/PP attributes, or *features*. Each of these features is identified by a name in the form of a URI (Uniform Resource Indicator). A collection of such names used to describe a client is called a *vocabulary*.

CC/PP describes a small, core set of features that are widely applicable and constitute the core vocabulary of CC/PP. In addition, it is anticipated that extension vocabularies also will be supported. You might recognize similarities here to the extensibility enabled by modularization of XHTML, which was described in Chapter 14, "XHTML Modularization," and Chapter 16, "Combining Custom Modules with XHTML." It is anticipated that the extension vocabularies might be standardized for, for example, imaging devices, voice messaging devices, and wireless access devices.

CC/PP vocabulary terms are expected to be constructed from a Namespace URI (see the introduction to XML Namespaces in Chapter 12, "XSL—Style the XML Way") together with a local attribute type to yield an attribute name URI of the following general form:

```
http://w3c.org/ccpp-core-vocabulary/type
```

Please note that, because the current documents are only a draft, the applicable URI might change.

Flexible, Extensible, and Distributed

The designers of CC/PP aim to make it flexible, extensible, and distributed.

It has to be flexible because, in practice, it isn't possible to predict all possible future user agents that might come into use.

It has to be extensible for similar reasons. It must be possible to add new types of profile.

It has to be distributed. A centralized register might suffer from system vulnerabilities that are contrary to the principles that led to the design of the Internet to ensure it was resistant to physical or other problems at any one location.

Current Scope of CC/PP

As currently drafted CC/PP does not fully describe the protocols or other means by which Preferences Profiles might be transmitted.

Currently no formal requirements document has been produced by the W3C working group, a situation that is a little unusual. Formal requirements documents have the potential advantage of sharply focussing thought.

However, there is a requirements summary that provides an overview of likely requirements.

The current drafts certainly recognize the need for security but more detailed consideration of such issues might be one benefit of developing a formal requirements document.

CC/PP and XML or XHTML

There are several ways in which CC/PP might specifically involve the use of XML and/or XHTML.

CC/PP is built on a foundation of the Resource Description Framework that is, of course, expressed in XML.

Use of RDF does not require that CC/PP be expressed in XML but it is possible, perhaps likely, that the CC/PP protocol itself (however its final version might look) will be available in an XML-compliant form.

CC/PP identifies the capabilities of the user agent together with how the user prefers to use them. XHTML Document Profiles express the required functionality for what the document author perceives as optimal rendering of the document. Hence, CC/PP and XHTML document profiles might, in certain settings, be compared when an origin server is considering the optimal type of content to be delivered to a user agent.

Background information on XHTML document profiles can be viewed at

http://www.w3.org/TR/1999/WD-xhtml-prof-req-19990906

Both CC/PP and XHTML document profiles can be considered as potential participants in the process of *content negotiation* in which the capabilities and preferences applicable to the user agent are compared to the capabilities or available document versions on the origin server.

After the preferences profile of a user agent has been identified, XML/XHTML might additionally be involved. For example, in some situations a suitable Web page might be created dynamically, using XSLT transformations and, perhaps, XSL-FO Formatting Objects that apply and extend the principles that were described briefly in Chapter 12.

The W3C Documentation on CC/PP

The W3C involvement in the development of Composite Capabilities/Preferences Profiles is part of the Mobile Access Activity within W3C, which is developing several initiatives relevant to mobile browsers.

At the time of this writing four Working Drafts relating to CC/PP have been made available to the public. If you are interested in coming to grips with this technology, familiarity with these documents, and succeeding documents which further develop these ideas, will be a must.

These are the currently available documents:

- Composite Capabilities/Preference Profiles: Requirements and Architecture http://www.w3.org/TR/2000/WD-CCPP-ra-20000721/

- Composite Capability/Preference Profiles (CC/PP): Structure http://www.w3.org/TR/2000/WD-CCPP-struct-20000721/

- CC/PP Attribute Vocabularies http://www.w3.org/TR/2000/WD-CCPP-vocab-20000721/

- Composite Capabilities/Preference Profiles: Terminology and Abbreviations http://www.w3.org/TR/2000/WD-CCPP-ta-20000721/

If you access these URLs, each page includes a link to the Latest Version near the top of the page, so that you might check if the drafts listed here have been superceded.

If you are not familiar with the typical process through which documents pass during their development at W3C, this is the hierarchy, in ascending order of importance:

- Working Drafts—These are draft documents that are subject to perhaps radical change or redrafting. Concepts or solutions can be added or removed. They are a snapshot of steps towards a hoped-for solution. When a Working Draft is nearing what is hoped to be its final form, a so-called "Last Call" Working Draft is issued. When a technology is particularly complex or the merits of a proposed solution are still being highly debated, it can happen that one "Last Call" draft is succeeded by another.

- Candidate Recommendation—Promotion of a document to Candidate Recommendation status is an indication that a document has successfully completed its Last Call process. Advancement of a document to Candidate Recommendation status is an explicit call to those outside of the related Working Groups or the W3C itself for implementation and technical feedback.

- Proposed Recommendation—If the feedback on the Candidate Recommendation is satisfactory, promotion to Proposed Recommendation is the next step. It is still possible for issues to be raised which, in a worst-case scenario, might result in the document being returned to Working Draft status for further development.

- Recommendation—For all practical purposes, this is a "fixed" standard—at least until a subsequent version is formally approved and issued. Because W3C is not an inter-governmental body, it cannot call its documents "standards" and therefore uses the term *Recommendations*. Recommendations are stable documents that might be cited as source material.

The W3C Documents of CC/PP are, at the time of writing, at the earliest stage—Working Draft.

Security

The use of a browser that might identify you personally and your location raises a number of security issues.

In at least some settings, it will be advisable or possible to conceal your identity (*anonymization*).

One issue that raises specific security concerns is mentioned in relation to position-dependent information.

Position-Dependent Information

Let's take a brief look at the pros and cons of the availability of systems that depend on knowing where you are; in the jargon, systems that operate using *position-dependent information*.

Imagine that you have a voice-enabled browser built into or plugged into your car that has capabilities (perhaps in conjunction with the electronic systems of the car) to determine your position and give you advice about suitable routes to your desired destination, perhaps with the ability to choose a scenic route, the fastest route, a route free of traffic jams, and so on. In that context the ability of your browser to transmit your exact position to others, and receive travel advice in return, has obvious benefits.

Similar benefits might arise if you are travelling and want to locate a hotel or other facility with criteria you want to define.

In practice, many of these processes, once they are fully developed, are likely not to involve direct human participation. However, it is quite possible that staff at the Web server company or others might be able to gain access to information about your location.

Because significant costs will be incurred in creating and maintaining such a system, it is unlikely to be free and thereby provide anonymous access. The fact that others might be aware of your geographical location might be viewed by you as an invasion of your personal privacy.

At first glance, others might say that there is no issue here. If you are acting lawfully and have nothing to hide, why should you object to others knowing your exact location?

Thinking beyond the principles of what are or are not the boundaries of legitimate personal privacy, some very practical issues arise. Suppose you are on a highway 300 miles from home, you transmit your position—for example, to find out traffic flows ahead—and that information is intercepted by an unauthorized person or is used unscrupulously by a member of the staff at a Web server company. Your position is known. You are 300 miles from home. A burglar has, at a minimum, four safe hours in which to invade your home and steal from it. The service that depends on knowing your geographical location has potentially exposed your property to crime.

Not surprisingly, issues relating to privacy and security are under active consideration in relation to position-dependent information.

Technical issues also are receiving consideration. For example, there is a need to develop an XML-compliant format for encapsulating position-dependent information.

Among the possible candidates as solutions are the NaVigation Markup Language (NVML) that Fujitsu submitted to W3C in June 1999:

http://www.w3.org/Submission/1999/10/

Another candidate is POIX (Point Of Interest eXchange) Language Specification proposed to W3C in May 1999:

http://www.w3.org/Submission/1999/06/

CC/PP and Web-Orientated TV

CC/PP provides a use-case scenario for TV-based Web access that will be described in the next section. In that scenario a server might broadcast a minimum set of content, because the TV-based browser might not be able to transmit its specific profile to the origin server.

TV and the Web

A number of initiatives are underway with a view to closer integration of television and the Web. These initiatives will spread more widely as more geographical areas convert television services from analog to digital signals.

Discussions on various developments are underway in a number of fora. The W3C is in discussion with a number of broadcasting standards bodies, both global and regional, with a view to exploring development of applicable standards.

Essentially, such developments involving TV and the Web seem likely to fall into one of two categories:

- Use of television, or associated devices, to browse the Web

- Addition of Web content to television, including making it a more interactive experience

Use of Television to Browse the Web

This has been possible for some time. For example Microsoft's WebTV service provides such a facility.

It is unlikely that TVWeb (a generic term for using television-associated devices to browse the Web, and not to be confused with the proprietary name WebTV) will require the full facilities of XHTML. Therefore the likely needs of TVWeb might lead to the adoption of only selected modules from the Modularized XHTML specification.

If widely applicable standards can be agreed as to which XHTML modules TVWeb will use, origin servers might choose to serve TVWeb-compatible documents as a default, in some circumstances.

As mentioned earlier in the chapter, the possible needs of television are one item being considered with the scope of establishing a CC/PP standard.

Addition of Web Content to Television

Many possibilities exist for the addition of Web-based content to television programs.

For example, during a sporting event it might be possible to include a clickable area of the screen that would call up background information about a sportsman or sports team. Given the limitations of some television systems, such information might be based on a limited range of XHTML modules.

Alternatively, background information could accompany a television broadcast without necessarily requiring viewer intervention, although such a text area also might include the possibility of advertisements for products related to the subject of the television program.

One issue that might require examination is to what extent viewers will find the presence of text areas of significant size a significant visual intrusion.

It is likely that televisions will not have computing power in set-top boxes that will be comparable to the computing power of a typical desktop PC. A consequence of that is television usage of the Web is likely to apply to a subset of Web content. Specifically, some of the modules of XHTML might be selectively used by television.

XHTML also was included as a component of the BXML (or BML)—Broadcast Markup Language—proposed as a possible standard by ARIB (Association of Radio Industries and Businesses).

Until recently, interactivity when watching television has primarily been limited to switching television channels using a remote control. However, the ability to click selected areas of a television screen to call up relevant information might add substantially to the range of entertainment or information, provision of which television is capable. With increases in bandwidth in Web-orientated media, the distinction between television and the Web might become significantly blurred.

It is by no means clear at the present time which of many standards under discussion by disparate broadcasting bodies will achieve critical mass to be considered to be a viable standard.

XForms

HTML forms were introduced to the World Wide Web in 1993. They and, more recently, XHTML forms, perform a pivotal role on many Web sites in the transmission of information from users of the World Wide Web to a variety of Web-based service providers.

The ubiquitous registration form, whatever its irritations on some sites, is an effective means of transmitting relevant personal information to permit registration on a Web site or to make online purchases.

Many e-commerce sites use HTML/XHTML forms to collect pieces of information that combine to form an online order, whether of items such as books at Amazon.com or Barnes & Noble, of other goods, or Web-based services.

However, despite the fact that they do provide useful functionality, traditional HTML/XHTML forms have a number of limitations that led the W3C to initiate an exploration of more advanced forms, which they call XForms. It is expected that XForms will be XML-compliant.

EXAMPLE

The development of XForms is, at the time of writing, at an early stage. So please be aware that the following code sample of an XForm from the W3C data model Working Draft, illustrating a sample purchase order using XForms, is subject to change:

```
<?xml version="1.0"?>
<!DOCTYPE html PUBLIC "-//W3C//DTD XHTML-XForms 1.0//EN"
"http://www.w3.org/TR/xhtml-forms1/DTD/xhtml-xforms1.dtd">

<html xmlns=http://www.w3.org/1999/xhtml
  xml:lang="en" lang="en">

<head>
<title>Purchase Order</title>
<xform xmlns=http://www.w3.org/2000/xforms
  action=http://www.my.com/cgi-bin/receiver.pl
  method="postXML"
  id="po_xform">
  <model>
    <group name="purchaseOrder">
      <group name="shipTo">
        <string name="name"/>
        <string name="street"/>
        <string name="city"/>
        <string name="state"/>
        <string name="zip">
          <mask>ddddd</mask>
        </string>
      </group>
    </group>
```

```
        </model>
        <instance>
          <purchaseOrder>
            <shipTo>
              <name>Alice Smith</name>
              <street>123 Maple Street</street>
              <city>Mill Valley</city>
              <state>CA</state>
              <zip>90952</zip>
            </shipTo>
          </purchaseOrder>
        </instance>
      </xform>
    </head>

    <body>
      <h1>Shipping Information</h1>
      <form name="po_xform">
        Name: <input name="purchaseOrder.shipTo.name"/><br/>
        Street: <input name="purchaseOrder.shipTo.street"/><br/>
        City: <input name="purchaseOrder.shipTo.city"/><br/>
        State: <input name="purchaseOrder.shipTo.state"/><br/>
        Zip: <input name="purchaseOrder.shipTo.zip"/><br/>
        <button onclick="submit('po_xform')">Submit</button>
      </form>
    </body>
  </html>
```

The Working Draft of the Requirements document for XForms is located at
`http://www.w3.org/TR/2000/WD-xhtml-forms-req-20000329`

In addition a Working Draft of a data model for XForms can be viewed at
`http://www.w3.org/TR/2000/WD-xforms-datamodel-20000406`

The XForms data model will include definitions of data types, data type facets, data model structures, and an XForms expression language. Because there are interdependencies between these aspects, and certain parts of the XForms data model are far from complete, there is little advantage in discussing here a draft that in all likelihood will change substantially in the coming months.

However, many of the more general issues relating to XForms are likely to be of more enduring relevance.

XForms relate, in part, to the two other initiatives mentioned earlier in this chapter because the requirements of handheld and television-based browsers are an explicit consideration in the development of XForms.

The W3C working group that is working to develop XForms has identified a number of key requirements for the next generation of Web forms that include

- Ease of migration
- Improved interoperability and accessibility
- Enhanced client/server interaction
- Advanced forms logic
- Support for internationalization
- Greater flexibility in presentation

In the current draft, the working group expresses the view that it will not be possible to maintain full backward compatibility with previous generations of Web browsers. Currently, it is not entirely clear to what extent and in what situations problems will arise because of such lack of backward compatibility.

In line with the principles of XML, increasingly being implemented in XHTML, it is desired that content and presentation within XForms be separated.

The increasingly global nature of e-commerce and e-business demands that internationalization of forms be achieved to a degree that would have been only of specialized interest only a few years ago.

It is likely that XForms will include capabilities for advanced forms logic, which are absent from the current generation of forms.

Because XForms will be based on XML and XHTML, the possibility exists of sophisticated use with other XML-based technologies such as the Scalable Vector Graphics (SVG) specification currently in "Last Call" Working Draft and the Synchronized Multimedia Integration Language (SMIL) Recommendation. Graphics-rich and multimedia-capable forms might provide user experiences that are currently difficult to envisage. Because all these technologies are XML-based, the possibility also will exist to use Cascading Style Sheets and Extensible Style sheet Language (XSLT and XSL-FO) to control aspects of presentation.

The facilities to be provided by XForms on different platforms will, quite obviously, differ greatly. On a mobile browser with a tiny screen, the priority might be to get an XForm to work at all, whereas on a large monitor attached to a computer with a high bandwidth connection to the Web a very rich graphical and multimedia user experience is likely to be possible.

As well as providing enriched output, at least for some users, it is likely that XForms will provide an increased number of options for data input. For example, it might be possible to input data using a voice-enabled browser, a facility potentially very useful for those with Repetitive Strain Injury or for call centers where employers want to avoid staff health problems of that type.

Currently many HTML and XHTML forms have either no error checking or custom scripting provides error checking. XForms aim to provide error checking by standard means that will, for example, reduce errors in inputting postal codes and telephone numbers. In e-commerce situations checking of credit card numbers for validity and so on also might be very useful functionality as a prelude to more definitive credit checking. The anticipated increased efficiency of forms development using XForms compared to using traditional forms plus custom scripting might produce both time and cost benefits.

The anticipated facility to manipulate XForms using the XML Document Object Model opens up new possibilities in data manipulation.

Another new capability that might be highly desirable in certain circumstances would be the ability to suspend the filling in of a form part way through the process. Imagine if you were filling your tax return online or a lengthy proposal form to obtain life insurance but were unable to complete it because one piece of information could not be found. With current forms, you either complete filling out the form or you lose the work already done. XForms might provide the capability to suspend form filling without losing data already entered.

XForms borrow a concept from client-server technology and split forms into three layers—presentation, logic, and data. This closely mirrors the concepts of n-tier server-based applications.

It is likely that work on XForms will result in the sequential production of various XForms modules, starting with a Core module. Such use of modules in XForms is likely to be associated closely with the modularization of XHTML, discussed in Part III, "Modularization."

In this chapter you have been given a taste of what might form part of the spectrum of future uses for XHTML and XML. Exciting new possibilities arise with such developments.

Part V

Appendix

A   XHTML Modularization Abstract Module Definitions

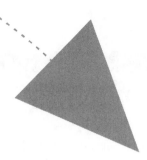
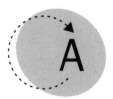

XHTML Modularization Abstract Module Definitions

This appendix contains the Abstract Module Definitions found in the W3C document Modularization of XHTML. It is provided here as a means of quick reference.

Some preliminary information is needed before the modules can be defined; specifically, syntactic conventions, attribute types, and attribute collection names.

Syntactic Conventions

The first thing that should be noted is that abstract module definitions are not written in a formal grammar. However, the W3C has borrowed conventions that should be familiar to the authors of DTDs.

Each module might be viewed as a table with three columns. In each row, you'll find an element, the attributes allowed within the element, and then the *minimal content model* for the element. A minimal content model might contain a list of elements, a content set (which is of itself a common list of elements), or a datatype such as PCDATA for the title element.

Occurrence indicators and other expressions will be found in the minimal content models as follows:

Expression	Meaning
Foo ?	Zero or one instances of *foo* are permitted.
Foo +	One or more instances of *foo* are required.
Foo *	Zero or more instances of *foo* are permitted.
A, B	A is required, followed by B.
A | B	Either A or B is required.
A - B	A is permitted, but omits elements in B that were otherwise found in A.
Parentheses	As in many mathematical operations, when an expression is contained within parentheses, evaluation of any subexpressoins within the parentheses takes place before evaluation of expressions outside of the parentheses. That is, evaluation starts at the deepest level possible.
Extending predefined elements	At times a module will add attributes to an element. When this occurs, the element name is followed by the ampersand (&) character.
Assigning type to attribute values	The type assigned to an attribute value is listed in parentheses after the attribute name.
Defining specific legal values of	If the module defines an attributes explicit list of legal values for an attribute, they are listed, enclosed in quotation marks and separated by vertical bars (|), inside parentheses following the attribute name.

Attribute Types

Each attribute listed in the module definitions will have an accompanying type definition in parentheses.

This first table holds attribute types as defined in the XML 1.0 Recommendation:

Attribute Type	Definition
CDATA	Character Data
ID	A document-unique identifier
IDREF	A reference to a document-unique identifier
IDREFS	A space-delimited list of references to document-unique identifiers
NAME	A name with the same character constraints as ID
NMTOKEN	A name composed only of name tokens as defined in XML 1.0
NMTOKENS	One or more whitespace-separated NMTOKEN values
PCDATA	Processed character data

The following table contains data types and their semantics as defined by XHTML Modularization. Links to ISO, RFC, and other references can be found in the Modularization of XHTML document on the W3C Web site:

Data Type	Description
Character	A single character from ISO10646.
Charset	A character encoding, as per RFC2045.
Charsets	A space-delimited list of character encodings, as per RFC2045.
Color	A color definition as specified in SRGB. It might be a hexadecimal number prefixed by a hash mark (#), or one of sixteen color names: Black = "#000000" Silver = "#C0C0C0" Gray = "#808080" White = "#FFFFFF" Maroon = "#800000" Red = "#FF0000" Purple = "#800080"

Data Type	Description
	Fuschia = "#FF00FF"
	Green = "#008000"
	Lime = "#00FF00"
	Olive = "#808000"
	Yellow = "#FFFF00"
	Navy = "#000080"
	Blue = "#0000FF"
	Teal = "#008080"
	Aqua = "#00FFFF"
ContentType	A media type, as per RFC2045.
ContentTypes	A comma-delimited list of media types, as per RFC2045.
Datetime	Date and time information.
FrameTarget	Frame name used as destination for results of certain actions.
LanguageCode	A language code, as per RFC1766.
Length	A value in either pixels or a percentage of the available vertical or horizontal space.
LinkTypes	A LinkTypes value refers to a space-delimited list of link types. Whitespace characters are not permitted within linktypes. The types are case-insensitive.
	The following link types are recognized, shown with their conventional interpretations:
	Alternate—Designates a substitute version for the document where the link occurs. When combined with the `xml:lang` attribute, a translated document is implied. When used with the media attribute, a version designed for a different medium (or media) is implied.
	Style sheet—Refers to an external style sheet. User-selectable alternate style sheets can be generated by using this together with the Alternative link type.
	Start—Refers to the first document in a collection. It is intended as a pointer to search engines.
	Next—Refers to the next document in a linear sequence of documents. Can be used to preload the next document to reduce perceived wait times.

Data Type	Description
	Prev—Refers to the previous document in an ordered series of documents. Synonymous to Previous where supported.
	Contents—Refers to a document that serves as a table of contents. Synonymous with ToC where supported.
	Index—Refers to a document providing an index for the current document.
	Glossary—Refers to a document providing a glossary of terms used in the current document.
	Copyright—Refers to a document containing a copyright statement for the current document.
	Chapter—Refers to a document serving as a chapter in a collection of documents.
	Section—Refers to a document serving as a section in a collection of documents.
	Subsection—Refers to a document serving as a subsection in a collection of documents.
	Appendix—Refers to a document serving as an appendix in a collection of documents.
	Help—Refers to a document offering help (more information, links to other sources of information, and so on).
	Bookmark—Refers to a bookmark. A bookmark is a link to a key entry point within an extended document. The `title` attribute could be used to label the bookmark. Also, more than one bookmark might be defined in each document.
MediaDesc	The MediaDesc attribute is a comma-delimited list of media descriptors. The following list contains recognized descriptors:
	Screen—Intended for non-paged computer screens
	Tty—Intended for media using a fixed-pitch character grid, such as teletypes, terminals, or portable devices within limited display capabilities
	TV—Intended for television-type devices (low resolution, color, limited scrolling)
	Projection—Intended for projectors
	Handheld—Intended for handheld devices (small screen, monochrome, bitmapped graphics, limited bandwidth)

Data Type	Description
	Print—Intended for paged, opaque material, and for documents viewed onscreen in print preview mode
	Braille—Intended for Braille tactile feedback devices
	Aural—Intended for speech synthesizers
	All—Suitable for all devices
MultiLength	The value might be a Length or a relative length. A relative length takes the form "i*" where "i" is an integer. When allotting space among elements competing for that space, user agents allot stated pixel and percentage lengths first, and then divide up remaining available space among relative lengths. Each relative length receives a portion of the available space, in proportion to the integer preceding the "*". The value "*" is equivilant to "1*".
Number	One or more digits.
Pixels	The value is an integer that represents the number of pixels on the canvas (screen, paper, and so on).
Script	Script data can be the content of the script element and the value of intrinsic event attributes. User agents *must not* evaluate script data as HTML markup but instead must pass it on as data to a script engine. The case sensitivity of script data depends on the scripting language. Script data that is element content might not contain character references, but script data that is the value of an attribute might contain them.
Text	Arbitrary textual data, likely meant to be human-readable.
URI	A Uniform Resource Identifier.
URIs	A space-delimited list of Uniform Resource Identifiers.

Attribute Collections

Five groups of attributes are used together frequently enough that they are placed into sets according to purpose, known as collections. The following table lists the collection name and each member attribute. Each attribute in the collection is further noted with its corresponding data type. The last collection, Common, is a superset of the other collections:

Collection name	Attributes
Core	Class (NMTOKEN), id (ID), title (CDATA)
I18N (Internationalization)	dir ("rtl"|"ltr"), xml:lang (NMTOKEN)
Events (each of type Script)*	onclick, ondblclick, onmousedown, onmouseup, onmouseover, onmousemove, onmouseout, onkeypress, onkeydown, onkeyup
Style**	style (CDATA)
Common	Core + I18N + Events + Style

* The Events collection is only defined when the Intrinsic Events Module is in use. Otherwise, the collection is empty.

** The Style collection is only defined when the Style Attribute Module is selected. Otherwise, the collection is empty.

The Core Modules

Each of the four modules defined here are required to be present for the document type to be Host Language Conformant.

Each table lists the elements, corresponding attributes, and minimal content model for each element in the module. The minimal content models might be expressed using EBNF notation.

Structure Module

The Structure Module defines the major structural components of all XHTML documents. The root element, html, is defined here:

Element	Attributes	Minimal Content Model
body	Common	(Heading|Block|List)*
head	I18N, profile (URI)	title
html	I18N, version (CDATA), xmlns (URI)	head, body
title	I18N	PCDATA

Text Module

As its name implies, the Text Module defines the elements used to structure text.

Four new content model sets are defined using the elements found in this module. The following table defines the content model sets and corresponding member elements. The fourth set is a superset of the previous three.

Content Model Set	Elements
Heading	h1|h2|h3|h4|h5|h6
Block	address|blockquote|div|p|pre
Inline	abbr|acronym|br|cite|code|dfn|em |kbd|q|samp|span|strong|var
Flow	Heading|Block|Inline

The member elements of the Text Module can now be defined:

Element	Attributes	Minimal Content Model
abbr	Common	(PCDATA|Inline)*
acronym	Common	(PCDATA|Inline)*
address	Common	(PCDATA|Inline)*
blockquote	Common, cite (URI)	(PCDATA|Heading|Block)*
br	Core	EMPTY
cite	Common	(PCDATA|Inline)*
code	Common	(PCDATA|Inline)*
dfn	Common	(PCDATA|Inline)*
div	Common	(Heading|Block|List)*
em	Common	(PCDATA|Inline)*
h1	Common	(PCDATA|Inline)*
h2	Common	(PCDATA|Inline)*
h3	Common	(PCDATA|Inline)*
h4	Common	(PCDATA|Inline)*
h5	Common	(PCDATA|Inline)*

Element	Attributes	Minimal Content Model
h6	Common	(PCDATA|Inline)*
kbd	Common	(PCDATA|Inline)*
p	Common	(PCDATA|Inline)*
pre	Common	(PCDATA|Inline)*
q	Common, cite (URI)	(PCDATA|Inline)*
samp	Common	(PCDATA|Inline)*
span	Common	(PCDATA|Inline)*
strong	Common	(PCDATA|Inline)*
var	Common	(PCDATA|Inline)*

Hypertext Module

Defining just a single element, a, the Hypertext Module allows links to other resources to be created. When present, and it must be in all XHTML Family conformant document definitions, the a element is added to the Inline content set from the basic Text Module.

Element	Attributes	Minimal Content Model
a	Common, accesskey (Character), charset (Charset), href (URI), hreflang (LanguageCode), rel (LinkTypes), tabindex (Number), type (ContentType)	(PCDATA|Inline - a)*

NOTE

a elements cannot contain other a elements. Because the a element is added to the Inline content set when the Hypertext Module is present, the minimal content model for a must be defined as Inline minus a.

List Module

The List Module defines the list containers and the corresponding item elements.

A new content model set, List, is defined in this module. The List set is then added to the Flow set defined in the basic Text Module.

Content Model	Elements
List	(dl|ol|ul)+

The List Module is defined as follows:

Element	Attributes	Minimal Content Model
dl	Common	(dt|dd)+
dt	Common	(PCDATA|Inline)*
dd	Common	(PCDATA|Inline)*
ol	Common	li+
ul	Common	li+
li	Common	(PCDATA|Inline)*

Optional Modules

The remaining 23 modules defined here are optional. They might be added in any combination as desired to the Core Modules set to create XHTML Family conformant document types.

Applet Module

NOTE

It should be noted that the Applet module, though provided by the W3C to describe behavior of these elements, has been deprecated.

The Applet Module provides a means for referencing and accessing external applications. When this module is present in a document type definition, the Inline content set is modified to include the applet element:

Element	Attributes	Minimal Content Model
applet	Core, alt (Text), archive (CDATA), code (CDATA), codebase (URI), height (Length), name (CDATA), object (CDATA), width (Length)	param?
param	id (ID), name (CDATA), type (ContentType), value (CDATA), valuetype ("data"|"ref"|"object")	EMPTY

Text Extension Modules

Three modules are defined here, using elements that manipulate the presentation of text.

PRESENTATION MODULE

When used, this module makes changes to two content sets, Block and Inline, as follows:

Content Model	Elements Added
Block	hr
Inline	b, big, i, small, sub, sup, tt

The Presentation Module itself is defined as follows:

Element	Attributes	Minimal Content Model
b	Common	(PCDATA|Inline)*
big	Common	(PCDATA|Inline)*
hr	Common	EMPTY
i	Common	(PCDATA|Inline)*
small	Common	(PCDATA|Inline)*
sub	Common	(PCDATA|Inline)*
sup	Common	(PCDATA|Inline)*
tt	Common	(PCDATA|Inline)*

EDIT MODULE

This module provides two elements used to show editorial changes in documents. When the module is in use, both elements are added to the Inline content set:

Element	Attributes	Minimal Content Model
del	Common, cite (URI), datetime (Datetime)	(PCDATA|Inline)*
ins	Common, cite (URI), datetime (Datetime)	(PCDATA|Inline)*

Bi-directional Text Module

The Bi-directional Text Module defines a single element, bdo, which controls the bi-directional rules for a given element's content. When the module is in use, the element is added to the Inline content set:

Element	Attributes	Minimal Content Model
bdo	Common	(PCDATA|Inline)*

Forms Modules

Two modules are defined in this section: a Basic Forms Module, which incorporates form features found in HTML 3.2, and the broader Forms Module, which provides the additional forms features introduced in HTML 4.0.

Basic Forms Module

When in use, this module defines two new content model sets, as follows:

Content Model	Elements Added
Form	form
Formctrl	input|select|textarea

Additionally, two existing content model sets are modified to include the new model sets:

Content Model	Content Model Sets Added
Block	Form
Inline	Formctrl

The Basic Forms Module is defined as follows:

Element	Attributes	Minimal Content Model
form	Common, action (URI), method ("get"|"put"), enctype (ContentType)	Heading|Block - form
input	Common, checked ("checked"), maxlength (Number), name (CDATA), size (Number), src (URI), type ("text", "password", "checkbox", "radio", "submit", "reset", "file", "hidden"), value (CDATA)	EMPTY

Element	Attributes	Minimal Content Model
select	Common, multiple ("multiple"), name (CDATA), size (Number)	option+
option	Common, selected ("selected"), value (CDATA)	Inline*
textarea	Common, columns (Number), name (CDATA), rows (Number)	PCDATA*

FORMS MODULE

The Forms Module is a superset of the Basic Forms Module. Accordingly, the new content model sets defined by the Forms Module are supersets of the sets defined earlier.

NOTE

The content model sets use the same name as the Basic Forms Module definitions in part because they are supersets, but also to allow easy substitution of forms modules in document type definitions. Any additional forms modules defined by the W3C will make use of these same content model set names, enhancing interoperability.

Content Model	Elements Added
Form	form|fieldset
Formctrl	input|select|textarea|label|button

As in the Basic Forms Module, the Form content model set is added to the Block content set, and the Formctrl set is added to the Inline set.

The Forms Module itself is defined here:

Element	Attributes	Minimal Content Model
form	Common, accept (ContentTypes), accept-charset (Charsets), action (URI), method ("get"|"put"), enctype (ContentType)	(Heading|Block - form|fieldset)+

Element	Attributes	Minimal Content Model
input	Common, accept (ContentTypes), accesskey (Character), alt (CDATA), checked ("checked"), disabled ("disabled"), maxlength (Number), name (CDATA), readonly ("readonly"), size (Number), src (URI), tabindex (Number), type ("text", "password", "checkbox", "radio", "submit", "reset", "file", "hidden", "image"), value (CDATA)	EMPTY
select	Common, disabled ("disabled"), multiple ("multiple"), name (CDATA), size (Number), tabindex (Number)	(optgroup|option)+
option	Common, disabled ("disabled"), label (Text), selected ("selected"), value (CDATA)	PCDATA
textarea	Common, accesskey (Character), columns (Number), disabled ("disabled"), name (CDATA), readonly ("readonly"), rows (Number), tabindex (Number)	PCDATA
button	Common, accesskey (Character), disabled ("disabled"), name (CDATA), tabindex (Number), type ("button"|"submit"| "reset"), value (CDATA)	(PCDATA|Heading|List| Block - Form|Inline - Formctrl)*
fieldset	Common	(PCDATA|legend|Flow)*
label	Common, accesskey (Character), for (IDREF)	(PCDATA|Inline - label)*

Element	Attributes	Minimal Content Model
legend	Common, accesskey (Character)	(PCDATA|Inline)+
optgroup	Common, disabled ("disabled"), label (Text)	option+

Table Modules

As with forms, two modules are defined in this section, a Basic Tables Module, providing the most basic table functionality, and the broader Tables Module, which has many more features and is a superset of the Basic Tables Module.

Whenever either module is present, the Block content set is modified to include the table element.

BASIC TABLES MODULE

Element	Attributes	Minimal Content Model
caption	Common	(PCDATA|Inline)*
table	Common, border (Pixels), cellpadding (Length), cellspacing (Length), summary (Text), width (Length)	caption?,tr+
td	Common, abbr (Text), align ("left"|"center"|"right"), axis (CDATA), colspan (Number), headers (IDREFS), rowspan (Number), scope ("row"|"col"|"rowgroup"|"colgroup"), valign("top"|"middle"|"bottom")	(PCDATA|Flow)*
th	Common, abbr (Text), align ("left"|"center"|"right"), axis (CDATA), colspan (Number), headers (IDREFS), rowspan (Number), scope ("row"|"col"|"rowgroup"|"colgroup"), valign ("top"|"middle"|"bottom")	(PCDATA|Flow)*
tr	Common, align ("left"|"center"|"right"), valign ("top"|"middle"|"bottom")	(th|td)+

TABLES MODULE

Element	Attributes	Minimal Content Model
caption	Common	(PCDATA|Inline)*
table	Common, border (Pixels), cellpadding (Length), cellspacing (Length), datapagesize (CDATA), frame ("void"|"above"| "below"|"hsides"|"lhs"| "rhs"|"vsides"|"box"| "border"), rules ("none"|"groups"|"rows"| "cols"|"all"), summary (Text), width (Length)	caption?,(col*| colgroup*),((thead?, tfoot?,tbody+)|(tr+))
td	Common, abbr (Text), align ("left"|"center"| "right"|"justify"|"char"), axis (CDATA), char (Character), charoff (Length), colspan (Number), headers (IDREFS), rowspan (Number), scope ("row"| "col"|"rowgroup"| "colgroup"), valign ("top"|"middle"|"bottom"| "baseline")	(PCDATA|Flow)*
th	Common, abbr (Text), align ("left"|"center"| "right"|"justify"|"char"), axis (CDATA), char (Character), charoff (Length), colspan (Number), headers (IDREFS), rowspan (Number), scope ("row"| "col"|"rowgroup"| "colgroup"), valign ("top"|"middle"|"bottom"| "baseline")	(PCDATA|Flow)*
tr	Common, align ("left"| "center"|"right"|"justify"| "char"), char (Character), charoff (Length), valign ("top"|"middle"|"bottom"| "baseline")	(th|td)+

Element	Attributes	Minimal Content Model
col	Common, align ("left"| "center"|"right"|"justify"| "char"), char (Character), charoff (Length), span (Number) , valign ("top"|"middle"|"bottom"| "baseline"), width (MultiLength)	EMPTY
colgroup	Common, align ("left"| "center"|"right"|"justify"| "char"), char (Character), charoff (Length), span (Number) , valign ("top"| "middle"|"bottom"|"baseline"), width (MultiLength)	col*
tbody	Common, align ("left"| "center"|"right"|"justify"| "char"), char (Character), charoff (Length), valign ("top"|"middle"|"bottom"| "baseline")	tr+
thead	Common, align ("left"| "center"|"right"|"justify"| "char"), char (Character), charoff (Length), valign ("top"|"middle"|"bottom"| "baseline")	tr+
tfoot	Common, align ("left"| "center"|"right"|"justify"| "char"), char (Character), charoff (Length), valign ("top"|"middle"|"bottom"| "baseline")	tr+

Image Module

The Image Module provides the ability to incorporate basic images in the document. Selecting the image module does not imply support for client-side image maps. Those are defined in a separate selectable module.

When the module is selected, the img element is added to the Inline content set:

Element	Attributes	Minimal Content Model
img	Common, alt*, height (Length), longdesc (URI), src* (URI), width (Length)	EMPTY

Client-side Image Map Module

This module provides elements required for client-side image maps, though it does not provide the img element itself. Therefore the Image Module (or another module that supports the img element) must accompany it.

When this module is in use, the map element is added to the Inline content set.

NOTE

The & notation after some elements indicates that the element is defined in another module, but the module defines new attributes. Accordingly, no minimal content model is defined here for those elements.

Element	Attributes	Minimal Content Model
a&	coords (CDATA), shape ("rect"*|"circle"|"poly"|"default")	n/a
area	Common, accesskey (Character), alt* (Text), coords (CDATA), href (URI), nohref ("nohref"), shape ("rect"*|"circle"|"poly"|"default"), tabindex (Number)	EMPTY
img&	usemap (IDREF)	When the Image Module is selected
map	I18N, Events, class (NMTOKEN), id* (ID), title (CDATA)	((Heading|Block)| area)+
object&	usemap (IDREF)	Note: only when the object module is included

Server-side Image Map Module

This module provides support for image selection and coordinate transmission. Like the Client-side Image Map Module, it requires that the Image Module or other img element–supporting module be present. This module only defines an attribute, no elements:

Element	Attributes	Minimal Content Model
img&	ismap ("ismap")	When the image module is selected

Object Module

This module is used for generic object inclusion, making no assertions about what type of object might be incorporated.

When the module is in use, the object element is added to the Inline content set.

Element	Attributes	Minimal Content Model
object	Common, archive (URIs), classid (URI), codebase (URI), codetype (ContentType), data (URI), declare ("declare"), height (Length), standby (Text), tabindex (Number), type (ContentType), width (Length)	(PCDATA|Flow|param)*
param	id (ID), name* (CDATA), type (ContentType), value (CDATA), valuetype ("data"*|"ref"|"object")	EMPTY

Frames Module

This module provides frame-related elements and modifies several previously defined elements with new attributes.

NOTE

When selected, this module makes a major change to the content model of the html element, which becomes (head, frameset).

Element	Attributes	Minimal Content Model
frameset	Core, cols (MultiLength), rows (MultiLength)	frame+, noframes?
frame	Core, frameborder ("1"|"0"), longdesc (URI), marginheight (Pixels), marginwidth (Pixels), noresize ("noresize"), scrolling ("yes"|"no"| "auto"*), src (URI)	EMPTY

Element	Attributes	Minimal Content Model
noframes	Common	body
a&	target (CDATA)	n/a
area&	target (CDATA)	Only when the Client-side Image Map Module is selected
base&	target (CDATA)	Only when the Legacy Module is selected
link&	target (CDATA)	Only when the Linking Module is selected
form&	target (CDATA)	Only when the Basic Forms or Forms Module is selected

Iframe Module

This module provides the definition for inline frames. It should be noted that it is not dependent on the presence of the Frames Module.

When this module is in use, the iframe element is added to the Inline content set:

Element	Attributes	Minimal Content Model
iframe	Core, frameborder ("1"|"0"), height (Pixels), longdesc (URI), marginheight (Pixels), marginwidth (Pixels), scrolling ("yes"|"no"| "auto"*), src (URI), width (Length)	Flow

Intrinsic Events

Intrinsic events are things that might occur when a user performs specific actions. This module defines attributes that are added to the attribute set for the listed elements *only* when the modules that define those elements are present in the DTD. This module makes use of the Events attribute collection defined at the beginning of this appendix.

Element	Attributes—All of Type (Script)	Notes
a&	onblur, onfocus	
area&	onblur, onfocus	When the Client-side Image Map Module is selected
form&	onreset, onsubmit	When the Basic Forms or Forms Module is selected

Element	Attributes—All of Type (Script)	Notes
body&	onload, onunload	
label&	onblur, onfocus	When the Forms Module is selected
input&	onblur, onchange, onfocus, onselect	When the Basic Forms or Forms Module is selected
select&	onblur, onchange, onfocus	When the Basic Forms or Forms Module is selected
textarea&	onblur, onchange, onfocus, onselect	When the Basic Forms or Forms Module is selected
button&	onblur, onfocus	When the Forms Module is selected

Metainformation Module

The single element in this module, meta, provides descriptive information in the declarative portion of the document.

When this module is present, the content model for the head element (as defined in the Structure Module) is changed to include the meta element.

Element	Attributes	Minimal Content Model
meta	I18N, content* (CDATA), http-equiv (NMTOKEN), name (NMTOKEN), scheme (CDATA)	EMPTY

Scripting Module

This module defines elements used to invoke or provide alternative content for executable scripts.

When this module is present, both elements are added to the Block and Inline content sets, and the script element is added to the content model of the head element in the Structure Module.

Element	Attributes	Minimal Content Model
noscript	Common	(Heading|List|Block)+
script	charset (Charset), defer ("defer"), *language* (CDATA), src (URI), type* (ContentType), xml:space="preserve"	PCDATA

> **NOTE**
>
> The language attribute is deprecated, and will not appear in future versions of the XHTML language.

Style Sheet Module

The Style Sheet Module defines a single element, style, used when writing internal style sheets.

When the module is used, the style element is added to the content model of the head element in the Structure Module.

Element	Attributes	Minimal Content Model
style	I18N, media (MediaDesc), title (Text), type* (ContentType), xml:space= "preserve"	PCDATA

Style Attribute Module

> **NOTE**
>
> This entire module is deprecated.

This module defines a single attribute, style. When the module is selected, it activates the Style attribute collection previously defined as part of the Common attribute collection. No other information is added.

Link Module

This module defines a single element, link, that can be used to define links to external resources (such as external style sheets or scripts).

When this module is used, it adds the link element to the content model of the head element in the Structure Module.

Element	Attributes	Minimal Content Model
link	Common, charset (Charset), href (URI), hreflang (LanguageCode), media (MediaDesc), rel (LinkTypes), rev (LinkTypes), type (ContentType)	EMPTY

Base Module

This module defines the element base, which can be used to define a base URI used to resolve all relative URIs in the document.

When this module is selected, the base element is added to the content model of the head element in the Structure Module.

Element	Attributes	Minimal Content Model
base	href* (URI)	EMPTY

Name Identification Module

NOTE

This module is deprecated.

This module defines a single attribute, name, for a collection of elements. It is provided for backward compatibility with user agents that identify specific elements within HTML documents based on the value of the name attribute. In XHTML, the id attribute has assumed this purpose. To retain compatibility where necessary, this module might be selected.

Use of this module carries several caveats:

- When including the module, both the name and id attributes must be defined for the elements listed in the following table.

- When appearing on these elements, the name and id attributes must have the same value.

- When documents using this attribute are served as Internet Media Type "text/xml" or "application/xml", the value of the name attribute cannot be used as a fragment identifier.

Element	Attributes	Notes
a&	name (CDATA)	
applet&	name (CDATA)	Only when the Applet Module is in use
form&	name (CDATA)	Only when the Forms or Basic Forms Module is in use
frame&	name (CDATA)	Only when the Frames Module is in use
iframe&	name (CDATA)	Only when the Iframe Module is in use
img&	name (CDATA)	Only when the Image Module is in use
map&	name (CDATA)	Only when the Client-side Image Map Module is in use

Legacy Module

This module defines elements and attributes that have previously been deprecated in earlier versions of HTML and XHTML. This module is provided to allow markup language authors the ability to support them, should they want to. It should not be inferred, however, that their use is encouraged or supported. The elements and attributes defined here remain deprecated.

When this module is in use, the base element is added to the content model of the head element in the Structure Module.

Element	Attributes	Minimal Content Model
basefont	color (Color), face (CDATA), id (ID), size (CDATA)	EMPTY
center	Common	(PCDATA|Flow)*
font	Common, color (Color), face (CDATA), size (CDATA)	(PCDATA|Inline)*
s	Common	(PCDATA|Inline)*
strike	Common	(PCDATA|Inline)*
u	Common	(PCDATA|Inline)*

Element	Attributes	Notes
body&	alink (Color), background (URI), bgcolor (Color), link (Color), text (Color), vlink (Color)	
br&	clear ("left"|"all"| "right"|"none"*)	
caption&	align ("left"|"center"| "right"|"justify")	
div&	align ("left"|"center"| "right"|"justify")	
h1-h6&	align ("left"|"center"| "right"|"justify")	
hr&	align ("left"|"center"| "right"|"justify")	
img&	align ("left"|"center"| "right"|"justify"), border (Pixels), hspace (Pixels), vspace (Pixels)	
input&	align ("left"|"center"| "right"|"justify")	Only when the Basic Forms or Forms Module is in use

Element	Attributes	Notes
legend&	align ("left"|"center"| "right"|"justify")	Only when the Forms Module is in use
li&	type (CDATA), value (Number)	
ol&	compact ("compact"), start (Number), type (CDATA)	
p&	align ("left"|"center"| "right"|"justify")	
pre&	width (Number)	
script&	language (CDATA)	Only when the Scripting Module is in use
table&	align ("left"|"center"| "right"|"justify"), bgcolor (Color)	Only when the Tables Module is in use
tr&	bgcolor (Color)	Only when the Tables Module is in use
th&	bgcolor (Color), height (Pixels), nowrap ("nowrap"), width (Pixels)	Only when the Tables Module is in use
td&	bgcolor (Color), height (Pixels), nowrap ("nowrap"), width (Pixels)	Only when the Tables Module is in use
ul&	compact ("compact"), type (CDATA)	

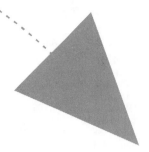

Index